Assessment in the Learning Organization

SHIFTING THE PARADIGM

T 84850

EDITED BY

ARTHUR L. COSTA

AND

BENA KALLICK

Association for Supervision and Curriculum Development
1703 N. Beauregard St.   Alexandria, VA 22311-1714 USA
Telephone: 1-800-933-2723 or 703-578-9600   Fax: 703-575-5400
Web site: http://www.ascd.org   E-mail: member@ascd.org

Typeset by Valerie Sprague.

ASCD publications present a variety of viewpoints. The views expressed or implied in this book should not be interpreted as official positions of the Association.

Printed in the United States of America.

ASCD member price: $21.95   nonmember price: $25.95   9/95s

ASCD Stock No.: 195188
ISBN: 0-87120-250-6

Library of Congress Cataloging-in-Publication Data
Assessment in the learning organization : shifting the paradigm /
  edited by Arthur L. Costa and Bena Kallick.
     p. cm.
   Includes bibliographical references and index.
   ISBN 0-87120-250-6 (pbk.)
   1. Educational evaluation—United States. 2. Work groups—United
States. 3. School supervision—United States—Evaluation.
4. Educational tests and measurements—United States. I. Costa,
Arthur L. II. Kallick, Bena. III. Association for Supervision and
Curriculum Development.
LB2822.75.A87 1995
379.1′54—dc20   95-32492
                                                            CIP

06 05 04 03 02 01 00   10 9 8 7 6 5 4 3 2

Assessment in the Learning Organization
Shifting the Paradigm

Introduction

ARTHUR L. COSTA AND BENA KALLICK

> I believe that we have only just begun the process of discover-
> ing and inventing the new organizational forms that will
> inhabit the twenty-first century. To be responsible inventors
> and discoverers, though, we need the courage to let go of the
> old world, to relinquish most of what we cherished, to aban-
> don our interpretations about what does and doesn't work. As
> Einstein is often quoted as saying: "No problem can be solved
> from the same consciousness that created it. We must learn to
> see the world anew."
>
> —MARGARET J. WHEATLEY

The design of most schools is based on the assumption that life proceeds in a linear fashion. For example, a strategic plan will outline a five-year design for a district, but it probably won't allow for more than one eventuality during that time. Because schools usually assume linear, certain paths in their work, assessment has always been designed to assume cause-and-effect relationships. As a result, we have been willing to use summative assessment as a final judgment rather than as a continuous feedback system based on a changing environment.

Although we recognize the nonlinear path of learning (whether by students or an organization), we continue to seek and use ways of assessment that ignore the realities of performance in a less predictable, nonlinear environment. This book describes a vision for "the world anew" based on both theory and practice regarding the role of assessment in school life. We will illuminate a new perspective for understanding what is meant by continuous improvement (Deming 1986) in a learning organization (Senge 1990).

Theoretical Background

To help us understand the nonlinear organizational world, we draw upon concepts by W. Edwards Deming as described in *Out of the Crisis* (1986) and Peter Senge's theories from *The Fifth Discipline: The Art and Practice of the Learning Organization* (1990).

Underlying our work is the idea that improvement is not a one-time effort. We must constantly seek ways of continual growth, renewal, and learning. As one of Deming's 14 principles states: "Improve constantly and forever the system of production and service." Also underlying our work are Senge's five disciplines. They are:

1. Systems Thinking: The discipline that integrates the others, fusing them into a coherent body of theory and practice.

2. Mental Models: The ability to unearth our internal pictures of the world to scrutinize them and to make them open to the influence of others.

3. Building Shared Vision: The practice of unearthing collective "pictures of the future" that foster genuine commitment.

4. Personal Mastery: Continually clarifying and deepening our skills toward improved practices.

5. Team Learning: The capacity to "think together," which is gained by mastering the practice of dialogue and discussion.

Organization of this Book

Parts I through VI describe how assessment is related to:

• Bringing congruence and integrity to organizational goals and assessments through **systems thinking** (Part I).

• The use of feedback spirals as a process design for **continued learning** (Part II).

• The need to change our existing **mental models** for the role of assessment in schools (Part III).

• How schools state their purposes and outcomes as their **shared vision** (Part IV).

• The power of **team building** and the role of

critical friends as resources for **continual learning** (Part V).

• A developmental continuum that helps us set milestones along the pathways to **personal mastery** (Part VI).

After an initial discussion of each paradigm, several authors discuss practical examples of the application of these concepts. These chapters have been contributed by outstanding educational practitioners, and they illuminate the realities and challenges of implementing the six concepts and shifting the various paradigms. The practitioners relate strategies from their districts, reflections on personal experiences with students in their classrooms and schools, and insights they have gained in working to create a renaissance in the assessment process. As you read these practitioner pieces, consider returning to the paradigm presented at the beginning of the chapter to gain the most meaning from each contribution.

Part VII concludes the book with a discussion of seven tasks that educators must confront and accomplish to implement shifts in the assessment paradigm and rebuild the school as a learning organization.

> Today, the ascendant nations and corporations are masters not of land and material resources but of ideas and technologies. ... The global network of telecommunications can carry more valuable goods than all the world's super tankers. Wealth comes not to the rulers of slave labor but to the liberators of human creativity, not to the conquerors of land but to the emancipators of mind.
>
> —PAUL DAVIES AND JOHN GRIBBIN

References

Davis, P., and J. Gribbin. (1992). *The Matter Myth*. New York: A Touchstone Book.

Deming, W.E. (1986). *Out of the Crisis*. Cambridge, Mass.: Massachusetts Institute of Technology Press.

Senge, P. (1990). *The Fifth Discipline: The Art and Practice of the Learning Organization*. New York: Doubleday, Current.

Wheatley, M.J. (1992). *Leadership and the New Science*. San Francisco: Berrett-Koehler Publishers.

PART I

Systems Thinking:
Interactive
Assessment in
Holonomous
Organizations

Systems Thinking: Interactive Assessment in Holonomous Organizations

ARTHUR L. COSTA AND BENA KALLICK

> The learning organization is "a place where people continually expand their capacity to create the results they truly desire, where new and expansive patterns of thinking are nurtured, where collective aspiration is set free, and where people are continually learning how to learn together."
>
> —PETER SENGE

As quoted above, Senge describes a learning organization with words and images such as create, new, expand, and nurture. His metaphors are quite different from those we currently use in schools, where teachers talk about "battling" the system for needed resources and administrators describe teachers as "in the trenches." A classroom is the "first line of defense," and students talk about "bombing out on a test." A school system's response to problems is "strategic planning" with new "tactics," an approach that implies a command/demand relationship.

All in all, such images suggest combative relationships among various parts of a system that is permeated by top-down authoritarianism and fragmentation. The farther away you are from students, the greater the inconsistency in principles and practices. Each part of the organization has little to do with other parts; each department works in isolation.

Instead of such a battlefield, imagine a garden where the interdependent balance of the system allows each plant to flourish. The gardener plants a seed in fertile soil, nurtures the seedling and its environment, and harvests with an eye to the future of the garden as well as to his or her immediate needs. The gardener cares for the whole to ensure the growth of each part. Such is the atmosphere of a true learning organization, where the paradigm of systems thinking encourages growth for all participants.

SYSTEMS THINKING

Systems thinking requires constant attention to the whole along with an analysis of whether its parts are, indeed, interdependent and interconnected. In his work on systems thinking, Senge conceives of an intentional connection and relationship among these parts and the organization as a whole. Members of systems need to learn how to map this whole and follow the connections. In classrooms, this is often referred to as interdisciplinary thinking; in organizations, we call it systems thinking.

Systems thinking fulfills a need to comprehend the boundaries, rules, and understandings within a part of the total system and, at the same time, to discern its interconnections. Although we often think of boundaries as ways of defining turf, systems thinking highlights the relationships among bounded groups. Data provide the energy source for continuous learning. Data are produced at the boundary of interaction between the unit and the larger environment. For example, Figure I.1 is a graphic organizer depicting one way a system functions. Circles delineate the boundaries of various groups, and lines connecting those circles demonstrate their interdependence.

Such systems maps serve as tools for understanding when we want to examine processes and interactions such as:

- how decisions are made,
- how disciplines work together,
- how new practices are initiated,
- how financial resources are spent,
- how time is managed, and
- how priorities are established.

For example, one district's overworked and exhausted administrative group faced the question: "How do we manage to get so many things on our plate every year?" They decided to map one innovation to understand how everything accumulated.

When they came together to address the question, each administrator individually mapped how he or she thought a particular decision was made: Who initiated the innovation? How was it discussed? Where did the discussions lead? Who finally made a decision? What were the consequences of the decision? Was there an anticipated sequel to the decision?

The maps were posted on the wall, and, interestingly, they showed a great discrepancy. The administrators studied each map and talked about the different perceptions. As a result of their analysis, they identified problems in the decision-making process as it was perceived and as it actually took place. This kind of analysis is an

FIGURE I.1

Graphic Organizer of System Functions

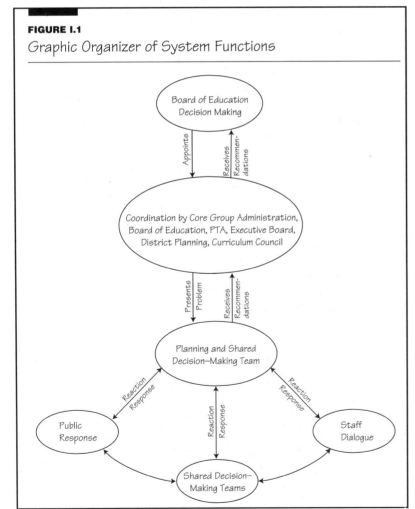

extremely valuable assessment tool when creating an environment for change.

We like to think of systems thinking in four ways:

- All the players are at once beneficiaries and leaders of the system.
- All players in the system see the parts-whole relationship, and they view their particular operation as part of a larger whole.
- Altered or innovative thinking in one part of the system affects the total system. If a creative idea or new approach is employed in one part of a system, it affects all other parts of the system.
- Everyone in the entire system is perceived to be a continual learner as well as a caring, thinking individual capable of complex decision making, creativity, problem solving, and continued intellectual development.

When adopting a new paradigm, all aspects of the system must change in accordance with the new perspective. Paradigm shifting, therefore, does not become fully operable until all the parts of the system are changed and aligned with the new paradigm. Any system is a synergistic relationship of interlocking parts; as one part changes, it affects the others. No one part can operate efficiently unless the other parts of the system work in harmony.

Wheatley observes that "organizations are conscious entities, possessing many of the properties of living systems." Therefore, every aspect of a learning organization—individuals, classrooms, schools, the district, and the community—needs to be dedicated to continual analysis, assessment, and reflection on system practices. The Japanese call this constant state of growth and self-renewal *kaizen*.

HOLONOMY: INTERACTIVE ASSESSMENTS IN THE LEARNING ORGANIZATION

Arthur Koestler (1972) refers to the parts-whole interaction as holonomy. The term "holon" comes from the Greek "holos," which means the whole, and the suffix "on," which means part. The holonomous organization, therefore, consists of two components: parts

and whole. One function of the holonomous organization is to support people in becoming autonomous and self-actualizing. This implies that each unit in the organization—individuals, classrooms, schools, districts, and the state—will become self-evaluating, self-renewing, and self-modifying.

Yet the concept of holonomy transcends individual autonomy and supplies a missing link between the individual and the larger organization. It supplants the dualistic thinking about parts and wholes that is so deeply ingrained in our mental habits and hierarchical metaphors. Autonomous individuals can be characterized as self-regulating, open systems governed by fixed rules that account for their coherence, stability, and specific pattern of structure and function. However, autonomous units cannot exist alone; they are always interacting with a larger unit or smaller units within. The concept of holonomy reconciles this parts-whole polarity and transcends the notion of an autonomous organism functioning only as a sub-part of a larger organization, which in turn is but a part of a still larger universe.

Koestler emphasizes that every individual part has the dual tendency to preserve and assert its individuality as a proud and quasi-autonomous whole, even while functioning as a humble part of a larger whole. This polarity between the self-assertive and integrative tendencies of organisms is inherent in the concept of hierarchic order and is a universal characteristic of life.

Consider the human heart, for example. It performs a unique function with its own intrinsic rhythm and pattern of functioning. The heart will assert this characteristic pattern of activity even when transplanted to another body. On the other hand, the heart's activities are initiated, inhibited, or modified by the autonomic nervous system, hormones, and other influences inside and outside the human body. Thus, the self-assertive tendency of the autonomous heart has its counterpart in its integrative function as a part of a larger system.

Likewise, in an educational community, each teacher may be thought of as a proud, autonomous individual: self-asserting, self-perpetuating, and self-modifying. However, the autonomous teacher is also part of a larger whole and is influenced by the attitudes, values, and behaviors of the school culture. In turn, the school is an autonomous unit, but it is organized around its own unique community, vision, and goals while maintaining an interactive relationship with the larger district and community (Costa and Garmston 1994).

FRACTALS: PARALLEL ASSESSMENTS IN THE LEARNING ORGANIZATION

> The very best organizations have a fractal quality to them. An observer of such an organization can tell what the organization's values and ways of doing business are by watching anyone, whether it be a production floor employee or a senior manager. There is consistency and predictability to the quality of behavior. No matter where we look in these organizations, self-similarity is found in its people, in spite of the complex range of roles and levels.
>
> MARGARET WHEATLEY

Many natural systems possess a fractal quality; that is, they share similar details on many different scales and levels (Briggs 1992). Consider the endless duplication of the patterns of a cauliflower or the repetitions in the shape of a fern. Focusing on any part of these systems reveals a reproduction of the larger system itself. Similarly, any one part of an organization will provide a lens into the whole organization.

We believe that assessment is a potent force in achieving an holonomous organization (one that is interdependent) and gives it a fractal quality (where examination of any one aspect offers insight about all aspects) by:

- providing data about the degree to which various parts of the school community interact in productive and interdependent ways;
- providing data about processes as well as behaviors that affect the school community;
- providing data about the degree to which processes in the school are evident and parallel regardless of position in the hierarchy; we expect

the same set of behaviors and values to be observed in the meetings of the board of education and faculty meetings.
- gathering, analyzing, reflecting upon, and acting on the data in a thoughtful way (see Feedback Spirals in Part II).

Only as these attributes become consistent throughout an entire system—self, classroom, school, district, and eventually the community—will it become

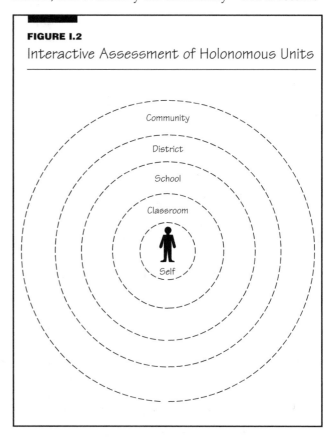

FIGURE I.2

Interactive Assessment of Holonomous Units

Community

District

School

Classroom

Self

an holonomous learning organization. So, for example, a system may consider a new form of assessment in several ways (Figure I.2):

- At the student level: "What constitutes evidence of outcomes achieved at the student level?"
- At the level of classroom teachers: "What might a teacher's portfolio contain?"
- At the school level: "What artifacts would go in a school's portfolio to show evidence of growth and change as a learning organization?"

- At the central office level: "How might administrators use portfolio assessment to demonstrate their growth?"
- At the superintendent's level: "How might the use of portfolios demonstrate accomplishments to the Board of Trustees?"
- In hiring practices and policies: "Do incoming candidates being considered for employment present their portfolios upon application?"

Because the concept of holonomy is interactive, no assessment of any one unit is complete without assessing the surrounding units. To assess student progress toward desired outcomes—cooperative learning, for example—the presence of that quality in classroom conditions must be monitored as well. To assess teacher performance, the quality of cooperation and collaboration in the school workplace must be examined. And to assess the quality of cooperation in the school district, community support and commitment toward collaboration and cooperation must also be assessed. Thus, a well-conceived assessment design includes a search for consistency, congruence, and integrity in the surrounding conditions and climate that directly influence each unit in the holonomous organization.

The word *dharmic* is Sanskrit for deep, deep integrity—living by your inner truth. *Dharmic Management* means bringing that truth with you when you go to work every day. It's the fusing of spirit, character, human values, and decency in the workplace and in life as a whole.

—JACK HAWLEY

References

Briggs, J. (1992). *Fractals: The Patterns of Chaos*. New York: A Touchstone Book.

Costa, A., and R. Garmston. (1994). *Cognitive Coaching: A Foundation for the Renaissance School*. Norwood, Conn.: Christopher Gordon Publishing

Hawley, J. (1993). *Reawakening the Spirit in Work: The Power of Dharmic Management*. San Francisco: Berrett-Koehler Publishers.

Koestler, A. (1972). *The Roots of Coincidence*. New York: Vintage Books.

Senge, P. (1990). *The Fifth Discipline: The Art and Practice of The Learning Organization*. New York: Doubleday, Currency.

Wheatley, M. (1992). *Leadership and the New Sciences*. San Francisco: Barrett Koehler.

From Paradigm to Practice I: Systems Thinking

Interactive Assessment in Holonomous Organizations

No single unit of an organization can function autonomously; rather, it is part of a larger universe and is composed of smaller units itself. Therefore, no single unit of an organization can be assessed without also assessing the larger universe of which it is a part. Coupled with Part II on Feedback Spirals, we now present three articles by administrators who constantly search their environment for indicators that their goals are being achieved: Diane Zimmerman, at an elementary school; William Sommers, at the secondary level; and Michael Couchman, at the district/community level. Each example illuminates the significance of developing a recursive process to continuously monitor the integrity of an organization by examining the alignment of purposes and outcomes with daily practice and the organization's culture.

1 A Systems Approach to Assessing School Culture

Diane Zimmerman

In our personal lives, we often choose hobbies that give us immediate feedback and satisfaction for a job well done, whether it's making a hole in one, knitting a sweater, or savoring the flavors of a new recipe. In contrast, principals often have difficulty finding ways to obtain specific feedback about their work, not to mention the satisfaction of completing something. We do, of course, receive a form of feedback in occasional praise from teachers, students, and parents. Though this reinforcement is gratifying, it is seldom specific enough to inform our practice.

Our first concern is knowing what we should assess. Albert Einstein once said, "Our theories determine what we measure." If we believe that efficiency is an important aspect of our job, we measure success with benchmarks such as completing tasks, meeting timelines, maintaining sufficient supplies, keeping computers in working order, or balancing the budget. These are important duties, and because they give

immediate feedback, we often use them to measure our success. But the challenge for principals is to devise ways to assess the whole building's effectiveness: the school culture. Although we may concentrate on one job at a time, our goal is to transform or maintain the entire professional culture of the school (Fullan and Stiegelbauer 1991). How do we move from a vague sense of improving school culture to an actual measure of change in the professional climate over time?

MENTAL MODELS

Principals must learn to focus their observations in a definitive way so they generate observable and measurable data over time. Sergiovanni (1987) states that the principal must develop "implicit and explicit mental frames of reference. These frame one's educational mindscape, provide the necessary rationale that enables principals to make sense of, and to justify, their decisions and actions" (p. 193).

One way for a principal to develop a mental frame of reference for school culture is to construct mental models from theory and put them into practice. Mental models are a kind of shorthand for describing and assessing our own behaviors, the behavior of others, or the behavior of a particular group. They provide us with a set of productive assumptions that help us focus our observations.

Principals must learn how to abstract key concepts from educational theories and use them to measure an organization and its ability to transform over time. If the application of a model yields useful data, it helps the principal inform his or her practice and provides a useful framework for guiding the collection of anecdotal information. Following are three different models I have used to analyze my school culture and collect anecdotal information about a professional organization, in this case an elementary school.

CULTURAL NORMS

A useful construct for measuring school culture is Saphier and King's (1985) list of cultural norms that affect school improvement (Figure 1.1). The authors suggest that these norms "can be supported where they exist and built where they do not exist by leaders and staff" (p. 67). In this case, not only did I wish to assess my school's culture, I wanted to raise the staff's consciousness of the elements that help build a strong culture.

The purpose of the assessment was to collect data that would demonstrate which cultural norms were strong and which were weak or nonexistent—not to generate statistical data. I had already determined that collegiality, experimentation, and humor were not high values in the school but that traditions and high expectations were.

At a staff meeting in my second year as a principal, I introduced the 12 norms and checked that all were understood. After questions, staff members were invited to cite examples of how these norms were evidenced in the school. To keep their focus on the norms and away from specific examples, I developed a simple

FIGURE 1.1

Cultural Norms That Affect School Improvement

1. Collegiality
2. Experimentation
3. High expectations
4. Trust and confidence
5. Tangible support
6. Reaching out to the knowledge bases
7. Appreciation and recognition
8. Caring, celebration, and humor
9. Involvement in decision making
10. Protection of what's important
11. Traditions
12. Honest, open communication

Source: Saphier and King 1985

bar graph, merely giving credit to an example rather than listing the specifics (Figure 1.2). (A more detailed anecdotal record of the examples could have given richer comparisons later.)

It took about 10 minutes for the group members to exhaust their ability to generate examples. I then asked them to reflect on the bar graph. What did it tell them about their school? This led to a rich discussion about why some norms were so strong and why others were not. This staff had been very independent and, as a consequence, they were somewhat isolated from each other. All agreed that the conversation had been useful in helping them focus on important aspects of school culture.

I continued to refer to these norms in my own assessment of changes in the school culture. I consciously worked on building humor and more collegiality. I went slowly to build trust. And as more trust was built, communication became more honest and open. About a year-and-a-half later, I could cite evidence of all of the norms except appreciation and recognition. I decided that it was time for the staff to reflect on and assess their own culture again (Figure 1.3).

As I suspected, examples in the area of appreciation were not evident. One teacher insisted that she felt

FIGURE 1.2

Bar Graph of Cultural Norms as Measured by a Staff *(Winter 1988)*

	Collegiality
	Experimentation
‖‖‖‖‖	High expectations
	Trust and confidence
	Tangible support
‖‖	Reaching out to the knowledge bases
	Appreciation and recognition
	Caring, celebration, and humor
	Involvement in decision making
‖	Protection of what's important
‖‖‖‖	Traditions
‖	Honest, open communication

appreciated but could cite no tangible examples. This time a meaningful conversation about appreciation ensued. One teacher suggested, "Perhaps part of the problem is that we haven't learned how to accept appreciation." Staff members again stated they had found value in reviewing the list. Another teacher suggested that the two surveys be compared. I printed the results in the staff bulletin so that all could see the changes in culture over time.

FIGURE 1.3

Bar Graph of Cultural Norms as Measured by a Staff *(Spring 1989)*

‖	Collegiality
‖‖	Experimentation
‖	High expectations
‖	Trust and confidence
‖‖	Tangible support
‖‖	Reaching out to the knowledge bases
‖‖‖‖	Appreciation and Recognition
‖‖	Caring, celebration, and humor
‖‖	Involvement in decision making
‖	Protection of what's important
‖‖‖	Traditions
‖	Honest, open communication

TEACHERS' CONCERNS

I have also applied a model for change based on teacher concerns described by Hall, Hord, Rutherford, and Huling-Austin (1987). In this model, teachers' levels of concern are ranked developmentally, beginning with awareness and concluding with refocusing (Figure 1.4). In fact, Hall and his associates have developed assessment devices in the form of questionnaires that can be used to assess change over time. These questionnaires were not available to me, nor was I interested in a long-term study of change. Instead, I was searching for a way to measure the changes in an incremental way.

FIGURE 1.4

Stages of Concern

IMPACT	Refocusing
	Collaboration
	Consequences
TASK	Management
SELF	Personal
	Informational
	Awareness

This mode proved useful for my own analysis and implementation plans. I found that by listening to and understanding the personal and mechanical concerns of teachers, I could help them move through the change process more smoothly. I began to see what might have been termed "resistance" as a normal part of an implementation curve. When teachers voiced emotional concerns, I helped them work through and clarify the sources of emotion. When mechanical issues proved difficult, I supported the implementation with dollars and time. The observation of teacher responses provided a useful guide to help differentiate responses.

SELF-EVALUATION MODEL

I have applied the two theoretical constructs described above to a real school as a way of collecting anecdotal information about the organization. On a more personal level, I use the mental model of cognitive autonomy—first conceptualized by Costa and Garmston (1989)—for my own self-evaluation and as a guide for helping me shape the staff's cognitive autonomy. Costa and Garmston (1994) describe cognitive autonomy as the ability to develop five different states of mind: efficacy, consciousness, flexibility, craftsmanship, and interdependence (Figure 1.5).

FIGURE 1.5

States of Mind for Cognitive Autonomy

Efficacy: People who have a sense of resourcefulness and optimism that creates a faith in their ability to solve their own problems. They are able to define problems within and outside their locus of control.

Consciousness: People who have an ability to think about their own thinking. They are aware of their own assumptions and the assumptions of others and how these affect communication.

Flexibility: People who can think of several ways to solve a problem and are not locked into rigid solutions. They are empathic in that they can think through the perspectives of others.

Craftsmanship: People who constantly strive to perfect their craft. They seek out specific feedback and use this to hone their abilities, knowing that they will never quite perfect human endeavors. Clarity is a hallmark of the precise person.

Interdependence: People who are autonomous understand that they are dependent on others. They have a highly developed sense of altruism and care deeply about others.

Source: Costa and Garmston 1994

My job is made of many complex interactions with others. Many of these interactions are stressful and difficult. Self-assessing my own states of mind has helped me build my resources and my ability to work

with diverse people. Some of the questions I might ask myself about a difficult or stressful situation are:

- What resources do I have and which ones did I use?
- What options did I consider?
- Are there other options I should have considered?
- What am I aware of about the other person's states of mind and my own?
- What could I have been more conscious of during the interaction?
- How clear and precise was my language?
- What specific feedback could have helped me know how to respond?
- How much trust exists between us?
- How can I increase our need for mutual interdependence and the need to work toward mutually beneficial goals?

The true power of this mental model, however, became evident when I used it to interpret events while working through serious problems with overcrowding. When the school grew by 150 students in a single year and did not have enough classroom space, the entire staff was mobilized to develop solutions to a serious crowding problem. I applied this mental model as a vision for how the staff might work together to develop solutions within their control and let go of conditions outside of their control.

I pushed staff members to be resourceful and to think of options rather than complain about someone else's poor planning. They quickly established priorities for space and how to be more precise in their scheduling of these spaces. Some of the teachers decided to team teach physical education to better use playground space and discovered that the interdependence built a better program than any of them had ever taught singly. A crowded staff room made them more conscious of what they valued in staff interaction. The mental model provided by these five states of mind helped me think about and talk with staff members about each new crisis in more productive ways. The staff began to talk about how these small crises had actually been gifts—gifts of chaos. And, because of these gifts of chaos, we had all learned more about how to work together toward a productive end.

These forms of assessment are admittedly quick and dirty. They do not depend on statistical analysis or rigid standards of research design. Put to stringent behavioral standards, much of the anecdotal information would be considered subjective. Still, focused observation can inform practice. If a principal intervenes and his or her observation does not yield a match to the mental model being applied, the principal can adjust and try a new path to reach the outcome. When principals apply theoretical constructs in practical ways, they develop benchmarks that can be used to measure change. What theoretical constructs have others adopted as mental models to inform their practice? We must begin to collect and share these mental models as a means for learning about how we assess our own efficacy as instructional leaders.

References

Costa, A., and R. Garmston. (1994). *Cognitive Coaching: A Foundation for Renaissance Schools.* Norwood, Mass.: Christopher-Gordon Publishers.

Costa, A., and R. Garmston. (1989). *The Art of Cognitive Coaching: Supervision for Intelligent Teaching* (Training Syllabus). Berkeley, Calif.: Institute for Intelligent Behavior.

Fullan, M., and S. Stiegelbauer. (1991). *The New Meaning of Educational Change.* New York: Teachers College Press.

Hall, G., S. Hord, W. Rutherford, and L. Huling-Austin. (1987). *Taking Charge of Change.* Alexandria, Va.: Association for Supervision and Curriculum Development.

Saphier, J., and M. King. (1985). "Good Seeds Grow in Strong Cultures." *Educational Leadership* 42, 6: 67-74.

Sergiovanni, T. (1987). *The Principalship.* Needham Heights, Mass.: Allyn and Bacon.

2. Examining One Practice As a Lens to the Whole System

WILLIAM SOMMERS

Ah, the sense of accomplishment we feel when we complete something to which we've dedicated a lot of effort. This feeling rings true in our professional as well as our personal lives. At the end of the school year, administrators often assess the quality of their school by the number of graduates walking across the stage, the achievement scores returned from testing centers, and the number of scholarships awarded.

These kinds of assessments are easy because they involve measuring, adding, and calculating percentages. In fact, most assessments of school quality have been linear, which works well for predictable patterns. But the simple fact is that life inside and outside of schools is no longer so predictable. Outcomes for graduates are moving from straight fact acquisition to more transferable process skills. To assess this new school organization, new forms of assessment are needed. But how can we find a sense of accomplishment when

trying to assess outcomes not easily seen or counted?

In my school, I try to observe a variety of system outcomes that tell me whether or not we are improving our practices. As part of my information gathering, I ask all members of our school community—teachers, administrators, secretaries, and custodians—the following questions.

1. Do you feel more resourceful in your ability to help others grow?

One way to receive feedback is through coaching. Rather than emphasize my role as evaluator, I join the staff in coaching relationships. Because coaching strategies emphasize a high degree of self-evaluation and reflection, colleagues tell me they have been able to develop their own thinking and see themselves as more efficacious.

Before they engaged in the process, teachers expressed concern over how much time coaching would take. At the end of the first year, however, they assessed coaching as not time-consuming. Staff members reported that they enjoyed talking to colleagues and suggested more of them should volunteer to participate.

A custodian has described how he is able to come up with more solutions by himself as a result of discussing problems in a coaching relationship. In a coaching session, a Spanish teacher would explain her teaching activities using story and metaphor. I would respond using the structure of the story or metaphor. She told me she never views the use of story the same way because she uses story and metaphor as a main source of teaching the Spanish language to students. She said the resource is endless, her students are not as intimidated when speaking about stories, and they make more meaning from metaphors than when using mainly drill and practice. One of our math teachers pursued and completed a Ph.D. degree. He had participated in the coaching program and used cognitive coaching (Costa and Garmston 1993) as a direct teaching method with his students. The students were observers while the math teacher was coached in front of the class by me as a direct teaching strategy.

Creative problem solving by teachers and principals results in new solutions. When principals practice coaching, they take active roles in helping teams form, supporting them, and providing times to meet for planning. Nadler and Hibino (1990) affirm that creative problem solvers are risk-taking nonconformists with the capacity to pursue untried solutions. The willingness to attempt new teaching strategies is evidence of the resourceful nature of some of our staff.

2. Do we have multiple options for ways to think and act as a supervisor, teacher, coach, or administrator?

Three years ago, a secretary named Hazel transferred a phone call from an irate parent to me. After I finished the conversation, Hazel asked, "How did that call go?" I said the parent was very upset, but at least he wasn't threatening to sue. Hazel then asked how I reduced the tension and anxiety with the parent, and I told her I had about 10 response strategies posted by my phone to look at during times of stress. She asked

me if I would teach her those techniques, and in the end I had four meetings with 11 clerical personnel to discuss strategies to handle stressful situations. Without Hazel, I don't believe I would have thought about expanding the repertoire of the clerical staff. And in working with them, I learned mountains of information about their daily jobs that stretched my knowledge base of school issues.

As leaders—whether administrators, teachers, or clerical workers—I think it is important to strike when such teachable moments arise. We all need to be committed to creating a learning environment. One way to affirm a learning environment is to extend repertoire and the flexibility to use that repertoire to anyone who can use the skills. Most times we think in terms of teachers teaching students, but the learning environment must encompass all staff members. For example, a secretary has coached me before I taught a lesson (Sommers 1990, Sommers and Costa 1992). If we cannot create an environment where every staff member can learn, it may be more difficult to create an environment where all students can learn.

People with a high degree of personal mastery are continually learning; they never arrive. Learning is a process, a lifelong discipline. To help fight against what Bardwick (1986) calls "content plateauing," leaders must motivate people to try different approaches, make it possible for everyone to be a follower and a leader, and be open to renewal. People, especially leaders, nurture learning behaviors by affirming and rewarding risk taking when it happens. Many breakthroughs occur by living on the edge, not staying on safe, predictable ground.

For example, two years ago a chemical dependency counselor and I started writing, assembling, and handing out condensed versions of literature about education. Now, half of the staff receives and contributes to the distribution of articles, book summaries, and new techniques about teaching and learning. This produces growth for everyone involved since sharing provides more resources. During the school year, I have observed many staff members using this literature to tap their natural talents and creative potential to develop new educational approaches.

Last year, an English teacher and a biology

teacher team taught their classes around the novel *Jurassic Park*. As a result of this teaming effort, the biology teacher now has students write in a journal a minimum of once per week, and the English teacher teaches writing as a problem-solving process. As part of the journal in biology, students must make connections between the content or the process and the outside world. Parents have commented to the biology teacher during conferences that the writings their children are doing and the connections they are making are more specifically related to their personal world.

The same biology teacher provides alternative ways to complete assignments. Instead of writing everything, some students create detailed mind maps or drawings to answer questions. Students can develop their own study guides with graphic organizers. The teacher also asks for a graphic representation of chapter summaries because he believes this helps all students develop their visual learning.

A calculus teacher asks students to keep journals and write in organized detail their processes of problem solving as well as find the answers on tests. Students initially resisted this assignment and asked, "What workshop did you go to?" But the teacher reports that calculus test scores are increasing and the percentage of students scoring a four or five on last year's Advanced Placement exams was higher.

The visual icons that began showing up in classrooms are another example of seeing thinking occur in our school. Several teachers met to discuss how they could create visible reminders relative to thinking skills. From that, a CAD drafting teacher took Art Costa's intelligent behaviors, enlarged the vocabulary and a short phrase, printed signs, and distributed them to interested teachers. A student stopped by my office a couple of months later and asked, "What's going on? These signs are all over the place!"

Several teachers enlarged an 8½" by 11" sheet of paper with the three-story intellect to a poster size. (The three-story intellect is a graphic model describing three levels of thinking: input-recall on the first floor, processing comparison on the second floor, and output-application on the third floor.) Those are now hanging in classrooms. Some have been translated into Spanish and German. Bookmarks with the intelligent

behaviors are given out to parents, students, and community members. Other bookmarks describe ways to extend student thinking, why teachers make a difference, and how to read a book. Any list or strategies that staff members are trying to integrate into their own thinking can be put on a bookmark or sign as a visual reminder while planning to teach, during the actual teaching, or in reflection about teaching after the lesson.

In Susan Rosenholtz's (1989) research, she discusses her findings that the greater the teacher's opportunity for learning, the more students tend to learn. When teachers have more opportunities to expand their own learning, their students show higher reading performances and greater accomplishments with basic math skills. Teachers who are involved with coaching or discussing alternatives in their teaching ask for more discussion time with colleagues. The teachers who have been involved with the most risk taking, more inclusion of process skills in their classrooms, and sharing of ideas are the staff members who expect and demand more ideas to continue working on their craft.

3. Is there precision in our ability to question and respond to others?

Professionals who ask questions about their craft are self-motivated learners. Teachers who participate in coaching are trying to learn more by asking for precise feedback. Trusting relationships provide a positive environment for specific feedback in collegial coaching. As trust increases, risk taking increases. For example, I had a teacher ask me to collect any evidence of racist or sexist language he used during his lesson. I was pleased that a teacher asked me, an administrator, to collect this kind of data.

Asking mediating questions to increase reflective thinking encourages, enhances, and sustains creative solutions. Using Cognitive Coaching questioning strategies helps staff members with mental rehearsal of lessons, creates alternative instructional processes, and clarifies student and teacher outcomes.

Another questioning strategy being used by our teachers is from LaBorde: the Meta Model. This questioning system is used to increase precision of language. By clarifying terms used by students, parents, teachers, and administrators, the communication among all parties has been more accurate and more focused on outcomes with less wasted time.

Though questioning strategies are vital, response behaviors can be more important. In fact, Lynch and Kordis (1988) say the quality of an experience is determined not by what happens to you, but by your response to what happens to you.

4. Are we conscious about our own thinking and the behaviors of others?

Teachers tell me that because I ask them questions about their instruction, they ask students the same kinds of questions and plan lessons with those questions in mind. Teachers say their students demonstrate more breadth and depth of understanding because of the questions.

My observations tell me I am hearing more efficacious talk, seeing an openness to diverse ideas, and meeting teachers who accept a class that does not work perfectly. I hear more discussion about the process of teaching and how staff members from different disciplines can work together toward common goals.

I have had to develop better listening skills to collect examples of the staff's thinking as it relates to the five questions. By listening better, I've become aware of more information. And when we're more aware, we all have an opportunity to process the information and then modify the result if necessary.

5. Is there collegial support and appreciation for our own and other's continued learning?

Coaching has become the number one way to reduce teacher isolation. After telling one teacher about a strategy I had observed in another teacher's classroom, he remarked that I had an instructional

overview that enabled him to obtain faster help with his unit. Those teachers started sharing ideas together.

Coaching reduces my isolation as an administrator. Teachers have told me they value discussion about instructional strategies instead of only talking about control or management issues. Being in classrooms provides me with more specific knowledge of content and instructional strategies.

Building connections within the building and throughout the district is an individual goal of mine. Senge (1990) describes this as "systems thinking." One of my goals this year has been to develop an appreciation of the interdependence of all staff. I think teachers are in the best position to determine what connections can improve education. As we all learn, we will all move ahead.

References

Bardwick, J.M. (1986). *The Plateauing Trap*. New York: Bantam Books.

Costa, A., and R. Garmston. (1993). *Cognitive Coaching: A Foundation for Renaissance Schools*. Norwood, Mass.: Christopher Gordon.

Lynch, D., and P. Kordis. (1988). *Strategy of the Dolphin*. New York: Fawcett Columbine, Inc.

Nadler, G., and S. Hibino. (1990). *Breakthrough Thinking*. Rocklin, Calif.: Prima Publishing & Communications.

Rosenholtz, S. (1989). *Teachers' Workplace*. New York: Longman, Inc.

Senge, P.M. (1990). *The Fifth Discipline*. New York: Doubleday, Currency.

Sommers, W. (November 1990). "Who's Coaching Whom?" *ECSU Newsletter*. 2, 2: 18

Sommers, W., and A. Costa. (September 1992). "Bo Peep Was Wrong." *MASCD Newsletter*. 9, 1: 2. Also in the *NASSP Bulletin*, December 1993, p. 110.

3 Assessing the Organization

MICHAEL COUCHMAN

osta (1991) summarizes his vision of "the school as a home for the mind" in this statement: "The school will become a home for the mind only when the total school is an intellectually stimulating environment for all participants; when all the school's inhabitants realize that freeing human intellectual potential is the goal of education; when they strive to get better at it themselves; and when they use their energies to enhance the intelligent behavior of others."

In Adrian, a rural southeastern Michigan community, this vision is becoming reality in the form of a seven- to ten-year project entitled "Communities for Developing Minds." This school improvement process moves beyond Costa's focus on the school to include the entire community, enabling citizens and school staff members to examine the needs of our student learners. Through collaborative training, study, and research, we are designing strategies that are intended to change the way our community facilitates learning for all students and adult residents.

FOCUS ON THE FUTURE

Communities for Developing Minds focuses on the future and the best a school and its community can become. By developing new learning traits as a part of a community, learners become more active participants in life rather than just recipients of more schooling. Communities for Developing Minds aims to make a difference for kids both in and out of the classroom. It also aims to enrich the daily lives of all district employees both professionally and personally. Finally, Communities for Developing Minds hopes to improve communication within the Adrian school community relative to exploring and studying topics that will initiate change in education.

One assumption underlying this project is that past efforts to install good ideas in schools have failed primarily due to inadequate implementation procedures. Thus, Communities for Developing Minds places heavy emphasis on the intelligent behaviors of all participants and on change processes that the Institute for Development of Educational Activities (I.D.E.A.) has researched and developed since 1968.

INITIAL TRAINING

In January 1991, Adrian Public Schools received formal notification that it had been selected as the only district in America to develop a prototype of schools of the future with the guidance of I.D.E.A. and Arthur Costa, Bena Kallick, and Marian Leibowitz. The goal was to put into operation all the desirable traits of a quality educational environment.

In August of that year, the project commenced with a week-long summer workshop. For two-and-a-half days, 126 community members representing every employee group within the school district along with parents, senior citizens, nonparents, business leaders, students, clergy, and government leaders came together as a School Community Awareness Team. These "community ambassadors" were instructed on how to acquaint other members of the community with the project. This initial training unveiled "three Cs" that became the cornerstones of our work together:

- Communication focused on how we talked with and listened to one another as a community.
- Collaboration highlighted how we worked together as a community.
- Cognition continually emphasized the role of thinking in our community.

During the remaining two-and-a-half days, 18 community members representing broad leadership roles within Adrian were convened as the "Vertical Team." They were instructed on how they could best support, provide understanding of, and be models of intelligent behaviors to the building facilitator and School Improvement Teams. Because of their various job roles, you might think these team members had

unlimited autonomy. In fact, they had neither authority nor jurisdiction over site improvement teams. The idea of the Vertical Team was to transcend all hierarchical barriers in the district and community to bring ideas and people together representing policy, practice, and management. Because of the tremendous success of this team during the first year of implementation, two Vertical Teams were developed for the following school year. Team C (continuing team members) was expanded to 25 participants and Team N (new team) had 26 representatives with two of the previous year's team members serving as co-facilitators. The 1995–96 Vertical Team will be expanded to include more community business people, with the Adrian Chamber of Commerce being the hub of activity.

Facilitator teams were developed at each site, composed of an administrator, a parent, a teacher, and a support person (for example, bus driver, custodian, secretary, or food service). They were instructed in the processes that would enable them to work with their individual School Improvement Teams. The processes evolved around shared decision making, brainstorming, problem solving, consensus development, vision building, and higher-order thinking—all in preparation for designing a plan of what their school might become. The buildings/grounds, maintenance, and transportation centers along with the central office and Head Start also have Improvement Teams for their sites with trained facilitators.

NINE PRINCIPLES OF EDUCATION

The characteristics of what human beings do when they behave intelligently (Costa 1991) played a major role in team discussions and practice. Through qualified research, it was found that community members from all walks of life who are effective thinkers share the same characteristics. The understanding, practice, and modeling of these behaviors have played a key role in the success of the different teams, and they have begun to permeate classroom strategies for teachers and students.

Also integral to the work of the facilitator teams are the nine principles of education developed after twenty years of research by I.D.E.A. These principles are:

1. Education is increasingly used to prepare students for successful life transitions.

2. Schools make every effort to link students with appropriate community resources that could make a positive contribution to the students' education.

3. Students become increasingly self-directed through planned activities leading to self-educating adulthood.

4. Schools explicitly teach and reward the agreed upon values of the school and community.

5. Parents are expected to be active participants in the education of their children.

6. Each student pursues excellence in an area of his or her own choosing.

7. Everyone affected by a decision is involved directly or representatively in the making of it.

8. Schools strive to integrate the interdependent educational efforts of home, school, and community.

9. Every participant involved in educating youth models the role of learner.

Eighteen to 25 community members were later convened per site as individual Site Improvement Teams. Using the nine principles as a context, they were instructed by Facilitator Team members from each site on how to think about and process ideal educational opportunities and intellectually stimulating working/learning conditions for all staff and students.

After approximately four principles had been comprehensively processed by the Site Planning Teams, a second facilitator training was conducted. The purpose of this training was to prepare for the Site Planning Team retreat and the ensuing Design Teams, which would be responsible for outcomes implementation.

To develop broad ownership in the vision, information about the ideas and discussions of the Site Improvement Teams needed to become common knowledge throughout the school staff and school community. Toward this end, as many discussion groups as necessary were convened in order to accommodate as many participants as possible. Fred Wood, Dean of the School of Education at the University of Oklahoma, has dedicated his sabbatical to working with the Discussion Group concept in Adrian.

The next phase of the project encompassed the Design Team. These teams were assigned to prioritize the outcomes developed at each site during one- to two-day retreats. It was the task of the Design Teams to develop a first-year implementation plan that would move a school toward its desired vision.

In his book *A Place Called School: Prospects for the Future*, John Goodlad (1984) talks about teachers being extremely isolated as they perform their craft behind closed doors. He goes on to say how little time they have within their rigid daily schedules to meet, plan, observe, and talk with each other. In our initial work with this project, we have learned that bus drivers, secretaries, custodians, food service people, instructional aides, and maintenance people also feel isolated. They have communicated a sense of confusion about their role in "schooling," but their voices have often gone unheard.

INDICATORS OF SUCCESS

As a result of the communication, collaboration, and thinking that is happening among both certified and classified staff, sharper images for a climate of thinking are being molded. School buses, classrooms, cafeterias, central offices, and maintenance workrooms are being celebrated as interdependent communities. For example, a high school custodian in her second year as a Vertical Team member recently worked with a chemistry teacher and his class by analyzing cleaning fluid.

Last year, a Vertical Team meeting centered upon a discussion of self-directed learning. Eighteen students from grades K–12 actively participated in the discussion. It was rewarding to listen to a 4th grader from one elementary school talk about the importance of decreasing impulsivity and being more persistent with his work. There was also a kindergartner from another school who talked about his action research project on bears, while his mother described how she worked with her son on using accurate information.

Further evidence of intelligent behaviors and

community was demonstrated during a recent budget reduction of $1.6 million. Since a broad base of staff and community had become participants in the project, it made good sense to design a process in which their input could be quantitatively, qualitatively, and objectively reflected in the budget.

More than 1,000 staff, students, and community members participated in a nominal group process of prioritizing reductions. Trust, problem solving, consensus development, brainstorming, listening to others, flexibility in thinking, and striving for accuracy and precision were readily observable during nine community meetings. Before Adrian's involvement in Communities for Developing Minds, budget reductions would have been determined in a central office meeting, making them the target of emotional reaction because of the traditional top-down approach. With the new process, intelligent community behaviors prevailed, and only 17 complaints about the reductions have been documented.

All of the Community Site Planning Teams have prioritized their outcomes. By the spring, how the outcomes will begin manifesting themselves in new traits of schooling will be more identifiable.

As for the role of curriculum, instruction, and assessment, those responsibilities remain solely in the hands of teachers and administrators for the time being. Due to the significantly increased participation of community members in our school district because of Communities for Developing Minds, I envision greater community participation in curriculum development during the next cycle.

It has became abundantly clear that noncertified staff members' knowledge and understanding have increased due to the systematic nature of this school improvement process. During the last six months, I have observed a growing number of classified staff and community residents becoming more aware of and interested in curriculum issues.

The integrity of our work will increase thanks to the prior knowledge that community members will bring to the curriculum development experience from their School Improvement Team research and study of educational topics. For example, math teachers taught with a slant on learners being mathematicians, and sci-

ence teachers taught as if children were going to be scientists. I believe knowledgeable community participation will create an influence on curriculum outcomes that reflect learners using math, science, social studies, and the arts in all professions.

Parents who are already participating on the various teams have become acutely aware of the terms interdisciplinary, tactile learners, kinesthetic learners, alternative assessment, experiential learning, and outcome based education. As their participation increases, I believe any teacher whose sole strategy is lecture will be challenged by parents whose background information on classroom strategies has been heightened. Though this may seem intimidating to some educators, it could have a very positive impact. The more a community understands the challenges, burdens, frustrations, triumphs, and hopes of the classroom practitioner, the more the seeds of a home-school partnership are likely to flourish.

The issue of alternative assessment may prove to be the most challenging for community and staff understanding. There appears to be a mindset that a learner's performance must be quantifiable in numerical terms only. But with the help of the past three summer workshops involving 381 community members in the strands of thinking, problem solving, coaching, assessment, parent involvement, and alternative schooling, the task may be easier than we first thought. With the guidance of Bena Kallick, 23 of the workshop participants convened as the assessment strand each morning. During the afternoon, members joined other strand representatives in designing lessons for grade-level clusters that would be taught to students later in the week. For example, I was teamed with representatives from the coaching, problem solving, and thinking strands for the purpose of designing and delivering a lesson to 21 early elementary students. The other groups were upper elementary, middle school, and high school. In all, 223 students have volunteered to give up two days of their summer vacation to work with us.

In work sessions on assessment with Kallick during the summer and throughout the year, we learned that effective performance criteria must lend greater clarity to instructional outcomes. In addition to professional educators, parents, students, and other community members can share in the responsibility of learning if everyone understands the performance standards that qualitatively and quantitatively measure a learner's progress.

As an Adrian community, how everyone becomes more knowledgeable of the standards against which learning is assessed is critical. To that end, the assessment strand formulated a series of questions within a context of community, some of which are:

- Does the community understand the whole as well as the parts with which they will be working?
- How do we work for more community inclusion/participation?
- What are the indicators of successful leaning?
- What will constitute evidence of successful learning?

As representative Community Teams, we are trying to focus on what is written as high achievement outcomes and expectations for students, what is taught, and what is learned. In order to examine this more closely, we are concerned with the juncture in which the print transforms into practice and when the practice results in improved learning as documented in multiple assessment.

Currently, 1,711 community members have participated or are participating in Communities for Developing Minds. For a school community of 25,000, I believe that to be significant. And as more Design Teams become operational, that number will increase. Even though specific results of Design Team work are not yet available, I know that a greater number of people within this community have learned how to talk with and listen to one another, to work better together, and to think about intelligent behaviors. I've worked in this community for 10 years, and I'm witnessing a genuine change of attitude from what was to what will be in relation to new traits of schooling as a community for the 21st century.

References

Costa, A.L. (1991). *Developing Minds: A Resource Book for Teaching Thinking*. Alexandria, Va.: Association for Supervision and Curriculum Development.

Goodlad, J.I. (1984). *A Place Called School: Prospects for the Future*. New York: McGraw-Hill.

PART II

Process Design: Feedback Spirals As Components of Continued Learning

Process Design: Feedback Spirals As Components of Continued Learning

ARTHUR L. COSTA AND BENA KALLICK

Autopoesis: (Greek) Self-production. The characteristic of
living systems to continuously renew themselves and to regulate
this process in such a way that the integrity of their structure is
maintained. It is a natural process which supports the quest for
structure, process renewal, and integrity.

—MARGARET WHEATLEY

Healthy learning organizations demonstrate a commitment to change by building critique and assessment into their everyday processes. By reexamining and clarifying various aspects of their vision, values, purposes, and outcomes, these organizations improve communication, share progress, and better align collective goals with those of individuals. But what process design best promotes this kind of feedback and continuous learning?

FEEDBACK LOOPS VS. SPIRALS

Originally, we considered using the concept of feedback loops as suggested by Argyris and Schön (1978). We were pleased with the concept until we decided loops imply that a learner is in the same state or condition at the "end" of a circle as at the beginning. Loops suggest returning to the same place.

Spirals, however, imply a recursive process. They are not intended to define bottom line, summative, or terminal conditions or behaviors. Instead, they can be cyclical guides to learning and continued progress. Feedback spirals are in and of themselves learning devices employed throughout a learning organization. They can easily describe the learning processes for a school's decision-making team, the professional teacher who continually improves instructional practices in the classroom, or a student working on a particular project.

As Heroclitus observed, "You can never step into the river of time twice." When a person steps into a river, neither the river nor the person will be the same again. They have both changed from the experience. A feedback spiral reflects this experience where a feedback loop does not.

Organizations and individuals employ feedback spirals by scanning the environment for clues about the results of their actions. For example:

Some feedback spirals are internal: An artist mixes colors on a palate. When the color for sea water is still not to her liking, she adds a little more blue. After using some of this new color, she stops to decide if she needs to make any more refinements. She re-mixes and stops several times during that day's session. The next morning, she decides the color still needs some adjustment. So she mixes the paint in a totally different way, which she hopes will better achieve the effect she's looking for.

Some spirals are external: A student artist displays his sculptures, then interviews patrons about their reactions. When he conducts another show later that month, he uses a similar interview technique to gather more information. In addition, he compiles newspaper and magazine reviews of the two shows. When it's time for the student and his professor to meet and decide on a focus for next semester, the student uses the interviews, the reviews, and his teacher's oral and written feedback to set new goals.

Some feedback spirals are intricately entwined: A teacher poses a higher-level question and then searches his students' verbal and nonverbal responses for evidence of mental engagement. As students offer responses, they search the teacher's face, verbal response, and body language for clues that may signal acknowledgment. This interaction occurs hundreds of times a day in a variety of subjects.

Some feedback spirals are grand in design: A school system implements a whole language program and designs a system for gathering evidence of its achievements. Feedback is gathered weekly and monthly. Information is considered at faculty meetings, in special committee meetings, and among small groups of teachers who are implementing the program in their classrooms. A variety of school and community representatives will be involved in a year-end review of the program, and they will also meet periodically over the summer to refine the program for the next school year, when the whole process will begin again with a variety of improvements and refinements.

Other spirals are enhanced with technology: A spaceship's sensors monitoring blast-off detect a liquid oxygen leak and the launch is scrubbed. Several teams of scientists go to their computers to compare this launch with previous launches that did and did not demonstrate this problem. Sophisticated diagnostic equipment is used to analyze the leak. When the launch finally takes place later that month, information from both the faulty and successful launches is saved for a new software program that will help scientists predict future launch failures.

Some feedback spirals are immediate: A thermostat monitors a room's temperature and turns the air conditioner on or off immediately upon reaching a preset reading of 72 degrees. When the temperature strays to 73 degrees, the air conditioner kicks back in. The air conditioner turns on and off all day in response to this preset temperature and changes from sunlight through a window, air currents, and thunderstorms.

Some spirals take years: Sociologists follow sets of identical twins from birth through age 40, searching for clues about the nature and influence of heredity and environment on human life.

Others may never be complete: Using highly sensitive equipment, geologists monitor the earth's slightest movements in search of patterns and stresses that will enable them to predict earthquakes. Though they have been gathering such information with continually refined equipment for more than 75 years, they're still searching for the combination of data that will enable them to correctly forecast shifts in the earth's crust.

EDUCATIONAL FEEDBACK SPIRALS

Ask teachers how they use achievement test scores, and they will often tell you that either they don't see them or they receive them after the school year is over. While some schools or districts communicate the data to the school and the teacher, scores are more often published in the newspaper in rank order by school or district. The data are used to compare and evaluate schools or to evaluate teachers. The feedback spiral is thus truncated, as it may not inform practice and discloses little to teachers or to students about teaching decisions, learning strategies, or their interests and achievements.

Schools need to incorporate feedback spirals not only to inform their practices but to guide the curriculum, instructional and staff-development decision making, and the expenditures of limited resources. More important, feedback spirals also serve as an environmental model for staff, parents, and students to emulate.

Consider, for example, a school system that implements a whole-language program and designs a system for gathering evidence of its achievements. Based on the results, more staff development in whole language is offered, and evidence of achievement is gathered again. Or imagine a board of trustees that allocates funds for curriculum materials and training teachers in strategies of conflict resolution. They seek records of the numbers of discipline problems in schools, classrooms, playgrounds, and school-related events. They analyze the data over a four-year period to determine increases or declines in reports of discipline, expulsions, and suspensions. Based on this analysis, they decide to expand, maintain, strengthen, or abandon their support of conflict resolution training.

Or consider a teacher who attends a staff development workshop on thinking skills. Theory, examples, demonstration, materials, and practice of higher-level questioning are provided. The teacher returns to the classroom and designs a lesson based on what was described in the workshop. When the lesson is taught, however, students ask why they are being asked those kinds of questions and why the teacher just doesn't tell them the answer. Driving home, the teacher reflects on her experiment. She revisits her values and goals of wanting students to think creatively and critically. Determined to stay committed to her values, she

designs another lesson incorporating higher-level questions. This time, she opens the class by explaining the lesson purposes, why she's asking those types of questions, what type of response is expected, and how such thinking will be rewarded not only in class but also in later life. She conducts the lesson again and observes for student participation and interest.

COMPONENTS OF FEEDBACK SPIRALS

As demonstrated above, feedback spirals depend on a variety of information for their success. In some cases, individuals make changes after consciously observing their own feelings, attitudes, and skills. Some spirals depend on the observations of outsiders (Critical Friends). And in other cases, those directly

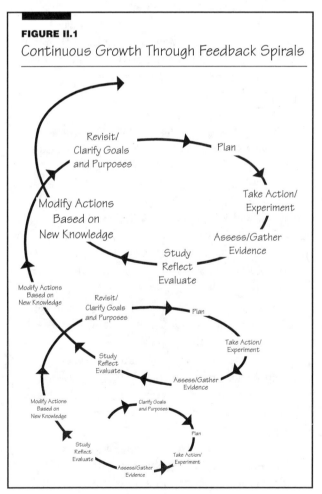

FIGURE II.1

Continuous Growth Through Feedback Spirals

involved in change collect specific kinds of evidence about what is happening in the organization's environment. Once these data are analyzed, interpreted, and internalized, actions are modified to more closely achieve the goals. Thus, individuals—and the organization—are continually self-learning, self-renewing, and self-modifying.

The components of a feedback spiral may be diagrammed as a cursive, cyclical pathway (Figure II.1):

Clarify Goals and Purposes: What is the purpose for what you are doing? What beliefs or values does it reflect? What outcomes do you expect as a result of your actions?

Plan: What actions would you take to achieve the desired outcomes? How would you set up an experiment to test your ideas? What evidence would you collect to help inform you about the results of your actions? What will indicate your outcomes were or were not achieved? And how will you leave the door open for other discoveries and possibilities that were not built into the original design? What process will you put in place that will help you describe what actually happened?

Take Action/Experiment: Execute the plan.

Assess/Gather Evidence: Implement assessment strategy.

Study, Reflect, Evaluate: Whether this is an individual or organizational change, how are the results congruent with stated values? What meaning can be make of the data? Who might serve as Critical Friends to coach, facilitate, or mediate your learning from this experience? What have you learned from this action?

Modify Actions Based on New Knowledge: What will be done differently in the future as a result of reflection and integration of new knowledge? Is this worthy of trying again?

Revisit/Clarify Goals and Purposes: Do the goals still make sense? Are they still of value or do they need to be redefined, refocused, refined? This returns to the first step in the spiral of goal clarification.

Participants in a true learning organization design feedback spirals by which to gather data through conscious observation of their own feelings,

attitudes, and skills; through observation and interviews with others; and through collecting evidence of the effects of their efforts on the environment. These data are analyzed, interpreted, and internalized. Based on this analysis, actions are modified in order to more closely achieve the goals. Thus, individuals and the organization are continually self-learning, self-renewing, and self-modifying.

FEEDBACK SPIRALS AND THE LEARNING ORGANIZATION

Feedback spirals create a situation in which people learn with a higher degree of rigor. Every experience in life can be a learning experience and involves not only action but meaning-making through reflection.

For example, John Longstreet, manager of the Harvey Hotel in Plano, Texas, employs what he calls the "lobby lizard" approach. Each day a member of his management team is in the lobby from 7 a.m. to 9 a.m. to serve coffee and interview departing guests about ways the hotel could improve. One member of the management team drives the courtesy van to the airport with the same purpose. Based on what they learn from the interviews, the team members share their findings, explore the implications of each, and develop strategies to implement the ideas from their guests.

Learning organizations like the Harvey Hotel have a willingness to change by building critique and assessment into their processes. Through those processes, they reexamine and clarify vision, values, purposes, and outcomes. Out of this clarity comes the capacity for individuals to communicate and share progress and to align the organization's goals with those of the individuals who compose the organization.

Organizations and individuals who do not think and act in terms of feedback spirals remain oblivious to the data coming to them. They are insensitive to feedback. They resist or avoid considering and reflecting on incoming data, and they lack the inclination for self-modification. Such individuals or institutions fail to meet our criteria and definition of a learning organization. They stagnate because they have no feedback spirals to guide self-improvement. Numerous organizations no longer exist because they were insensitive to feedback from their customers, they disregarded market trends, or they failed to keep a close inventory of their merchandise.

Such individuals and organizations can learn to think in terms of feedback spirals and to employ them in their processes of self-renewal. We believe it is crucial that everyone—schools, communities, teachers, administrators, students—engage with trusted others to recognize the need for and learn how to design and employ the products of feedback spirals.

> Most ailing organizations have developed
> a functional blindness to their own
> defects. They are not suffering because
> they cannot resolve their problems but
> because they cannot see their problems.
> —John Gardner

References

Argyris, C., and D. Schön. (1978). *Organizational Learning: A Theory of Action Perspective*. New York: Addison Wesley.

Gardner, J. (1965). *Self Renewal*. New York: Harper and Row.

Wheatley, M. (1992). *Leadership and the New Sciences*. San Francisco: Berrett-Kohler.

From Paradigm to Practice II: Process Design

Feedback Spirals As Components of Continued Learning

Borrowing from Deming's principle of continuous improvement, a centerpiece of our thinking about the new role for assessment is focused on feedback spirals as a strategy for continual growth, learning, and improvement. Feedback spirals are more than a theoretical model for achieving change. They're already being used in a variety of schools and districts, as detailed in the following chapters.

Alison Preece describes how educating children in feedback spirals begins early in a child's education as a basis for continual self-referencing, self-evaluation, and self-modification. Jane Fraser demonstrates the collaborative role of parents in encouraging feedback spirals for themselves, their children, and the teacher. Theodore Czajkowski and Margo Montague provide an illustration of the way feedback spirals inform decision making about a change in district assessment practices to replace standardized tests.

4 Self-Evaluation: Making It Matter

ALISON PREECE

The purpose of evaluation is to enable students to evaluate themselves.

—ARTHUR L. COSTA

Until we realize that the student is the best evaluator of his or her own learning, we will never know what our students really know or are able to do.

—LINDA RIEF

One significant aspect of our shifting conception of evaluation is a recognition of the foundational and key role of self-evaluation. We have come to realize that opportunities for self-critical review and reflection are no longer an extra or an enrichment activity reserved solely for the "more able," but are necessary and desirable components of the educational experi-ence for *all* learners (Anthony, Johnson, Mickelson, Preece 1991; Barell 1991; Costa 1991). Autonomous, self-directed, and self-confident learners can realistical-ly and constructively judge the merits and shortcom-ings of their own efforts and productions. Realizing this, teachers at all levels are seeking ways to meaning-fully involve their students in reflectively reviewing their work; in identifying their strengths, preferences, and accomplishments; and in determining areas need-ing support or attention. If these efforts to engage stu-dents in the evaluation process are to be productively exploited and move beyond the superficial, however, a number of guidelines must be kept in mind (Figure 4.1). In the discussion that follows, each of these points is presented along with examples of practical strategies for supporting self-evaluation in elementary class-rooms.

FIGURE 4.1

Self-Evaluation: Stacking the Deck for Success

1. Point out the payoff. Ensure that your students understand and actually experience the value of self-evaluation. Help them discover and prove to themselves how it can make a positive difference to their learning.

2. Start small and keep things simple. Self-evaluation, like anything else, needs to be learned. Expose students to a variety of techniques and meaningful opportunities to practice, apply, refine, and personalize them.

3. Build it in. Self-evaluation needs to become a natural and habitual component of day-to-day learning activities, rather than an exercise or an event.

4. Use it; make it useful. Help students link the insights gained to personal goal setting and activity and program options so that areas of strength or interest can be capitalized upon and areas of perceived need provided for. Make it lead somewhere. Make it necessary. Make it matter.

5. Clarify criteria. Help students articulate, render explicit, vary, and elaborate the criteria they apply when evaluating their performance, productions, progress, and accomplishments. Assist them gradually to enlarge their repertoire of ways of thinking about their learning and the vocabulary needed to talk about it.

6. Focus on strengths. Place the emphasis on the positive. Self-evaluation should be a constructive, confidence-building, affirming experience. Shortcomings and areas in need of support and attention are best dealt with when balanced against an honest acknowledgment of strengths and accomplishments.

7. Encourage variety and integrate self-evaluation strategies with peer and teacher evaluation. Avoid having self-evaluation activities become tedious, onerous, or overly routinized. Periodically undertake perception checks to determine student opinions of their effectiveness and value. Act on feedback received.

8. Grant self-evaluation status and a high profile. Self-evaluations should figure prominently in goal setting when making individualized instructional decisions and when reporting to parents. It needs to be valued, and students must see it as such.

PERCEIVING THE "PAYOFF"

Teachers and students need to understand and appreciate the purpose and value of self-evaluation if it is to be successfully integrated into instructional practice. Both need to understand why the ability to self-evaluate is crucial to successful learning as well as exposure to concrete evidence of the relevance and utility of self-evaluation in their own situations.

In practical terms, this means students need to experience for themselves how systematic self-review of their efforts, performances, products, and accomplishments can have a positive impact on their learning and on their sense of self. Unless self-evaluation is experienced as a plus by students, taken seriously by teachers, and recognized by both as a valued attribute in the world beyond the classroom, it will be dismissed as "just another exercise in doing school."

STUDENT EXPERIENCES AS EVALUATORS

Students can be eased into self-evaluation by having them first evaluate the materials and activities to which they're exposed. This grants them experience as evaluators—a role they are rarely invited to assume in school—while offering a less intimidating focus than themselves. For example, students can be asked to think back over the day's or week's activities and indicate or vote for what they found the most challenging, involving, or frustrating. Then they can elaborate on the reasons for their choices.

Students can be invited to rate and respond to books, films, illustrations, advertisements, projects, and field trips in terms of previously agreed-upon or—better yet—jointly developed criteria. Then they can explain and justify their ratings. "Top-Ten" lists of recommended books in various categories can be generated, and students can lobby for their choices (for example, Best Bets for Younger Buddies, Best Illustrated, Best Nonfiction, Best Textless). As demonstrated in Figure 4.2, instructional materials, texts, videos, and units can be critiqued for appeal, quality of content, and presentation effectiveness.

A teacher might ask, "From which of these two descriptions of the life cycle of butterflies did you learn the most, and why?" Or, a teacher might ask for suggestions for improvements: "If I were to teach this same unit to next year's class, what do you think should stay the same, and what should be changed?"

Peer audiences can be taught how to respond to the work of their classmates by first offering specific

FIGURE 4.2

Student Evaluation of Instructional Units

(a.) Well to tell you the truth I thought it was kind of boring NO efence or anything It's just kind of boring! We could have really carved a tree, build a long house together and even try to weave the way they did.

(b.) Chocolate Unit

I would like to keep the TV things the same. I want to keep the poster the same and the graph the same.

I would like to add a recipe book on the choc. bars I would like to add if we went to a factory and also if we could make a choc bar

My reaction;

Was that I really enjoyed and I hope we do it again.

The first example (a) refers to a study of the Haida. The second example (b) refers to a unit that examined the manufacture and marketing of chocolate bars.

Courtesy of Andrea Lees, Grade 3/4, Chartwell Elementary, West Vancouver, B.C., Canada.

33

SELF-EVALUATION: MAKING IT MATTER

acknowledgments of what is effective before giving one or two constructive suggestions for changes or additions. Peer-editing sessions can be structured so that the editor's first responsibility is to inquire of the author just what he or she wishes feedback about. The editor's job then involves focusing on the specified areas to offer support and practical advice.

Even young children can provide perceptive and revealing evaluations. I once recorded a 7-year-old's spontaneous and thoughtful analysis of the shortcomings of a workbook intended for preschoolers. Rating it "not a good book for little guys," she pointed out numerous places where instructions were misleading, the tasks unnecessarily simplistic, and the layout potentially confusing.

For example, on a page that contained a numbered dot-to-dot exercise, she demonstrated how the page number could easily be mistaken for one of the numbers to be linked up. In every case, the points she raised were flaws overlooked by teachers who had earlier rated the same workbook. Children are natural evaluators, and we need to find ways to capitalize upon, extend, and refine these abilities in the classroom.

CLARIFYING CRITERIA

Experience gained from evaluating materials and activities, and from structured opportunities to offer constructive responses to the work of classmates, provides a solid base upon which to build the skills and habits of self-evaluation. Activities such as those listed above can be easily and routinely incorporated into the daily classroom agenda. Their value lies in the evaluative experience they afford students who are expected and helped to articulate and apply relevant criteria in the process of making and defending judgments.

Learning how to evaluate involves learning how to identify, generate, remember, and apply appropriate criteria so that judgments are reasonably based. By regularly making their own criteria explicit, public, and open to discussion, teachers provide instructive and illuminating models of how judgments are made. By providing many in-class opportunities for students to apply a limited but evolving set of criteria, teachers

help students not only to make judgments but also to clarify, refine, and expand the basis for those judgments. For example:

- How did Jason make the characters in his story believable?
- This author is famous for her precise and unusual descriptions of insects and animals. Can you find some passages that would justify her fame?
- Directions need to be accurate, clear, and concise. Are these?

By routinely requesting that students justify and explain the reasons for, and the thinking behind, their ratings and judgments, teachers encourage a thoughtful, analytical, and responsible stance toward evaluation. As students gain experience, global, "one-adjective-fits-all" ratings like "It's good," "It's interesting," and "I like it" gradually should be replaced with more elaborate, specific, and subtle analyses.

Expectations need to be realistic, however. When young students are first asked to comment on the quality of their work, answers tend to be brief, guarded, general, and seemingly lacking in depth and substance—at least from the adult perspective. Encountering this, some teachers conclude that self-evaluation is beyond the reach of young children and move on to other things.

Like anything else that is learned, children need multiple opportunities to observe others productively and routinely engaged in self-evaluation. For example, a teacher might say, "I'm not happy with the introduction I've written to our class newsletter; it's too formal. I need to make the tone more inviting. Do you think it would be better if I worded it like this?" Students also need to try a variety of strategies such as learning logs, conference records, response journals, self-report sheets, attitude surveys, and portfolio annotations. Gradually, they will adapt and modify those strategies until they have an individual "fit" and personal utility.

Learning how to effectively self-evaluate is an incremental process, and it needs to be approached as such. It's important not to expect too much at first, nor to give up if initial attempts seem contrived or labored. It's equally important that self-evaluation activities not be tedious, burdensome, or ends in themselves.

Children will get better at evaluation the more they engage in it—as long as the purpose is clear to them, guidance and support are provided, and sharing their opinions and judgments does not leave them feeling unduly vulnerable or open to criticism.

START SIMPLY AND USE IT

To successfully build self-evaluation into classroom practice, teachers need to make it useful and use it regularly. Rather than occasional or stand-alone events, self-evaluation activities should be part of dynamic feedback spirals that link and inform goal setting, instructional choices, and reporting to parents.

The easiest way to begin is to start posing and inviting questions that focus attention on the learning process. This need be no more complicated than asking students at the end of a lesson, a day, a unit, or whenever makes sense to think for a moment about something they do particularly well, an activity they try to

avoid, a recent instance where they demonstrated creativity, or a situation where they successfully overcame an obstacle.

If appropriate, they can share their observations with a partner. Questions should be limited to one or two on each occasion, and they should be varied to encourage students to view their learning from a range of perspectives.

Sharing their responses with each other helps students realize they're not alone in their feelings, and it alerts them to alternative strategies they might adopt. If handled orally, the process demands little time and sidesteps the labor of always having to write things down. While it's appropriate and desirable to have students periodically record their responses in learning logs or personal journals (Figure 4.3), the important thing is that students become used to thinking explicitly about their learning.

As is evident in Figure 4.4, children's comments and observations can be impressively perceptive.

FIGURE 4.3
Student Journal

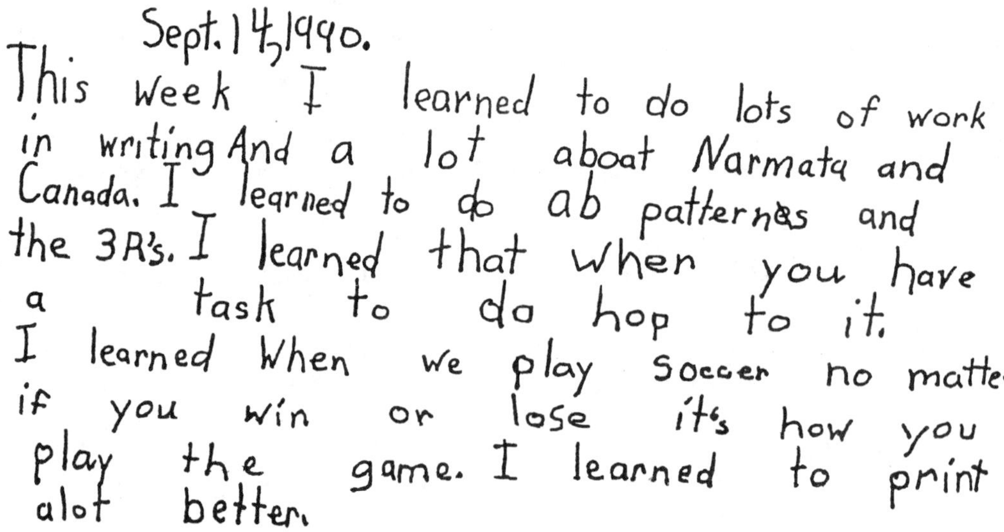

Sept. 14, 1990.
This week I learned to do lots of work in writing And a lot aboat Narmata and Canada. I learned to do ab patternas and the 3R's. I learned that when you have a task to do hop to it. I learned When we play Soccer no matter if you win or lose it's how you play the game. I learned to print alot better.

Weekly "stock-taking" by an 8-year-old in her journal.

Courtesy of Myrtle Miller, Lavington Elementary, Vernon, B.C., Canada.

Written by primary children in response to a request to describe "what learning is," these particular statements reveal an active, optimistic orientation toward learning. For some, this task proved quite difficult and abstract, and their answers consisted of little more than naming subject areas such as "reading and writing" or "doing hard numbers." Students learn a great deal about learning, however, when they share and discuss

answers. The important thing is that such questions are posed and that the invitation to think about learning is extended.

A technique called "Ticket-Out-The-Door" has proven particularly successful with young children. A question intended to encourage reflection is posed orally or printed on a "ticket" that contains space for a written answer. For example:

- I know I'm learning when . . .
- One thing I could teach a friend is . . .
- One strategy I use when I don't understand something is . . .

As the children are dismissed at the end of the day, each in turn offers an answer or hands the completed ticket to the teacher. Some teachers date and file these tickets and use them to help monitor students' developing self-awareness as learners. Another technique for sharing reflections is to divide the children into small groups and give each group a "Thinking Rock" (Davies, Cameron, Politano, and Gregory 1992). The rock is then passed from child to child, with the person in possession granted the right to respond to the question posed or to share insights and observations about learning strategies and successes. Children can pass if they wish. Initially the questions can be quite straightforward; as the children become familiar and comfortable with the process, questions should become more probing and challenging:

- As a learner I'm outside my comfort zone when . . .
- When I need to concentrate I . . .

Much is gained when students are involved in generating as well as responding to these questions. By encouraging them to come up with questions that focus on attitudes, strategies, stumbling blocks, and indicators of progress or achievement, students can construct a rich understanding of just what learning entails.

FIGURE 4.4
Young Children's Definitions of Learning

Lorning Meens that your geting beder each time

Lorning mehs to me. finbing owt Samthing you dont ho abawt Yat.

I think learning means that I teach mysofe somthing

I think learning means tinding out remorckabill things to keep life going.

Courtesy of Diane Cowden, Hillcrest Elementary, Victoria, B.C., Canada.

One-to-one check-in conferences offer obvious opportunities for students to update their teacher about the work they're engaged in and their perceptions of how they're doing. In most instances, conferences of this sort are characterized by a stream of teacher-posed queries designed to efficiently ascertain what's been accomplished and where the student needs to be directed next. Although such individualized monitoring is unquestionably valuable, it can be made more so if the exchange is structured so that the student takes the lead. If the teacher clearly signals the expectation that the student will come prepared to describe what's being worked on, what's going well, and what's causing difficulties, then a subtle but crucial shift of responsibility occurs. It's very easy for teachers to inadvertently dominate these mini-conferences. However, much more is learned if, instead of doing all the diagnosing and evaluating for students, we support them in their efforts to do it for themselves.

By requiring students to keep a record book in which they note books read, assignments completed, projects-in-process, personal goals, accomplishments, challenges, and any difficulties encountered, we help them understand that keeping track of their learning is their responsibility as well as ours. A record book of this type can become a genuine vehicle for reflection if we treat it seriously, expect it to be kept up-to-date, record our own observations or suggestions for the student in it, and refer to it when trying to determine progress made and instructional needs. As with any tool, its value lies in the use that's made of it.

VOCABULARIES FOR TALKING ABOUT LEARNING

Children unaccustomed to talking about their learning initially may need some help finding the words that make such talk meaningfully specific. Terms such as imaginative, creative, reflect, review, hypothesize, analyze, initiative, thoughtful, strategy, and plan need to be consciously introduced, defined, and discussed with concrete illustrations drawn from experiences familiar to the students. Often, little more is required than making explicit the terms and processes we tend to take for granted.

Barell (1991) recommends that "at every opportunity, especially when introducing new ways of thinking (e.g., problem solving, classifying) we should show students how we employ the process or skill using the precise vocabulary of the processes we are modeling (e.g., generating alternatives, comparing, evaluation)" (p. 79). Teacher modeling of this sort provides a powerful and instructive scaffold for students. We demonstrate and provide the tools for talking about learning by describing our own thinking, by thinking out loud as we work through a problem or activity, and by sharing our reasoning when we engage in evaluation.

GOAL SETTING

As soon as children are comfortable discussing their learning, they should be encouraged to set personal goals. Goal setting provides a natural and purposeful opportunity for taking stock as well as incentive for directing and focusing efforts. Obviously, goals should be closely related to students' perceptions of their strengths, interests, needs, and ambitions.

Long lists of resolutions can be overwhelming and, ultimately, self-defeating, so it's wise to limit goals to one or two that are genuinely meaningful. Students will probably need help setting priorities and narrowing their focus. There are a number of ways to achieve this without inadvertently taking over the task and suggesting the goals you would have them choose. One method is to brainstorm with the class a list of all the different subject areas and learning activities in which they're currently engaged. Students are then asked to select no more than two areas from this list and to formulate one or two goals related to each that they seriously want to work toward achieving.

An alternative focus is provided by eliciting different characteristics, qualities, or dispositions that are significant for successful learning in any subject or endeavor (for example, initiative, risk taking, perseverance, flexibility, or thoughtfulness). Some time should be invested in demonstrating precisely why these attributes are important and valued; students need evidence that such things matter. The task then becomes selecting one (or more) of these characteristics and determining specific ways to monitor and strengthen those qualities in day-to-day performance (Figure 4.5). It helps if teachers model the process by setting goals for themselves at the same time.

Another approach is to provide students with a sheet on which they're asked to identify a single goal and to propose some strategies for accomplishing it. On this same sheet, space is allocated for the teacher to select one goal for the student; the student then is asked to determine and record what he or she needs to do, or is willing to attempt, in order to realize the goal (Figure 4.6). An advantage of this approach is that it provides the student ownership of a goal while simultaneously leaving room for the teacher to suggest areas in need of focus. It also highlights the reality that goals need to be grounded in concrete plans of action if anything is to come from them.

A variation that has proven popular with parents involves including them in the goal setting. All that's needed is a form with space for recording the student's, the teacher's, and the parent's school-related goals (Figure 4.7). Forms can easily be completed and updated during the parent-teacher reporting conferences, or they can be sent home with an explanatory note.

Mutual goal setting of this sort signals that the activity is taken seriously. It focuses all involved on things they care about and rallies and coordinates support for the learner.

Experience suggests a number of cautions. First, unless students perceive that the goals will actually make a difference in some way to what they do in school, many will merely go through the motions. Some will dutifully generate goals designed to please the teacher. Others will write down the first thing that comes to mind just to get the task over and done with. To avert this, it's important that meaningful follow-up occurs. It's a good idea to negotiate check-in times when progress toward the goals will be reviewed and discussed.

To help ensure that the goals truly represent something of significance to the student, periodic opportunities to reconsider, refine, or replace them must be built in. Also, there are many small but important gestures that indicate to students their aspirations are valued. One is simply to become familiar with each child's goals so that you can quietly acknowledge and support them when appropriate occasions arise. Instructional options, activities, and projects that would provide students with opportunities to address their goals can be suggested and selected. The importance you place on the goals is clearly evident when you note and refer to students' self-evaluations, goals, and efforts during parent-teacher conferences or in comments written on the report card. To put it baldly, something useful has to happen if goal setting is to be anything more than just another assignment.

To ground the goals in reflective self-appraisal, it's helpful if students are encouraged to ask themselves questions such as:

- What am I good at, that I want to get better at?
- What do I want to be able to do really well?
- What do I need to work on?
- What am I especially interested in?
- What would help me do better in _____?
- Which activities do I avoid or have difficulty finishing? Why?
- What have I not tried yet—and why is that?

To prevent the goals from being overly global, encourage students to specify concrete things they can do right now that will help them make progress. For example, if the goal is "I want to be a better writer," assist the student to reframe the aim more precisely so that an actual plan is developed: "I will spend at least 15 minutes every day on my writing, and I will get my ideas down before I worry about correcting my spelling." Well-formulated goals lead to action; they offer more than wishes and hope.

Initially, students' goals may seem simplistic, shallow, or far off the mark from what you consider they should be attending to. For example, goals recently generated by a class of 6- and 7-year-olds include:

- My goal is to score goals in floor hockey.
- My goal is to write lightly.
- I want to type fast on the computer.
- I am working on speaking louder.
- I am trying to make my drawings realistic.

The critical thing to remember is that these are early attempts and that goal-setting competencies are refined with practice, experience, and exposure to use-

FIGURE 4.5

Student Self-Evaluation

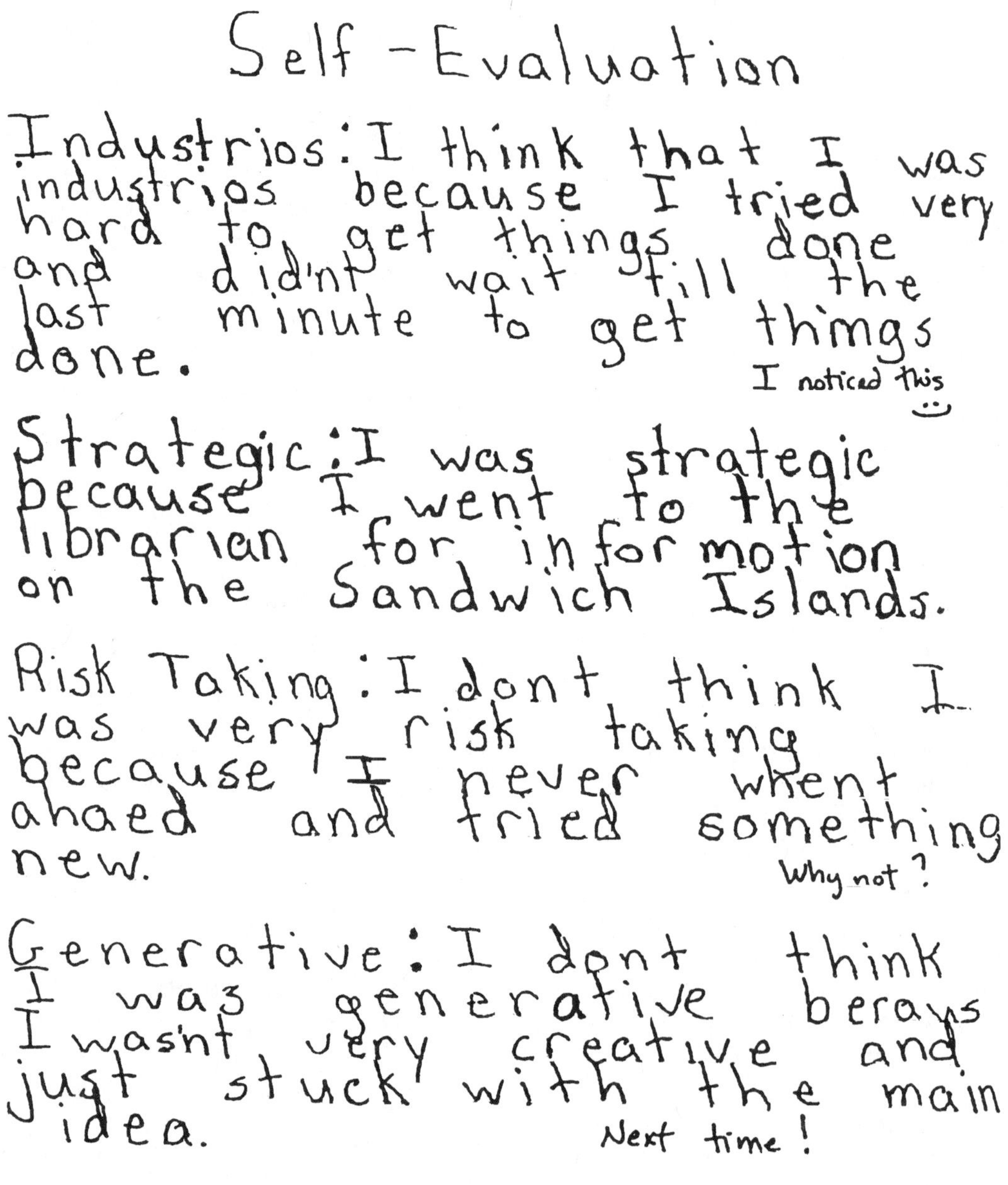

Self-Evaluation

Industrios: I think that I was industrios because I tried very hard to get things done and didn't wait till the last minute to get things done.

I noticed this :)

Strategic: I was strategic because I went to the librarian for informotion on the Sandwich Islands.

Risk Taking: I dont think I was very risk taking because I never whent ahaed and tried something new.

Why not?

Generative: I dont think I was generative berays I wasn't very creative and just stuck with the main idea.

Next time!

Self-evaluation becomes more informed if students are encouraged to consider specific criteria and qualities. This example was completed by a 4th grade student after a novel study.

Courtesy of Sue Smith, Harrison Hot Springs, B.C., Canada.

I I I I I I I I I I I I I I I I I I I

FIGURE 4.6

Student Goal Setting

Planning Ahead

NAME: _____ DATE: _____

MY GOAL IS TO:	SO I PLAN TO....

A GOAL MY TEACHER WANTS ME TO FOCUS ON IS. . . . . .

GOAL	SO I WILL NEED TO ....

I WILL TRY MY BEST TO WORK TOWARDS THESE GOALS.
CHECK IN TIMES WILL BE: _____ 199 __
and _____ 199 __.

Signature: _____

Teacher's Signature: _____

PARENT'S COMMENTS AND SUGGESTIONS FOR SUPPORT:

Careful selection and strategic, realistic planning is the key to successful goal setting. This form was adapted from a model Louise Soar used with her 7th grade students at Doncaster Elementary, Victoria, B.C., Canada.

ful models. The other thing to keep in mind is that the whole point of the exercise is to help students focus on what matters to them so that they gain a sense of being in control of their learning. What might strike us as trivial may be supremely important to a child for reasons we will discover only if we take the trouble to ask why they've chosen the goal.

It would be difficult to overstate the importance of students' feeling some sense of control over their learning. One of the defining characteristics of students who experience prolonged difficulty and defeat in our schools is the absence of both a feeling of control and the belief that anything they do will make a positive difference. All students—and especially those in diffi-

culty—need to set things up so they feel they're working for themselves and directing their energies toward things they value, want, and recognize they need.

INVOLVING STUDENTS IN ONGOING REVIEW

It's not easy to gain a critical perspective on one's own work, and this is especially true for children. A number of easily managed strategies can facilitate the process in an accessible and straightforward fashion. For example, Two-Stars-and-a-Wish, a response guideline usually applied in peer-editing situations, can be adapted to support self-evaluation. Children are encouraged to respond to their work by paying themselves two compliments (Two Stars) and then indicating one thing they could improve or strengthen (a Wish). Easily remembered, the jingle emphasizes the positive while nudging children to consider ways to make what they've done even better.

The Travelling Sticky (a.k.a. the "Peripatetic Post-It Note") is a simple yet powerful technique for encouraging students to meaningfully review the work they've produced and to comment on the patterns of growth they perceive. The procedure, which has great appeal and infinite flexibility, consists of nothing more complicated than issuing every student a sticky or Post-It Note and asking them to examine the work they've produced over a certain period of time. They should place the sticky note on the sample they feel best reflects the highlighted criterion.

For example, students might be asked to review the contents of their writing folders to determine the piece they consider their best to date, or to find evidence of personal risk taking or inventiveness. Math notebooks could be scrutinized for an example of thoughtful problem solving or creativity. Reading-response logs can be examined for entries that reveal interpretation or making personal connections.

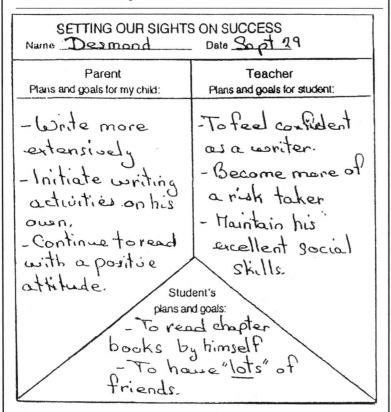

FIGURE 4.7
Joint Goal Setting

SETTING OUR SIGHTS ON SUCCESS
Name: Desmond   Date Sept 29

Parent	Teacher
Plans and goals for my child:	Plans and goals for student:
- Write more extensively - Initiate writing activities on his own. - Continue to read with a positive attitude.	- To feel confident as a writer. - Become more of a risk taker - Maintain his excellent social skills.

Student's plans and goals:
- To read chapter books by himself
- To have "lots" of friends.

From Alison Preece and Diane Cowden, Young Writers in the Making: Sharing the Process with Parents *(Portsmouth, N.H.: Heinemann, 1993).*

The descriptor is written on the sticky note, and the note positioned. Once the sticky note is in place, the student is then expected to explain the reasons for the placement to a partner, small group of peers, or the teacher. After a suitable period has elapsed (depending on the age of the students and the nature of the work), students can be asked to reconsider the location of the sticky note to determine whether, in view of the work produced in the time since, it should remain or be moved to another piece that better represents the criterion being applied. If students can manage it, two or three notes of different colors can be distributed at the same time, each one representing a different quality or characteristic. For example, a blue sticky might be placed on "my best," a yellow on "my most creative," and a green on "most polished." Obviously, the criteria chosen need to be appropriate to the context, and students need clear definitions and examples before being expected to apply them. It's the teacher's responsibility to ensure that the criteria are significant, relevant, and informative, and that students are focusing upon things that genuinely matter.

This review tactic has a number of obvious advantages. It can be employed in any subject area and with learners of any age. It requires little in the way of preparation, yet it meaningfully involves students in reviewing and examining their work over time with a particular focus in mind. Students for whom writing is difficult are not placed at a disadvantage. It makes it easy for teachers to feature and familiarize students with specific criteria, but it grants students the opportunity to determine if and where these are exemplified in their own productions. Finally, the activity is satisfyingly concrete. A child experiences tangible evidence of progress when moving the sticky from work previously rated as "my best" to another piece produced more recently.

PORTFOLIO ANNOTATIONS

The traveling sticky provides a natural bridge to portfolio annotations. Although portfolios are as individual and varied in form and function as the teachers and students who keep them, there is considerable consensus that portfolios should be judicious selec-

tions, rather than simple collections. It is now common practice to have students play central and active roles in choosing the work samples included in their portfolios. The responsibility for indicating the reason for the choices, and for pointing out any particular qualities or features of the selected items, also rests with the student.

Teachers facilitate and focus this in a variety of ways. Some make small, duplicated sheets with different stems readily available in a "Portfolio Center" equipped with staplers, hole-punchers, and glue-sticks:

- I chose this because . . .
- This shows I am able to . . .

Other teachers schedule regular time blocks for students to review their work, complete their commentaries, and update or add to their portfolios. Some direct students' attention to particular characteristics (Figure 4.8) and request they find examples for their portfolios that exemplify qualities such as originality, perseverance, humor, personal reflection, an area of strength, or an area where improvement is evident. However it's handled, the value lies in the students' opportunity to view their work from different perspectives, to make decisions about those pieces they feel are representative of their efforts, and to explain and justify their choices (Figure 4.9).

Some teachers provide scheduled class time for the informal sharing of portfolios with a partner or an older buddy. This grants children an audience to whom they can present their work as well as an opportunity to seek and receive affirmation and specific feedback. It also provides a rehearsal for sharing the portfolios with parents. There are all sorts of creative ways to facilitate such sharing without adding unreasonably to the already heavy workload demands on teachers.

At designated points during the year, portfolios can be sent home with an accompanying cover letter requesting parents set aside some time for their child to present and explain the contents along with his or her learning and progress. To facilitate a focus on the learning demonstrated *by* the products rather than *on* the products per se, self-evaluation and goal sheets can be included in the portfolios (Figure 4.10). Parents are then asked to respond to the child, usually on a prepared comment sheet that is returned to school with the portfolio.

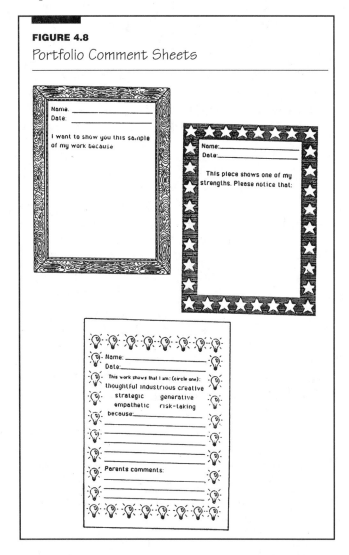

FIGURE 4.8
Portfolio Comment Sheets

Some teachers prefer to invite parents to view the portfolios at school, either by arranging individual appointments during class time or by hosting an after-hours open house at which students present their work. Others involve students in the parent-teacher reporting conferences and build in time for youngsters to present their portfolios and discuss their progress and goals. When portfolios are used in this way, they provide strong support and incentive for self-evalua-

tion and simultaneously provide parents with a rich and personalized frame of reference for understanding what their children are accomplishing and how they feel about it. By the same token, peer and parental responses can provide students with affirmation, confirmation that progress has been made, and specific feedback and suggestions that lead naturally to setting new goals or endorsing current ones.

SELF-EVALUATION AND REPORTING

Ironically, and all too often, students are virtually excluded from the reporting process. Happily, this is changing. The procedures and assumptions surrounding report cards and the form and focus of parent-teacher conferences have undergone healthy reassessment in many schools in recent years. In many ways, the process has become a more open, inclusive, reciprocal, and genuinely communicative exchange (Anthony et al. 1991). Increasingly, students are sharing responsibility for summarizing and interpreting performance and progress. Recognizing that the learner is uniquely positioned to comment on the progress he or she has made, more and more teachers are seeking ways to include student perspectives in the reports provided to parents. If given support and guidelines, even young children can profitably participate and contribute.

One of the easiest and most obvious ways to include students in the reporting process is simply to ask for their input. Some teachers arrange for this by asking students to respond either orally or in writing to a lead-in phrase such as, "An important thing to say about me on my report card is. . . ." Others share the contents of the report cards privately with each student before sending them home to the parents, taking advantage of the occasion to clarify any comments or judgments not understood and to invite students to note anything overlooked. I recently observed 6- and 7-year-olds consulting with their teacher in this fashion. While a student teacher read the class a story, individual children were called to a table at the back of the room where their reports were quietly read and explained. After confirming that each child was clear about the meaning of the comments, the teacher asked

FIGURE 4.9

Student Comment Sheet

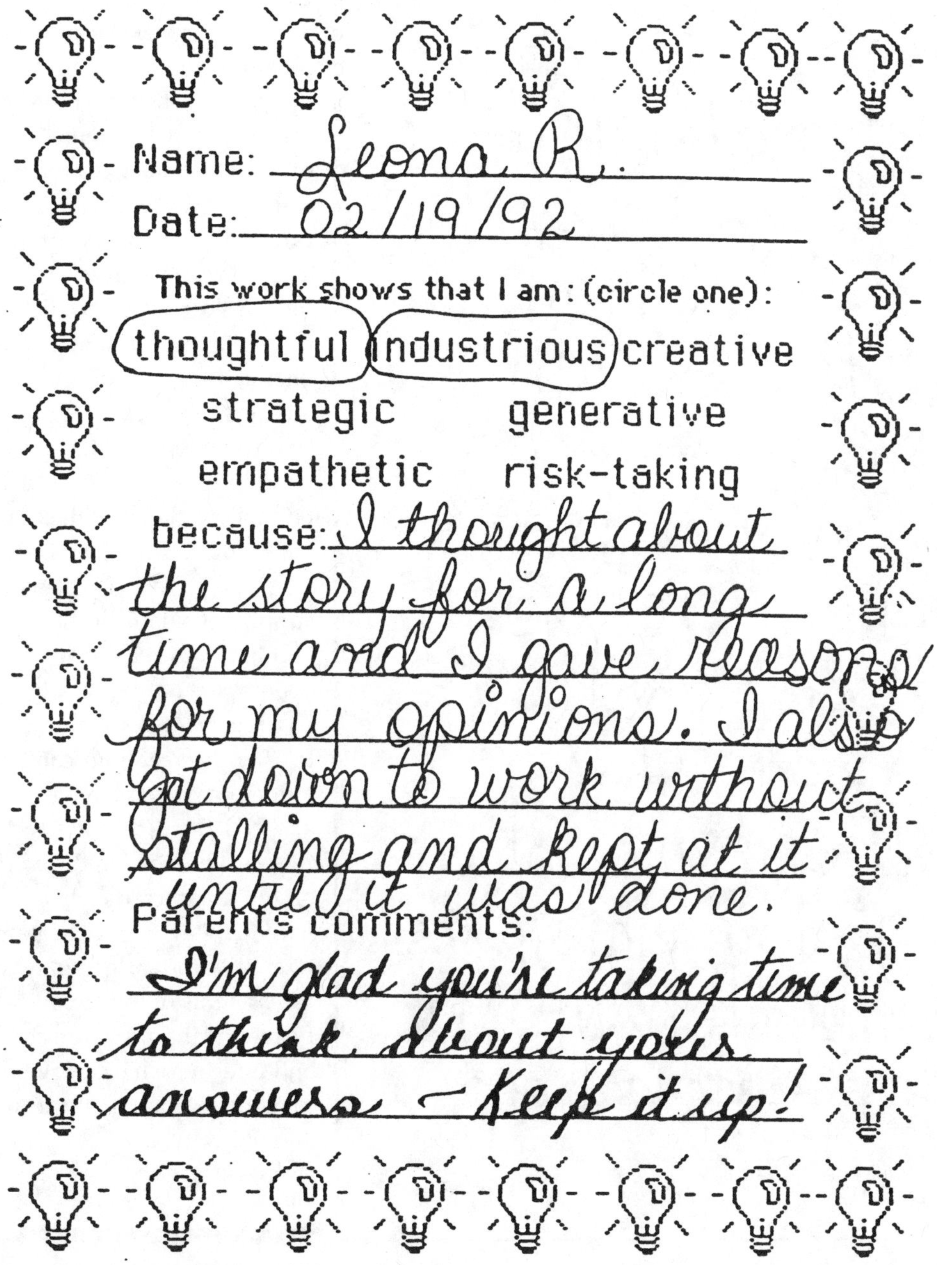

Name: Leona R.

Date: 02/19/92

This work shows that I am: (circle one):

(thoughtful) (industrious) creative

strategic   generative

empathetic   risk-taking

because: I thought about the story for a long time and I gave reasons for my opinions. I also got down to work without stalling and kept at it until it was done.

Parents comments:

I'm glad you're taking time to think about your answers — Keep it up!

Courtesy of Sue Smith, Harrison Hot Springs, B.C., Canada.

44

ASSESSMENT IN THE LEARNING ORGANIZATION: SHIFTING THE PARADIGM

FIGURE 4.10

Student Note to Parents

1. When you see my math drill book notice that I got a lot of questions right.
2. When you look at my snow storm picture notice that it's a good sky.
3. When you look at my Journal notice it's better writing then September.

Courtesy of Andrea Lee, Chartwell Elementary, West Vancouver, B.C., Canada.

the bottom of their reports. The respect embodied in this courteous and inclusive gesture was impressive; clearly, in this classroom, evaluation is something done with children, not to them.

Before report cards are written, and periodically throughout the school year, students can be asked to comment on how they think they're doing in general terms, in terms of any personal goals that were set, and with respect to specific activities and subjects. This can be handled as a learning-log entry, or students can be given an open-ended recording sheet (Figure 4.11). Older children can complete these independently while younger ones can respond orally and have their answers recorded on audiotape or written by an adult. Steps should be taken to protect privacy and to assure students that they can be frank in claiming their accomplishments and in indicating areas of concern.

Observations elicited this way can supply invaluable insights into the learning that has occurred as well as students' feelings about what has or has not been achieved. Discrepancies between the student's and the teacher's perceptions can be discussed and judgments and criteria clarified (Anthony et. al. 1991). Some teachers include quotes from these evaluations in the comments they write on the report cards while others make reference to them during the parent-teacher conferences. Student-generated summative assessments of this type lead naturally into further goal setting; the activities support and inform each other, with both operating to make evaluation a learning experience in and of itself.

STUDENT-LED REPORTING CONFERENCES

Student-led conferences, a recent and increasingly popular innovation in reporting, offer a powerful

if the student had anything to add. Without exception, every child volunteered information he or she wanted included, and this was carefully written for them on

| | | | | | | | | | | | | | | |

FIGURE 4.11

Student Self-Reports

I really liked my confrince very much My mother was really happy with my work. I'm going to keep up the good work.

I liked my confrise because my mom and dad rot good comints on there letter to me. I also liked it because I was in controll.

I think it is a good idea because you and your parents get to know each other better and they learn what you have been doing in school.

On my confrence I felt verey comitable because I always talk about this at home. I felt that I did great! My dad made me laf during it. But other than that it was good.

I thought my confrence went well! My mom was really proud! She was really, really proud

Excerpts from the summary self-reports of three children in 2nd grade.
Courtesy of Diane Cowden, Hillcrest Elementary, Victoria, B.C., Canada.

example of how student self-evaluation can be richly extended to meaningfully and coherently link ongoing learning with the reporting process. Students play no active role in conventional parent-teacher conferences, apart from serving as the subject under discussion. Even when they're invited to attend, students' participation is minimal and usually limited to the role of audience member. In contrast, student-led conferences are organized so that students rather than teachers report their progress to their parents.

Clearly, this doesn't happen without a great deal of teacher planning, preparation, and support. Detailed descriptions of recommended procedures are provided by Little and Allan (1988), Anthony and colleagues (1991), and Davies and colleagues (1992). When well set up, the conferences represent a culmination of numerous experiences of self-evaluation, of selecting and annotating work samples, and of discussing work both with peers and the teacher.

Although different teachers organize for student-led conferences in somewhat different ways, preparations usually involve the following steps. Well in advance of the conference date, students are encouraged to start thinking about how they could demonstrate their learning to their parents. Lists of possibilities are brainstormed and considered. A special folder is created in which carefully selected samples of work are accumulated, each one bearing a student-written note documenting the features thought to be worthy of notice. Some teachers guide the selection but leave final decisions up to the students; others permit students to select most of the items to be presented but also choose several themselves to ensure a representative array. Just before the conference, students review their folders and write a letter to their parents. This letter, which stays with the folder, points out particular aspects of their work they wish to have noticed, summarizes areas of strength, and indicates things they are working to improve. For example, one 3rd grader wrote:

> I want you to notice these things about my work: 1. How neat my printing is. 2. How well I'm doing in art. 3. I'm thinking more so I write more. In math I'm having

problems with carrying, but only sometimes.

As a final, and vital, preparatory step, students rehearse the procedure with a classmate or an older buddy. These rehearsals contribute dramatically to building children's confidence, providing them with peer feedback and pointers, and giving them valuable experience in presenting themselves.

Invitations are sent and appointments scheduled. Because the conferences are primarily conducted by the student, several can be scheduled simultaneously. This means that parents and students benefit from an extended period in which to discuss the contents of the folder (conferences commonly last from 45 minutes to an hour) without necessitating an extension of the total period of time allocated for conferencing. The teacher is present in the room and may join the conference if invited. However, because the whole point of the exercise is to grant students the key role in reporting progress, the teacher maintains a low but supportive profile.

At the close of the sharing session, parents are asked to respond to the child by writing a comment or brief letter. ("Two Stars and a Wish" is useful here as well.) Sensitivity to parental literacy skills may be necessary. If so, casually make clear that parents may respond orally or in their first language should that differ from the language of instruction. They may also write their letters at home. As they leave the classroom, parents are invited to sign a guest book in which they may, if they wish, add a comment for the teacher. On the first school day following the conferences, students are asked to talk about the process and share their feelings about how things went (Figure 4.12).

This way of reporting has proven to have powerful appeal for parents and students alike and to richly complement the information contained in the formal report card. Parental attendance rates are strikingly higher than for conventional conferences (100 percent is common), and guest book comments and satisfaction ratings by parents and teachers are glowingly positive. Rather than being passive recipients of others' judgments, students assume some of the responsi-

---

FIGURE 4.12

Comments on Student-Led Conferences

Reading I am gating good at my reding becose When I whas a littl yougger I guost What thuru the pichers. I yousto red Ficton books but now I am reding non ficton anml books.

Arithmetic My arithmetic is quite good at my point of view. My goals are to not rush my work (the answers come out wrong if I do) and to work on my multiplying and Division. I think I'm usauly good at learning new things.

Writing I'm getting better at my writing. Somtimes I'm careless like at recess when I wont to get out sied but other times I'm not.

Excerpts from the comments made by 9- to 11-year-old students after their student-led conferences.
Courtesy of Shari Vander Velde and Chris Hobbs, Thunder Mountain Elementary, Grand Junction, Colorado.

bility for evaluating and interpreting their own learning in terms of criteria they understand. Students are participants, not bystanders. The process exemplifies authentic, personal accountability in a context designed both to provide and further learning.

PERSONAL ACCOUNTABILITY

Zessoules and Gardner (1991) point out that evaluation should be experienced as "a moment of learning" (p. 51), and its potential as a learning tool should be richly and imaginatively explored and exploited in classrooms. The capacity for constructive, informed, self-critical judgment is fundamental to learning. It is essential, therefore, that we respect and nurture this capacity in our students. Although we will always and necessarily be responsible for evaluation in our classrooms, a key part of that responsibility involves teaching students how to evaluate themselves.

The goal is to graduate students who are confident they can rely on their own judgment rather than be dependent on the judgments of others. If this goal is to be realized, opportunities for self-evaluation need to be built into the school experience and instructional fabric from the very beginning. Self-evaluation is one of the learning basics, and it needs to be a core component of any sound and balanced program of classroom evaluation. Self-evaluation matters—and it can make all the difference.

References

Anthony, R., T. Johnson, N. Mickelson, and A. Preece. (1991). *Evaluating Literacy: A Perspective for Change.* Portsmouth, N.H.: Heinemann.

Barell, J. (1991). *Teaching for Thoughtfulness.* White Plains, N.Y.: Longman.

Costa, A.L. (1989). "Reassessing Assessment." *Educational Leadership* 46, 7: 2.

Costa, A.L. (1991). *The School as a Home for the Mind.* Palatine, Ill.: Skylight Publishing.

Davies, A., C. Cameron, C. Politano, and K. Gregory. (1992). *Together Is Better.* Winnipeg, Man.: Peguis.

Little, N., and J. Allan. (1988). *Student-Led Teacher Parent Conferences.* Toronto, Ont.: Lugus Productions.

Rief, L. (1992). *Seeking Diversity.* Portsmouth, N.H.: Heinemann.

Zessoules, R., and H. Gardner. (1991). "Authentic Assessment: Beyond the Buzzword and into the Classroom." In *Expanding Student Assessment*, edited by V. Perrone. Alexandria, Va.: Association for Supervision and Curriculum Development.

5 Making Parents Partners in Encouraging Intelligent Behavior

JANE F. FRASER

Teachers have many different kinds of evidence showing what individual students have learned in the classroom. Much of this evidence can be shared with parents as a demonstration of "the having of wonderful ideas" (Duckworth 1987). In using certain communication strategies, teachers may play off the very same intelligent behaviors they are attempting to enhance in the classroom, and they can help parents understand what these behaviors are so they can be reinforced at home.

COMMUNICATING CHANGE

Today's world of parenting is often characterized by mini-moments with sound-bite kids who play video games and watch television. Of necessity, parents attempt to find shortcuts for tuning in to their children's school lives. Unlike Albert Shanker (1993), who has contended that many parents do not take an interest in their children's education, I find that parents are deeply interested in what is happening at school. They want to know how their kids are doing in relation to others as well as to themselves. Thus, teachers are challenged to help students learn how to convey the world of school to those who are not participating in it and may not even be familiar with it.

School life has changed. Many classrooms are profoundly different from those in which parents sat 30 years ago. The adult is no longer the single authority figure imparting wisdom to the uninitiated. Students often command authority with their knowledge. There is a focus on talk as students share and learn from each other.

Communications within the classroom and between school and home may be visualized through a Venn diagram of the three sets of participants: students, parents, and teachers (Figure 5.1). Each intersection represents mutual interactions. All of these intersections are needed to create a whole when thinking about quality communications both in and out of school.

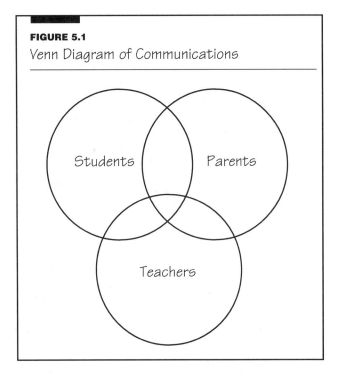

FIGURE 5.1
Venn Diagram of Communications

In the theater of school, all actors enhance their performance through feedback spirals by communicating needs, desires, thoughts, achievements, aspirations, and expectations. Thoughtful listening to both students and parents can inform the teacher's actions and decisions. The teacher will know when to intervene, focus, or stimulate the conversations. The quality of the dramatics are further refined when students learn to listen to and learn from each other. And by encouraging parents to participate in the drama, both students and teachers will have additional insights and thoughts upon which to act. The lasting effects of learning will be increased for the student who enjoys being the teacher at home—summarizing, synthesizing, and sharing with parents.

PARENT CONFERENCES AND PORTFOLIOS

Conferencing with parents has long been a part of regular communication between school and home.

Twenty-five years ago, teachers simply sent home letters containing times for conferences that were scheduled for their own convenience. Now it's necessary to schedule these conferences at the convenience of the parent, often at night. While teachers have discovered new and more insightful ways to share student work, such as the student portfolio, this sharing must of necessity occur at a time that fits into a busy parental life.

When I was a beginning teacher, I knew that it was important to share student work with parents. I now realize that the collection of work was haphazard and sometimes without a theme or clearly understood purpose. I looked for work that pleased me and I thought would please the parent.

Today, sharing student efforts is purposeful. I select some works; students select others. The students' selections are accompanied by a written explanation of why they chose a particular item. This explanation may reveal how the work reflects the student's view of himself as a learner. It may tell why the particular piece of work is important to him or why he believes it is his best. Such evaluation helps students develop feedback spirals by becoming self-critical and reflective while it also leads toward further learning. Sharing the student's thoughts with parents brings them into the feedback spiral of reflection and learning.

Now, the portfolio pieces I select demonstrate how a student met certain outcomes. Whether I am teaching 2nd or 5th grade, I can select pieces of writing that demonstrate a knowledge of metacognition and flexibility of thinking. A piece with revisions may demonstrate persistence in solving a problem. When sharing such works at a conference, I can bring parents up to speed by the way I discuss the reasons for my selections. I can help them join discussions both with me and with students at a level far different from "What did you do in school today?"

REHEARSAL FOR SHARING

While some students are natural communicators, others are not. It's not unusual for parents to ask, "Did you have a good day at school?" Yet many say their children do not wish to share. Others say their children simply talk about a problem on the playground. While it may be psychologically healthy for a parent to listen to talk about a recess argument, this kind of conversation doesn't meet a parent's need to understand how a child is doing academically. Because of this, I developed the following rehearsal strategy to process the day at school prior to dismissal.

For five minutes at the end of the school day, it is helpful to sit in a circle and specifically discuss the day's events. This gives the teacher insight into what is important to each student and what has been learned. It gives students the opportunity to hear each other's voices and learn from their peers (Harste, Short, and Burke 1988; Newkirk 1992). The question changes each day, although repeated practice with a relevant question is beneficial. The question is focused on what I consider central to thinking about the day. Posing the question early in the school day highlights and encourages actions and thoughts that lead to desired behaviors. Questions I might pose are:

- What was the most important thing that happened to you in reading today? Why?
- Why did we have a 10-minute silent writing period today, and what did you do during that time?
- Explain in three or four sentences what you read during silent reading today.
- What did your reading response group discuss today? Did the discussion help you understand your reading, and why?
- What did you write about in your reading journal today, and why?
- When you teach the poem "Lazy Witch" by Myra Cohn Livingston, what will you say is your favorite part, and why?

Some useful rules for these conversations are:

- It is important to listen to each other.
- Try to say something that no one else has said.
- Focus on the question.
- Plan ahead what you wish to say.
- Two or three sentences is the maximum.
- You may pass when it is your turn.

My regular questioning techniques use wait time and follow-up questions designed to focus a student's comment to make it more specific. This includes the frequent use of cues such as "because," "why," "in addition to," "give evidence," and "be specific."

This processing encourages students' synthesis, metacognition, and evaluation at the conclusion of the day. It puts closure on the day, helps students remember what has occurred, and enables them to hear the thinking of others. It refocuses thoughts and sets the stage for school-home-school communication as well as for the next step in learning.

Feedback from parents about this strategy has been encouraging. For example, one said that she felt it was helpful for her son to listen to classmates. Another noted that her daughter had begun to talk with more insight about her day in school and was now willing to add details about specific things she had done in class. Keeping parents linked to the classroom gives them a definite feeling of participation.

FOCUSED WRITTEN SHARING

The strategy of focused written sharing is a variation on the verbal rehearsal. I put up a large piece of newsprint at the beginning of an academic period. The question I plan to pose before dismissal is written at the top of the paper. This question is discussed earlier in the school day, giving an opportunity for students to rehearse for the activity. At an appropriate time, everyone writes a memo on the paper that is focused on the question. Examples of questions are:

- Today I observed and drew my tree in science. I noticed the following changes: . . .
- Here are three things I learned about Martin Luther King . . .
- The best language I used in my writing today was . . . because . . .
- I predict that the next thing Wilbur will do in *Charlotte's Web* is . . . because . . .
- What I learned when I used pattern blocks today was . . .

The completed chart is given to a student to take home for sharing. This strategy enables parents to focus their discussion about school. I make sure that everyone has a turn to take a chart home by using a class list as a check-off sheet.

NEWSLETTER OF STUDENT COMMENTS

At the conclusion of a favorite read-aloud, I record students' comments in my journal as they discuss their reactions and evaluations of the book. I use these comments to compose a circular for parents. One purpose is to share student thoughts with them so they gain a sense of what we do when we finish reading a book. It also helps parents join in discussion at home.

After reading aloud *The Little House in the Big Woods* (Wilder 1953), students in my 2nd grade classroom shared the following thoughts that were then typed and sent home:

- I liked how Pa told stories to Laura and Mary. He had a good imagination.
- I heard this book before. I didn't remember it. I was really little.
- You learn stuff from this book. And I learned that reading a book twice is better than reading it once.
- I learned how they made bullets.
- I really like this book because of the long chapters. The author made them really interesting because you felt you were there.
- My favorite part was the characters. I liked Laura best. She had some of the same problems I do because I am also a middle child.
- I learned how to make cheese and how to take corn off the cob.
- It leaves you in suspense. You don't know what will happen next. I made a lot of predictions.
- It is fun to hear what the next chapter title is. It gives you clues about what is going to happen.
- I liked baby Carrie. She is cute and everyone likes her.
- I like to read about colonial [sic] times. They couldn't have as much fun as we do on Sunday. They had a job to do everyday.
- My favorite characters were Pa and Laura. I think they were the main characters, partly because Laura wrote the story. I liked Pa's stories. They were funny.

"ROOM 13 NEWS"

Another type of newsletter is written by students. "Room 13 News" is an experience chart written by the class. The writing has two purposes. The first is to serve reading instruction; the second is to inform parents. We write the newsletter often in September and October. Later in the school year, it is written after a special experience that warrants pulling together the thoughts of the group to create a totality.

We may write "Room 13 News" following a field trip, an assembly program, a new lesson such as learning a solitaire game to teach math facts, a science experience, the completion of a class project, a special visitor, or a rewarding writing period. "Room 13 News" pulls parents into the classroom life and summarizes the purpose of an activity for students. It encourages synthesis, metacognition, and evaluation while helping the teacher understand what students value in a particular activity, what they have learned, and how they are responding in terms of intelligent behaviors.

LETTERS TO PARENTS

A new student is a tabula rasa for a teacher in September. That's when I write letters to the parents of my students. The purpose is to bring me closer both to parents and my new students. I ask parents to answer three questions:

- What would you like me to know about your child?
- How does your child spend time on his/her own at home?
- What are your goals/expectations for your child this year?

The answers can be extremely thought provoking. They pull me into alignment with parental views early in the school year as well as give me information I would not have otherwise. They open a dialogue between home and school at a different level than before I wrote the letters.

For example, Richard's mother wrote, "Our major concern is for Richard to develop as a person. We know he's intelligent and is eager to learn the academics—but we're more concerned with his self-esteem. If he has good self-esteem, we feel everything else will fall into place. . . . Our goal is for Richard to be a well-rounded, curious, expressive, and most of all HAPPY child at the end of 2nd grade."

Kari's mom said, "She hides her feelings about most things. She is very sensitive. She is the peace-maker if someone is upset or hurt."

And Jim's mother reported, "He is very concerned about obeying regulations, and he never likes to do anything out of line. On the other hand, he is upset by regulations that make no sense to him. It is very important to him that everything be fair."

PHONE CALLS TO PARENTS

Phone calls are a quick way to enrich school-home communication. I use them for positive communication, phoning home when something special has occurred, no matter how small it may seem. Perhaps Paul has never before made a positive comment to Brian about his behavior. Amy may have made a great inferential comment in her reading response group. Andrew may have contributed a personally sensitive thought to the reading share to which Michael responded positively.

Some schools have institutionalized such phone calls by asking teachers to phone two parents each day. Parents say these comments help them feel a part of that mystery time when their children are away from home.

PARENTAL HELP WITH PUBLISHING

Parents can be especially helpful with classroom publishing. I have taught parents to help with this very time-consuming activity. Training parents to help with student editing, for example, helps them understand what is expected of a child in the classroom. Parents also assist with typing and binding student writing. They enjoy spending time working in the classroom during Writer's Workshop to see how I help my students and how their own children work. Some teachers prefer privacy and set up a computer work station in the hall once parents understand what is expected.

PARTIES

I have worked to find ways to contain and focus the excitement before and during a class party. To do this, I include a student activity such as a short play, some choral reading, poetry recitation, or Readers' Theater. This becomes a short-and-sweet culminating activity that is naturally related to the days and weeks preceding the party. We do not spend much additional time preparing a performance because it is informal and is something that has already been done successfully.

Parents who come to the party enjoy seeing how their children function in the group. Also, they may not otherwise be aware of the fact that the class has learned something like the metaphorical poem "Spring Is . . ." by Bobbi Katz. Dialogue at home is a natural follow-up to these kinds of party activities.

READING RESPONSE JOURNAL

The homework in my school includes reading for pleasure 20 to 30 minutes daily. A response journal for home begins halfway through the school year, after students have the opportunity to learn some strategies for responding to books. This activity is voluntary.

Many families find the response journal a constructive way of reading together. I make a notebook with perhaps a dozen pages and bind it together with an oak-tag cover, which students love to illustrate. The notebook goes home on Monday and is returned to school on Friday. A letter to parents suggests that they may enjoy reading with their children. Inside the cover of the journal I staple a list of possible ways to respond to reading. This same list—which has been written over a period of time by the class—is posted in the classroom.

I ask students and parents to read a book of the child's choice together. When the chapter or the book is finished, students and parents each write a brief response to the book in the journal. When these journals are returned, I write my response. This is done weekly for a month or so. Parent feedback is excellent. The journal encourages fulfillment of the homework and helps parents understand how books are discussed in the classroom. A parent learns that we don't simply say, "I liked the book." Instead, they discover that we attempt to state concisely what we liked and why with specific references to the text and illustrations. Or, we may compare this book with another we have read.

OTHER CELEBRATIONS

Inviting parents to an Authors' Share is another way of reporting good news. This activity especially helps educate parents about how the classroom operates differently since they were in school. On this occasion I take the opportunity to speak to parents briefly about my educational beliefs, including the purpose of the gathering, the close connection between reading and writing, the importance of choice, and the importance of student questions and comments. This helps parents understand the writing process as well as some of my goals and expectations.

This type of sharing is appropriate several times during the year. I find it more meaningful than the traditional play performance because it is an opportunity to share the daily functioning of the group. Children choose which pieces of writing they wish to share. A dress rehearsal alleviates nervousness. The room can be made festive with decorations and refreshments, and chairs are arranged so visitors sit on the perimeter of a circle or oval. It is helpful to provide time to visit informally at the conclusion of the share.

I also invite parents to Poetry Shares. A variety of activities can take place. Children recite their own poetry or that of published authors. They recite alone, with a partner, with several people, or as a class. This is a little closer to a play performance, but I feel it is important to allow students to plan, rehearse, and critique this activity with my guidance.

CLASSROOM PRESENTATIONS BY PARENTS

If a family has had a unique experience or taken a special trip, this may provide an occasion for a visit. For example, the father of one of my students named Michael was born in Egypt. The whole family spent a month in Egypt the summer after Michael completed

1st grade. At the beginning of 2nd grade, Michael wrote a book, *My Trip to Egypt*. Many children were intrigued, and we invited Michael's parents to visit our classroom. They brought artifacts, coins, and library books for the children to use—plus that all-important item of food. After their exciting visit, several students became interested enough to do some research and writing. These 2nd graders were especially intrigued with ancient Egypt, the tombs, mummies, the gods, and legends. Michael's parents had given the impetus to some excellent classroom research, and it was possible for me to teach research skills to those who were interested. "Room 13 News" let everyone know what happened.

FAMILY MATH

The Family Math program devised by the EQUALS Project at the University of California, Berkeley, is another concrete example of how teachers can educate parents about school curriculum and newer ways in which concepts are taught. My school invites children at a particular grade level to attend school with one parent one night for approximately an hour-and-a-half. Teachers organize four or five activities for their classrooms. Attendees are divided into groups and rotate among the classrooms with each parent and child visiting several classrooms together.

All activities focus on teaching mathematical concepts through games and manipulatives. Each classroom may focus on a different concept such as estimation, measurement, graphing, problem solving, or probability. At both the beginning and end of the evening, our principal speaks to the group about the purpose of teaching math using manipulatives with an emphasis on thinking skills.

Mathematics instruction now concentrates on concepts using manipulatives and on mathematical reasoning. I have often heard parents say they don't understand math, especially the way it is being taught today. Family Math Night is a way of helping them feel more familiar with what is going on in their children's schools.

"PICTURE PEOPLE"

My school has a series of laminated art posters from museums. They are kept in the school library, where parent volunteers choose a picture and learn about the artist. Then the parent comes to the classroom to make a short presentation, which may be combined with some kind of activity.

A parent in my classroom who was extremely interested in quilts used her own pictures to talk with children about that special art form. I prepared some geometric shapes with construction paper, and students enjoyed creating their own quilt patterns. The children learned about the geometry of quilt making using manipulatives. What I find most fascinating about this program is that students use the strategies they have learned to talk about children's books, authors, and peer writing when they discuss art and the artists. Sample comments from a presentation about Joan Miró included:

- I wonder where he got that idea?
- He made them to look not realistic. He is different from other artists in that way. He draws flat like a kid would.
- It looks like he let his imagination run.
- I can't figure out how he did it.
- I don't think it is meant to be anything. He just painted what he was feeling.

The children felt free to speculate. They noticed details and were responsive to the art in the same ways in which they had learned to respond to their books and illustrations. Having a parent lead this activity permitted me to observe my students and revel in their learning.

VIDEOTAPING

Using videotape is a telling strategy to help parents understand what is going on at school and how their children are functioning. Each child brings in a videotape, and I make individual recordings that are sent home at intervals and are a record to keep at the end of the year.

I tape individual reading once a month. I also tape students sharing an Author's Share. Science lessons, reading response groups, math classes, and writing workshops can be recorded. A Poetry Recitation or a Reader's Theater performance make good viewing. I find the most difficult aspect of taping is to have the room quiet enough so a child's voice can be heard well on the tape. We worked on achieving a quiet room and not walking in front of the camera.

No matter how teachers choose to share with parents, I feel it is important to take into account the fact that they are extremely busy and not conversant with the practices in today's classrooms. Since we ourselves are also overloaded with the pressures of our profession, it is important for us to find ways to accomplish our goals in an integrated way.

When thinking about parent communication, I have found it beneficial to look for strategies that not only help me but, more importantly, help students become self-analytical and reflective. In doing this I have tried to become an educator on several levels. Integrating classroom strategies that encourage intelligent behavior with teaching parents how to encourage these behaviors in their children is a powerful goal for home-school communication.

References

Duckworth, E.R. (1987). *The Having of Wonderful Ideas and Other Essays on Teaching and Learning.* New York: Teachers College Press.

Harste, J.C., K.G. Short, and C. Burke. (1988). *Creating Classrooms for Authors.* Portsmouth, N.H.: Heinemann.

Newkirk, T. (1992). *Listening In.* Portsmouth, N.H.: Heinemann.

Shanker, A. (February 7, 1993). "Where We Stand." *The New York Times News of the Week in Review.*

Wilder, L.I. (1953). *Little House in the Big Woods.* New York: Harper and Row.

6 Preparing for Change: Standardized Tests or Authentic Assessment?

THEODORE CZAJKOWSKI AND MARGO MONTAGUE

Over the last few years, our district teachers became dissatisfied with using standardized tests to measure learning growth. Instead of approaching change with the traditional process of hours of discussion followed by committee decision making, we decided to use the model of a feedback spiral. We started by examining the purpose for our work, then moved to planning for change based on careful study of knowledge in the field. We used focus groups and action research groups to develop a more refined knowledge of our community of teachers, learners, and parents. Then we studied, reflected, and evaluated the results of our investigation.

After two years of thoughtful research and experimentation, we designed portfolios to collect evidence of student work. We also designed a new report card that is carefully aligned with those portfolios. As we made our way through the feedback spiral, we realized the value of thinking about change as a recursive process that can lead to continuous improvement.

GOALS AND PURPOSES

As we began this process, our district teachers wanted to find answers to the following questions:

- How well are students performing relative to our curriculum goals?
- How well are students performing relative to some standard of quality?
- How can we improve instruction for groups and individual students based on good information about student progress and performance?

These questions defined our purpose: to refine our assessment practices so we could discuss and report on student progress with a larger understanding than our current informal system provided. We decided that we had several goals:

- To serve student learning,
- To improve teacher decision making about instruction, and
- To improve our ability to report progress to parents.

Prior to undertaking this task, we had found little support among our primary teachers for developing new assessment procedures, but it seemed at least necessary to get some substantive measure of achievement at or about the end of 2nd grade to verify that our instructional programs were successful. We extended our state-mandated 4th and 8th grade Metropolitan Achievement Tests down to 2nd grade. Our primary teachers were quite displeased with this solution. In fact, they felt that adding standardized tests—especially at that stage of development—would create developmentally inappropriate conditions for measurement, possibly doing more harm than good. They now seemed ready to help develop an alternative more consistent with their professional beliefs about children.

It is against this backdrop that our district sought assistance from Bena Kallick and began an exciting adventure to develop our own authentic assessment procedures in the language arts. We had long been proponents of developmentally appropriate instruction, particularly in the kindergarten program. We knew at this point that standardized tests were not the answer, but we couldn't specify what the alternative should look like.

USING ACTION RESEARCH

We asked a variety of primary classroom teachers, reading teachers, and Chapter One teachers to join a committee that would design a process for rethinking our assessment practices. This group became knowledgeable in the research and practices of assessment, especially focusing on authentic assessment. After careful study of the work of others, they decided to experiment with new assessment practices in their classrooms.

Their plan was to set up action research teams. Each team agreed to focus on an aspect of assessment they believed would answer the teacher questions

detailed above. One team focused on using a running reading record and miscue analysis. Another team decided to design a method for collecting evidence of student performance in the play area. Still another team decided to develop portfolios.

As our work progressed, we found that what began as a search for appropriate assessment procedures for students in primary language arts expanded into aligning our written, taught, and learned curriculum and instruction. As we began to describe literacy for primary children in language arts, it became clear that the student activities in the classroom should have enough breadth, depth, and integrity to also function as assessment.

IMPLEMENTATION, STUDY, REFLECTION

Committee members returned to their school buildings with an enthusiasm and vigor for experimentation. They invited colleagues to join their research teams on a voluntary basis, and many did. They agreed on their practices and what they would collect as evidence of student learning.

Months later, each research team brought to a meeting the work they had collected from students. We spent a considerable amount of time studying the work and discussing its meaning for us as teachers and for students as learners. After much consideration, we decided the running reading record was a powerful tool for assessing reading, but miscue analysis seemed too difficult at this time. We decided to offer workshops on the running reading record for any teacher who would like to learn the technique, and we agreed that it would be a useful districtwide tool when all teachers were ready to use it.

The team that tried to develop prompts and assessments in the area of play reported a series of frustrating attempts. We discussed what they had learned from their experimentation and decided that observation was the best way to record the work of play. The group members felt that they were not prepared to formalize their observations for the purpose of a districtwide assessment.

Finally, the portfolio team was most enthusiastic about what was happening as a result of collecting student work and talking with students about their work. As a result, the group opted to further develop this strategy. Since we were already adopting a new integrated language arts series—as well as crafting essential learnings in language arts—we felt that piloting portfolios would provide a way to organize student work as it related to our essential learnings as well as show student work over time.

The portfolio helped us tie our K–2 developmental continuum of essential learnings to the integrated language arts curriculum that specifies the skills, knowledge, and attitudes of student learning. We decided that the ongoing portfolio would be multi-faceted and would contain selected student work samples that placed the learner at the center of the assessment process. The portfolio would act as the active medium to demonstrate the alignment among our philosophies, written curriculum, teaching practices, and authentic assessment. Students' daily work would become the basis for assessment.

REVISION BASED ON NEW KNOWLEDGE

At this point, we had learned a great deal about assessment and, specifically, portfolios. Many of us had gone to workshops, experimented in our classrooms, and met with the consultant. We were not the same group that entered the process one year ago, and we needed to revisit our purposes in light of our realization that we were going to use portfolios.

As we returned to our original objective, we realized that we had not yet discussed how we would align the portfolios with a strategy for reporting to parents. We all felt dissatisfied with the current report card, and we redefined our purpose: How can we make certain that we have aligned the essential learnings, the portfolios, and the report cards?

We had now completed one year's loop in the spiral and were once again engaged in planning. We identified the new knowledge we needed to acquire. We realized that we would have to learn how to grade/score and how to develop criteria for performance. This new venture took us through another loop in the spiral. We attended workshops, looked at the work of other school districts, met with our consultant,

and finally decided to develop criteria and rubrics that describe our students developmentally.

USING FOCUS GROUPS

We felt that reports to parents should be informative and communicate essential and understandable information about student progress and performance. Just as it was our goal to validate student work by aligning what is learned with what is taught and written, our intention for reporting to parents was to communicate student progress in a comprehensible manner that was accurate, concise, and constructive. By design, the portfolio would function as the system to enhance an interactive exchange of information about student work.

Primary teachers agreed that they wanted to show student growth over time and report where students performed on a developmental continuum. But in many ways, they still viewed themselves as separate entities at a given grade level: kindergarten, 1st, 2nd. The new reporting system dictated that K–2 teachers see themselves as interactive and widen their reporting audience to colleagues, parents, and students. Teachers also had basic management needs. The report cards needed to be less time consuming and give a fair, accurate assessment of students' work along with a critique of their performance.

The system we used to build our new report to parents involved both content and process. We not only had to decide what information the document would contain and how it would be designed, but we needed a way to involve all primary teachers and to work together collaboratively.

COMMITTEE WORK WITH COLLEAGUES

Our process was cooperative and consensual. Each committee member was responsible for updating the primary staff in his or her building and bringing recommendations back to our working committee. This way, all primary teachers felt they were informed and had input into the process.

For the content of the card, we began reviewing

many examples of report cards from around the country. After reviewing our essential learnings for the integrated language arts (What do we want our students to know at each level?) and the skills and strategies associated with those, we identified the major concepts that fit K–2 developmentally. Additionally, we examined projects and activities in the primary grades and agreed on those that included the content, skills, and strategies we believed to be inherent in a performance-based outcome. Our new approach to grading indicated a student's level of independence, individual growth, quality of work, and consistency of performance.

LISTENING TO THE "CUSTOMER"

When we began to evaluate the new report card at the end of the first pilot year, we found we could not complete our task without the help of parents. Each committee member asked two parents to assist us in the revision. Parents were invited to help design the "Dream Report Card." They were familiar with the new pilot report card because it had been reviewed with them during November Parent Conferences and a second report sent in March.

Upon completion of our evaluation of the K–2 report card we found that parents supported:

- A developmental performance key.
- A multigrade (K-1-2) report card.
- Work habits and personal development coming before language arts (reading, writing, listening, and speaking).
- A place for comments.
- Knowledge, skills, and strategies presented in a developmental fashion.
- The student's progress reported as development or growth over time rather than compared against the rest of the class.

Parents also requested that we provide:

- An optional place for family goals. (At conference time, parents and the classroom teacher have the opportunity to set goals specific to a child's learning needs.)

- A brochure explaining our assessment philosophy, assessment and evaluation techniques, and the reading and writing strategies taught.
- Ways for parents to help their children at home.

We also found that parents were very pleased to be asked to participate in this process. We now know the report card belongs to all of us: students, parents, and teachers.

During the 1992–93 school year, we designed a developmental report for grades 3–5 using the same process we used to with the K–2 report card. Because we found parental input so valuable, we had parents assist us in revising the intermediate report card.

As parents and teachers have worked collaboratively to build a new assessment system, our report cards have gone through many changes. We found that the report card cannot stand alone. It needs the support of the portfolio, which documents authentic student performances over a period of time. Also, parents and students are an important part of the grading process. Parents need to know the philosophy and belief systems that drive our educational system. If they are to support and work as partners in our educational system, they need to clarify how their children are progressing toward developmentally appropriate outcomes in all areas of growth: academic, social, physical, and emotional. As students learn to become self-evaluators, they develop a sense of their own capacities for learning and become active participants in their education.

We will continue to refine our reporting system by finding ways to enhance communication among parents, teachers, and students with the timely exchange of information. Working our way through the feedback spiral has provided us with a framework for continuous improvement in our district. We now realize that there is no end to new knowledge and new understandings. Therefore, any change we make needs to be subject to revision on the basis of assessment information gathered from the parties who are most affected by the change. Figure 6.1 shows the most recent version of our report card, which we continue to assess even as you read this.

FIGURE 6.1

Bellingham Public Schools Report to Parents

KEY: N - November M - March J - June

READING

N M J

☐ ☐ ☐ **PRE-READER**
Enjoys being read to; looks at pictures in books but does not yet make the connection to print; exhibits limited attention span during shared reading and may not participate; limited experience with letters and sounds; inexperienced book-sense (left to right, front to back, right side up)

☐ ☐ ☐ **EMERGENT**
Enjoys being read to; participates in shared reading; memorizes and repeats oral language patterns, but does not yet connect to print; knows some letters and sounds; understands book-sense (left to right, front to back, right side up).

☐ ☐ ☐ **BEGINNING**
Makes the connection between oral language and written material; begins to read own writing; reads patterned text from memory; knows most letters and sounds; "pretend read" and retells familiar literature; beginning to have one-to-one correspondence with words and a developing awareness to self-correct; reads some words in isolation; uses memory and pictures to gain meaning from material.

☐ ☐ ☐ **DEVELOPING**
Begins to read familiar stories and predictable literature with accuracy, is developing confidence; has command of letters and sounds; understands the sound-symbol relationship; begins to use context, picture clues, phonics and knowledge to decide new words and derive meaning from familiar books; consistently uses one-to-one correspondence and self-corrects.

☐ ☐ ☐ **CAPABLE**
A strong reader who approaches familiar material with confidence but still needs some support with unfamiliar materials; beginning to make predictions and draw inferences from books and stories read independently; chooses to read independently; self-corrects for meaning; greater confidence in utilizing a variety of reading strategies.

☐ ☐ ☐ **EXPERIENCED**
Confident and independent reader who reads and understands familiar and unfamiliar material that is age appropriate and above; enjoys pursuing own interests independently; can summarize; uses a wide range of strategies to deal with difficult text.

PANEL 1

WRITING

N M J

☐ ☐ ☐ **PRE-WRITER**
Communicates using pictures; using scribble writing or letter-like marks; text conveys no meaning to reader; may dictate sentence to teacher.

☐ ☐ ☐ **EMERGENT**
Drawing conveys message may copy letters, words or sentences from the environment; beginning to use familiar letters and words as labels; writes some familiar words from memory.

☐ ☐ ☐ **BEGINNING**
Writes with guidance; beginning to use spacing to define word boundaries; may use beginning, middle, and ending letters to represent words; writing begins to convey a comprehensible message but may be difficult to read; complete framed sentence patterns meaningfully; may copy words, phrases and sentences from class-generated tasks.

☐ ☐ ☐ **DEVELOPING**
Developing fluency; writes competently with guidance; text beginning to reflect logical sequence; uses inventive spelling to convey the message; observes word boundaries; writing contains more apparent meaning; sentence structure may be simple and repetitive; and begins to correctly spell high-frequency words.

☐ ☐ ☐ **CAPABLE**
Competent and confident, fluent writer; writes independently; begins to use conventions of print in spelling, punctuation and grammar; text conveys the message; begins to use some techniques to engage reader; writing reflects logical sequence.

☐ ☐ ☐ **EXPERIENCED**
Enthusiastic, fluent, writes independently; has command of many conventions of print in spelling, punctuation and grammar; demonstrates sentence sense; may use a variety of techniques to engage reader; writing shows originality and an organizational plan.

PANEL 2

MATHEMATICS

N M J

☐ ☐ ☐ **EXPLORATION**
Becoming aware of math concepts; interacts with materials.

☐ ☐ ☐ **EMERGENT**
Benefits from monitoring and help in problem solving; is beginning to understand math concepts; needs assistance to produce work.

☐ ☐ ☐ **BEGINNING**
Solves problems with assistance; needs assistance learning math concepts; needs support to complete math tasks successfully; beginning to learn and use math facts.

☐ ☐ ☐ **DEVELOPING**
Solves problems with occasional assistance; understands math concepts; usually completes math tasks accurately; can recall and use some math facts.

☐ ☐ ☐ **CAPABLE**
Solves problems independently; applies previously learned math concepts; shows accuracy on math tasks; recalls and uses math facts.

☐ ☐ ☐ **EXPERIENCED**
Uses a variety of strategies to solve problems independently; independently applies previously learned math concepts; demonstrates high accuracy on math tasks, confidently recalls and uses all math facts.

Student Name _____

PANEL 3

The Bellingham Public Schools Report to Parents is printed on two sides of an 8½" x 14" sheet of paper. Each side is divided into three equal panels, as shown on these two pages. Panel 3 is folded onto panel 2, and then panel 1 is folded onto panel 4, (which is the reverse of panel 3), producing a compact yet informative report to parents.

BELLINGHAM PUBLIC SCHOOLS

REPORT TO PARENTS

Kindergarten, First and Second Grades

PLAY

"Play is viewed as fundamental to children's learning, growth and development, enabling them to develop and clarify concepts, roles and ideas by testing them through use of open-ended materials and role-enactment. Play further enables children to develop fine and gross motor skills, to learn to share with others, to see others' points of view and to be in control of their thoughts and feelings." (*Moyer et al., ACEI position paper, 1987*)

You child is expected to initiate play, communicate with others during play, and sustain play.

Comments: (Optional)

"Teachers and parents can never know all that a child knows. A report card is merely a snapshot–a tiny slice of a child's learning over a given period of time. It is through talking with a child, looking at what a child creates, and watching the child in action that we gain a clearer, more comprehensive understanding of a child's progress."

Student is assigned to the _____ grade next year.

Student was present _____ days and absent _____ days.

PANEL 6

Performance Key:
C: consistently
M: most of the time
S: some of the time
N: not at this time
x: not applicable

WORK HABITS & PERSONAL DEVELOPMENT

N M J   N = November   M = March   J = June

N	M	J	
☐	☐	☐	Shows positive attitude
☐	☐	☐	Interacts cooperatively with others
☐	☐	☐	Demonstrates self-confidence
☐	☐	☐	Respects the rights of others
☐	☐	☐	Practices self-control
☐	☐	☐	Follows classroom rules
☐	☐	☐	Follows school rules
☐	☐	☐	Works independently
☐	☐	☐	Asks for help when appropriate
☐	☐	☐	Attends to and completes tasks
☐	☐	☐	Uses time effectively and efficiently
☐	☐	☐	Works carefully
☐	☐	☐	Uses materials appropriately
☐	☐	☐	Cleans up
☐	☐	☐	Willingly shares ideas
☐	☐	☐	Makes relevant contributions to class discussions
☐	☐	☐	Responds appropriately to oral directions
☐	☐	☐	Attentive to speaker and discussions

These are areas in which your child participates and beginning concepts are introduced:

☐	☐	☐	Social Studies
☐	☐	☐	Science/Health
☐	☐	☐	Art
☐	☐	☐	Physical Education
☐	☐	☐	Music

PANEL 4

FAMILY GOALS

(Optional)

PANEL 5

PART III

Shifting the
Paradigm:
Giving Up
Old Mental Models

Shifting the Paradigm: Giving Up Old Mental Models

ARTHUR L. COSTA AND BENA KALLICK

> Insanity is continuing to do the same thing over and over and expecting different results.
>
> —ALBERT EINSTEIN

The 19th century British physicist and mathematician William Thomson Kelvin is quoted as saying, "When you cannot measure it, when you cannot express it in numbers, your knowledge is a very meager and unsatisfactory kind."

Based on this archaic, technological, and reductionist theorem, we have tried to translate educational goals into observable, measurable outcomes. We have become fascinated and enamored with:

- amount of time on task;
- numbers of questions asked at each level of Bloom's Taxonomy;
- gain scores on achievement tests;
- class size, including numbers of students and the ratio of students to adults;
- length of time in school;
- I.Q. scores as a basis for grouping;
- numbers of days in attendance;
- minutes of instruction;
- percentages of objectives attained;
- numbers of competencies needed for promotion;
- school effectiveness based on published test scores; and
- numbers of As and Bs on report cards.

These obsessions reflect the statement by Irish social commentator George W. Russell that "when steam first began to pump and wheels go round at so many revolutions per minute, what are called business habits were intended to make the life of man run in harmony with the steam engine, and his movements rival the train in punctuality." Yet we agree with William Glasser (1992): "What is most needed in the public school is not new personnel or equipment but a new philosophy and a new structure for using what we have." And as Jacob Viner observes, "When you can measure it, when you can express it in numbers, your knowledge is still of a meager and unsatisfactory kind!"

THE PARADIGM SHIFTS

> As we let go of the machine models of work, we begin to step back and see ourselves in new ways, to appreciate our wholeness, and to design organizations that honor and make use of the totality of who we are.
>
> —MARGARET WHEATLEY

Wheatley (1992) agrees that up to this time, all our organizations have been constructed on notions derived from 17th century Newtonian physics and on cherished assumptions that ours is a world of things, mechanics, leverage, hierarchies, and rigid organizations. We are being challenged to reshape these fundamental world views, however, through new sciences and fresh discoveries and hypotheses in biology, chemistry, and quantum physics. We are discovering that this is not a world of things but a world of relationships. As Wheatley points out, "To live in a quantum world, to weave here and there with ease and grace, we will need to change what we do. We will need to stop describing tasks and instead facilitate *process*. We will need to become savvy about how to build relationships, how to nurture growing, evolving, things. All of us will need better skills in listening, communicating, and facilitating groups, because these are the talents that build strong relationships" (p. 38).

We are learning that power in organizations—power to get work done, to teach, to learn, and to transform lives—is energy. Energy needs to flow through the entirety of organizations. It cannot be con-

fined to positions, functions, levels, titles, or programs. As Wheatley contends, "What gives power its charge, positive or negative, is the quality of relationships. Those who relate through coercion, or from a disregard for the other person, create negative energy. Those who are open to others and who see others in their fullness create positive energy" (p. 39).

A quiet revolution is taking place. It is a revolution of relationships and a revolution of the intellect, placing a premium on our greatest natural resource— our human minds in relationship with one another. We are increasingly recognizing and accepting those attributes of a climate conducive to intellectual growth and self-fulfillment. The conditions that maximize creativity are being described, understood, and replicated in classrooms, schools, districts, and communities. The new paradigm of industrial management emphasizes a trusting environment in which growth and empowerment of the individual are the keys to unlocking corporate success. This view provides a new paradigm with which to consider the mission, vision, outcomes, and assessment of schools.

In his book and video programs on paradigm shifts, Joel Barker (1989) develops a convincing scenario about how we develop mental models from which we interpret the world. The process of building these models is what we, as educators, refer to as constructivism. We know also that people support what they create. And we have learned from the work of Piaget that when we are placed in a state of disequilibrium with our existing mental models, we construct new ones. Typically in our society, however, people await the new model. They express frustration that a new recipe has not been formulated. Their traditional paradigms have "plateaued" (Bardwick 1986). As we hear in school life, "Show me the new model; prove that it works first before I will believe you."

A change in mental models, for most people, implies the unknown. It implies psychologically unknown risks of a new venture, physically unknown demands on time and energy, and intellectually unknown requirements for new skills and knowledge. In addition, people who are invested in their present ways of working believe that if they can just do what they are currently doing better, everything will

| | | | | | | | | | | | | | | | | | | |

improve. Part of this notion is supported with a current interpretation of continuous improvement: Work toward higher quality by cutting the number of errors.

We have clearly entered the information age, and we face a two-fold dilemma in a world that is constantly redefined through increased information technology. One dilemma is identifying practices that we should not change but work to improve. The second dilemma is to invent new practices that are reengineered in fundamental ways that change the way we operate. With increased technology, we will be able to enhance our practices through the use of databases that can be synthesized, tracked, and reorganized as never before. Clearly, such new databases will dramatically change the role of assessment.

The system that has served us in an industrial age now needs to be reexamined. In order to change mental models, we must first examine the assumptions of our present models. For example, we have assumed that there is a need for highly specialized work; each department represents a discipline that has its own order of business. This is true from the perspective of the classroom as well as from the central office. We assume that those who are responsible for accounting are quite separate from those who are responsible for curriculum and instruction. As a result of this specialized and often fragmented organization, assessment has also become narrowly defined. Our present assessment breaks apart knowledge and skills and, in the most narrowly defined way, tries to produce information for instruction.

An additional assumption is that we will be able to create incentives for workers—children as well as adults—by creating stronger relationships between work and inspection of it. We believe that we can better educate students when we develop better means for checking and controlling. Our assumption has been that the fear instilled by the threat of "if you don't do this, you won't get in" will serve as a strong incentive. We also assume that making learning exclusive (only a few will make it) will serve to motivate.

The concepts in this book are based on new assumptions that shift our present paradigm. They will be confusing and counterproductive under the old paradigm of education. Figure III.1 describes the exist-

ing state of educational thinking and the desired state with which the concepts of educational change and assessment must be viewed.

In order to adopt this new vision, educators will need to experience a paradigm shift. Some of our traditional ways of viewing schools, education, learning, teaching, achievement, and talent will be found obsolescent and will demand replacement with modern, relevant policies, practices, and philosophies that are consistent with the view of multiple intelligences in a quantum world.

For example, as our paradigm shifts, we will need to let go of our obsession with acquiring content and knowledge as an end in itself and make room for viewing content as a vehicle for developing more complex, higher goals such as personal efficacy, flexibility and adaptability, craftsmanship and high personal standards, consciousness and metacognition, and interdependence and sense of community (Costa and Garmston 1994). We will dismiss uniformity in deference to valuing diversity; we will reduce our emphasis on "parts" and increase our emphasis on relationships—the true source of power in today's world.

Additionally, student evaluation will be as significant an influence as external evaluation. We will balance external rewards with intriguing activities that spark internal motivation. We will devalue competition and enhance interdependence. We will redefine "smart" to mean having a repertoire of intelligences and knowing when to use each.

Barker (1989) suggests that when adopting a new paradigm, all aspects of the system must change in accordance with the new paradigm. Paradigm shifting, therefore, does not become fully operable until all parts of the system are changed and aligned with the new paradigm.

Changing our mental models, a first step in changing paradigms, requires time as well as courage. Administrators, teachers, and parents often feel bound by traditions, laws, policies, rules, and regulations that tie them to past practices, obsolete policies, and archaic metaphors. As the late President Dwight D. Eisenhower stated, "Things are more like they are today than they ever have been."

FIGURE III.1

Existing and Desired States of Change and Assessment

From the Existing State. . .	**. . .To a Desired State**
Bureaucratic institution that fosters dependence based on external evaluation offered as summative rather than formative. The assumption that change takes place by mandating new cognitive maps and training people to use them. Assessments that limit the frame of reference by which people will judge the system.	A system that recognizes the necessity for those who are being assessed to be a part of the evaluation process, to become self-evaluating. A system that encourages continuous external feedback to be used for ongoing, self-correcting assessment. Operating within people's maps of reality (personal knowledge) and creating conditions for people to examine and alter their own internal maps. Assessments that assist learners in understanding, expanding, and considering alternative frames.
Assessments that impose external models of reality. Assessments that communicate that knowledge is outside the learner. Assessments that signal that personal knowledge and experience are of little worth. The conception of curriculum, instruction, and assessment as separate entities in a system. Each aspect of the system that is assessed is considered to be separate and discrete. Individual and organizational critique perceived as negative and a barrier to change.	Assessments that allow different demonstrations of strengths, abilities, and knowledge. Assessments that allow the capacity to make meaning of the massive flow of information and to shape raw data into patterns that make sense to the individual. Assessments of knowledge being produced from within the learner. Communicating that the learner's personal knowledge and experience is of great worth. Assessment is an integral component of all learning at all levels and for all individuals who compose the system. All parts of the system are interconnected and synergistic. Critique is perceived as a necessary component of quality for individual and organizational decision making.

A CATALYST FOR CHANGING MENTAL MODELS

The question most frequently asked about changing mental models is, "How do we help people realize the need to do this? "After all, unless there is a real need to change, change will not take place within the entire system.

Consider that growth and change are found in disequilibrium, not balance. Order is built out of chaos, learning takes place, understandings are forged, and, gradually, organizations function more consistently as their vision is clarified, their mission is forged, and their goals operationalized.

Wheatley reminds us that reality is actively constructed, and this construction occurs most effectively when the whole system is in the room generating information and thinking about what it wants to be. In schools that operate in this fashion, codes of discipline, school rules, and policies are assessed for their consistency with the organization's new mission and goals of interdependence, self-evaluation, and self-modification. Kriegel and Patler's *If It Ain't Broke, Break It!* is a wonderful title that elegantly sums up what school leaders do with crystallized, plateaued organizational thinking. Numerous strategies can be employed to break mental models:

- Create school climate conditions in which people can take risks and experiment.
- Rotate job assignments with tasks assigned to stretch the imagination and cognition of staff.
- Research alternate classroom and instructional strategies.
- Experiment with various lesson designs, instructional sequences, and teaching materials.

The classroom climate, too, can foster risk taking as students experiment with ideas, share their thinking strategies with each other, and venture forth with creative thoughts without fear of being judged. Value judgments and criticism are replaced with acceptance, listening, empathy, and clarification of each other's ideas. Students learn, use, and assess their skills of communication.

In the past, archaic compartmentalization of the disciplines kept school staffs separated. But traditional content and subject matter boundaries are being selectively abandoned and replaced with relevant, problem-centered, integrative themes that are chosen because of their contributions to the thinking, learning, and community-building processes.

When a system seeks ways of knowing whether it is, in fact, accomplishing its mission, it turns to assessments. Assessments are tools for measuring; they are ways to gather information about the success of a practice. Unfortunately, in the past we have too often assumed that assessments and tests are synonymous. We now realize that there are many ways to measure, only one of which is a test. We now have tools such as portfolios, exhibitions, and observations (see the matrix in the introduction to Part IV). Our measures are no longer limited. As a result, we find that we can gather information about success in areas that we always claim to value but find few ways to evaluate. These areas include the capacity to collaborate and work on a team; the capacity to communicate effectively in ways other than writing; the capacity to solve complex problems and offer multiple solutions; and the capacity to perform as a scientist, artist, mathematician, or historian.

New measures give us a window through which we can examine how well we are working toward the goals most systems have embraced, such as problem solving, effective communication, and critical and creative thinking in all subject areas. When teachers open these windows, they find change inevitable. The assessment data strongly suggest the need to change instructional practices.

For example, a teacher decides that students will keep portfolios as a way of collecting information about mathematical problem solving. She wonders first what will go in the portfolio to reflect the student as problem solver. She initially decides to have students collect sheets of problems that have mathematical operations such as multiplication and division. As she reviews these sheets, she realizes the information is insufficient. She knows that problem solving should be a demonstration of what the student does when faced with a complex situation in which the answer is not immediately apparent or cued by the instructions.

Simply knowing that a student can perform an operation is not sufficient data.

The question she asks next is, "Does the student know which operation will be most appropriate to apply when faced with a new situation?" The portfolios now start to include the results of complex problems. As she finds increasingly more complex problems to present to students, they complain, "This work is too hard. "They are accustomed to being placed in situations that do not call for persistence (another quality she highly values). We see this teacher's paradigm shift as she struggles with:

- convincing herself that she must provide instructional situations that offer students more opportunities to be self-directed, work in teams, and solve complex problems;
- staying the course when students observe that the "game" is changing; and
- finding appropriate measures that continue to refine her understanding of student learning as well as provide rich feedback for class members so they take responsibility for their learning.

There is a necessary disruption when we shift mental models. If there is not, we are probably not shifting; we may be following new recipes but we will end up with the same stew!

Of all forms of mental activity, the most difficult to induce . . . is the art of handling the same bundle of data as before, by placing them in a new system of relations with one another by giving them a different framework, all of which virtually means putting on a different kind of thinking-cap for the moment. It is easy to teach anybody a new fact . . . but it needs light from heaven above to enable a teacher to break the old framework in which the student is accustomed to seeing.

—ARTHUR KOESTLER

References

Bardwick, J.M. (1986). *The Plateauing Trap*. New York: Bantam Books.

Barker, J. (1989). *Discovering the Future: The Business of Paradigms*. St Paul, Minn.: Infinity Limited Incorporated Press.

Costa, A., and R. Garmston. (1994). *Cognitive Coaching: A Foundation for Renaissance* Schools. Norwood, Mass.: Christopher Gordon Publishers.

Glasser, W. (1992). *The Quality School*. New York: Harper Collins.

Koestler, A. (1972). *The Roots of Coincidence*. New York: Vintage Books.

Kriegel, R.J., and L. Patler. (1991). *If It Ain't Broke, Break It!* New York: Time/Warner Books.

Wheatley, M. (1992). *Leadership and the New Science*. San Francisco: Berrett-Koehler Publishers.

Shifting the Paradigm: Giving Up Old Mental Models

As described in Part III, it is difficult to observe change unless you have a sense of what preceded the change itself. We have provided a "from-to" chart (Figure III.1) to help define the basic shifts we are seeking. Ann Johnson and Kathryn Schladweiler describe a process they use in staff development to help teachers shift their mental model of limited paper-and-pencil testing to performance-based tests. Patricia Hoffman describes the struggle to form a new mental model of the role and function of meaningful report cards intended to communicate student progress toward the district's new goals. Charlotte Danielson explicitly describes changing the assessment practice by examining the old paradigm for testing in light of a new one. Robert Swartz clarifies the picture through his concrete examples of the shift from limited and narrowly defined questioning to questioning that requires critical and creative thinking.

7 The Challenge of Revising Report Cards

Patricia J. Hoffman

In September 1990, my district's Assessment Task Force was given a charge: align district assessment and reporting measures with district goals and objectives. An initial review of K–12 report cards revealed the greatest need to be at the elementary level, so work focused there (although the computerized report cards of grades 6–12 presented great challenges that the Task Force did not address).

Increasingly, principals, teachers, and district office personnel had called for a revision of the current report cards used in the Burlington Area Schools. Burlington is a small K–12 district in Wisconsin with approximately 3,000 students, and its report cards reflected a multitude of approaches. Each grade level and school had individualized cards, added special inserts and checklists, and developed unique approaches to communicate with parents. The call for revision originally came from a need to standardize and modernize design and graphics. District office staff

members broadened that purpose to develop a system to reflect district goals and the evolving strategic plan. That plan was emerging with a strong emphasis on all students achieving at high levels, on results that could be measured and reported, on thinking skills as central to every child's education, and on student accountability and parental involvement.

At the same time, district curriculum was in transition from a segmented/isolated, skill-based program to a process-oriented thrust with much greater awareness of the complex demands an information society places on citizens and workers. Key words to the Task Force throughout this time were "emerging, evolving, transitioning, developing." So much was changing so quickly that capturing the current reality and planning for the hoped-for future was frustrating and divisive as well as exciting and challenging. Shifting paradigms is easier said than done. Since many audiences had much at stake in the realm of report cards and grading systems, the route to change was never direct, simple, or universally embraced.

A VARIETY OF AUDIENCES

Parents did not cry out for change. Survey results showed that 38 percent would favor some change, but 62 percent thought our report cards were fine. However, parents voiced a strong desire for more direct communication with the classroom teacher—longer, more frequent conferences and more information about students' social skills, attitudes, work habits, and thinking skills. It also seemed clear that parents did not agree regarding what should be reported. Some wanted strict academic progress while others were more interested in social development. One group wanted to know about thinking skills and learning processes, and another seemed most interested in employability skills. Certain parents wanted to compare their students with others in the class, the same grade, or the nation. Some only wanted to have their children's growth over time reported at an individual level.

Teachers were no more unanimous in their directions to the Task Force. When asked what they wanted in a report card, the responses ranged from objective (not too cumbersome), to checklists that covered curriculum objectives, to an inventory of skills along with some way to assess children's thinking ability, to a way to communicate a child's overall ability and attitude. Other recommendations included forms that were not complicated to fill out, report cards with no grades nor a lot of writing, total narrative reports, positive instead of negative comments, and letter grades for academics and for effort. Suggestions went on to list evaluating the growth of the child; carbonless paper; a simple, developmental instrument that parents can understand; avoiding a lot of checklists; emphasizing attitudes; and on and on and on.

All of the report card's audiences are affected when the child receiving the card has an exceptional educational need. Thus, special educators were active in all discussions and on the Task Force itself. The problems that report cards pose for mainstreamed exceptional-need youngsters are thorny. Regular education teachers have many ways of accommodating the needs as well as the self-esteem of their special education students. Trying to systematize years of individual approaches challenged the Task Force.

District office personnel were interested in both logistics (carbonless form, one page, easy to access, identical K–5 format) and the philosophical base (developmentally appropriate, focused on thinking skills and learning-to-learn processes, positively oriented, and reflective of best educational practices). Of course, personnel at this level also disagreed as to the value of report cards, the political issues involved, and the reality of what was doable by elementary teachers given classes of 25–32 students, limited prep time, and constant demands to change instructional practices. New approaches to reading, writing, and math instruction were introduced within the same two years that report cards were being studied and revised.

Finally, the school board had a very real interest in the district's reporting systems. The majority of board members knew only grade-dependent report cards: either A-B-C or percentage scales. Board members were keenly aware of the lack of reliability of teacher grading. From personal experience and from parent complaints, they knew that different teachers graded differently. The same exact work could merit an A from one teacher and a C from another.

The school board had adopted goals and a strategic plan that focused on thinking skills. They had been very involved in discussions of school-to-work transitions. They were very sensitive to the criticism that "kids today can't even read or add or speak politely." They wanted a report card that communicated expectations to students and parents and provided meaningful information to teachers and principals for improving instruction.

THE CHALLENGES OF REVISION

Clearly, arriving at districtwide consensus was a monumental—probably impossible—challenge. It was decided that a Task Force made up of teachers, administrators, counselors, parents, and students would take input from everyone throughout the revision process, but the Task Force would make all final decisions (subject to acceptance by the school board).

Throughout the 1990–91 school year, the Task Force met, studied, conferred, attended conferences, argued, developed prototypes, and revised, revised, revised. The process was neither simple nor painless. The Task Force was criticized and praised by all parties. Members grew frustrated and discouraged. Some quit. Some renewed their interest in districtwide issues and became very active in the process. It was a student who told us of the "second-class program" you get if you aren't in the top groups. A parent reminded us that she just wanted to know if her son could read. A teacher brought in a note from a 3rd grader that said, "And when I get bad grades I feel sad and sometimes I don't want to come back to school."

As the Task Force struggled to develop a report card that would serve the needs of students, parents, teachers, administrators, and the school board, it became apparent that what was reported and how it was reported would communicate expectations to teachers about what was being taught and how it was being taught. When report cards called for a letter grade in reading or math or social studies, there was never a clear definition of what that course involved. But when a teacher reports on the frequency with which an entire list of skills, attitudes, or behaviors are used, the course content is very clearly defined. This made the development of the new report card much more difficult and much more important.

After a full year of struggle and hard work, the new report card eliminated letter grades for kindergarten through grade 3, with a transition year for 3rd graders. It instituted checklists of skills in language arts and math. It reflected the Wisconsin Department of Public Instruction's definition of reading as constructing meaning from print. It reflected the National Council of Teachers of Mathematics standards and a process approach to writing.

Most interestingly, the top of the report card featured 10 intelligent behaviors. These had been selected by the district's K–12 teachers and building-level teams after extensive study by a core Thinking Skills Team

working with Art Costa. In the original format, each teacher rated individual students on behaviors from "usually" to "sometimes" to "working on it" to "not yet." The 10 behaviors were divided into "Habits of the Mind" and "Social/Personal Growth." They were: perseverance, curiosity, flexibility, precision, transfer, responsibility, independence, respect, cooperation, and expressing feelings appropriately. Wording was developed to define the terms for students and parents, but the same 10 behaviors were on each report card from kindergarten through grade 5. The language arts and math checklists varied from grade to grade to reflect the goals at each level.

The pilot year was 1991–92. Teachers had the opportunity to become familiar with the system and find the problems with it. The Task Force believed that at the end of year one, the report cards could be finalized and transferred to carbonless paper to ease record keeping. That wasn't the case. The end of year one saw widespread discontent from teachers and calls for major revisions.

The Task Force struggled with feelings of frustration and rejection until a wise member finally suggested that maybe this was a two- or three-year process, and we should see it as an opportunity for growth. The entire area of intelligent behaviors was at risk during the revision. Teachers found them difficult to mark. They said students changed from day to day and from subject to subject. Teachers found they were not consistent in their own evaluations of the same student or between students. The process was very time-consuming, and the rating scale wasn't clear. Discussions with parents about the intelligent behaviors were uncomfortable because teachers held many different interpretations of the behaviors.

The report card for 1992–93 did not satisfy all requests for change nor did it sacrifice the intelligent behaviors nor was it seen as a final copy. The revised card listed only eight intelligent behaviors. Cooperation and expressing feelings were subsumed under responsibility and respect. Teachers marked only the four areas that were most concrete and observable, and they marked them only if attention was needed. Parents were given the responsibility for addressing the other four intelligent behaviors in the context of how they saw their child demonstrate these behaviors in the home and community. Other adjustments were made to the checklists, generally paring down and simplifying them.

The Task Force has accepted an ongoing responsibility to monitor teacher and parent response to the cards and to keep them current with the emerging trend in the district to performance-based education. Recently a school/community group developed a set of eight Essential Learner Goals that will soon be adopted by the school board as the underlying philosophy in curriculum development. Although most of these goals are already reflected in the curriculum and report cards, it is clear that some adjustments will be necessary. As the focus of the educational effort is clarified, the Task Force will be charged with ensuring that the report card reflects those goals and clearly reports progress to parents.

It is clear that the painful process of changing something so fundamental as an elementary report card is valuable and worth the price. It's also essential if we are to shift the paradigm governing how we do business in the Burlington schools. The very process becomes the curriculum of change and allows a district to educate the many audiences of the report card. At one point early in the Task Force's work, it became clear that parents, teachers, and students had many different perceptions of what was worth reporting and what format was best. One member facetiously suggested that multiple report cards be developed and parents be allowed to pick the best one for their child. As the laughter died, it was clear that a seed had been planted. Someday, we may be capable of responding to the unique needs of each child and each family, and report in a way that is both honest and personally meaningful.

8 | Developing Writing Prompts for Assessing Thinking and Content Learning in Science Classrooms

ROBERT SWARTZ

cience education is changing. We still see many classrooms where students passively learn information about the natural world from written texts. However, we also see a growing emphasis on helping students achieve a deeper connection to the natural world through active and constructive learning. With this approach, students are the center of the science classroom. Teachers and texts facilitate the process of active learning instead of merely providing students with its inert products. Figure 8.1 outlines how these two types of science classrooms differ.

To be sure, scientific principles and information about the natural world must play a role in the new science classroom. But rather than give such informa-

tion to students as the focus of their learning, it should be available to students who will seek it as they actively construct new understandings. In the new science classroom, emphasis is placed on the development of:

- processes through which students can construct meaning,
- processes students can use to validate their understandings, and
- strategies through which students can use their insights in constructive problem solving.

Basic concepts of science together with scientific principles that flesh out these concepts are valuable in the new science classroom only insofar as they are appropriately embedded in these processes.

As instructional goals change, so too must assessment of whether we are achieving these goals. We must not only change what we assess but how we assess it. Relying primarily on standard ways of assess-

Note: This article is an adaptation of Chapter 1 of a longer monograph by Robert Swartz in *New Ways to Assess Learning in Science*, edited by S. Loucks-Horsley (Miami, Fla.: Miami Museum of Science, 1991). Copyright 1991 by Miami Museum of Science. Reprinted with permission.

FIGURE 8.1

Traditional Science Class vs. New Science Class

TRADITIONAL CLASS
- Students are told what others think the natural work is like.
- Students are told how science works.

- Students are told about contemporary issues in science.
- Teachers and texts give students information to learn.

NEW CLASS
- Students are guided to developed their own conception of the world.
- Students test and modify their constructs through scientific thinking.
- Students make use of their understanding in science to think through issues.
- Teachers and texts facilitate understanding and are resources for information students use in problem solving.

---

ing whether students retain basic information is no longer appropriate. Modes of assessment that reveal and enhance the use of the processes listed above must replace more traditional modes of assessment.

This means that the primary emphasis in assessment must be on student performances that demonstrate the use of these active processes. This chapter explains how teachers can prompt extended written (or oral) responses by students in ways that bring out their active thinking and learning so that its quality can be assessed. In emphasizing the design of assessment prompts of this sort, we in no way wish to suggest that these modes are preferable to using students' active performance in science activities or to using a classroom system where students keep a portfolio with self-evaluation of relevant work. All three of these modes of assessment should mesh in the science classroom. We concentrate here on ways of prompting extended written or oral performances because it is the natural next step to move to from assessing learning solely with multiple-choice items and because it is an efficient way of determining the level of student understanding in day-to-day classroom situations.

The mode of assessment we describe in this chapter uses pencil-and-paper assessments of student learning in a fairly traditional testing situation. However, this is not the only—nor oftentimes the best—purpose for such assessment. Rather, assessment should be viewed as a much broader enterprise.

Ongoing, informal assessment using these techniques, for example, is important to planning classroom instruction. It is also a wonderful vehicle for helping students learn to monitor their own learning.

Our primary message in this chapter extends to all levels of science instruction. However, the focus here is on assessment for the elementary and middle grades. This is because we believe that if new science teaching is to influence the attitudes of students toward science in their lives and in the classroom, it is critical to begin early. This said, secondary school teachers should certainly find useful ideas here as well.

TWO CONTRASTING ASSESSMENT EXAMPLES

Between grades 3 and 6, many elementary science programs introduce children to the concepts of endangerment and extinction of species. Dinosaurs are often used as an example of a species that is extinct. Students also learn that some species, such as the African elephant, are threatened with extinction primarily because of hunting, while others are threatened with extinction because man has disrupted their habitats so severely that they no longer can find food. It is in this context that students are usually introduced to the concept of a species. In particular, the implications of the extinction of a species are typically contrasted with the death of one individual in a species.

Here are two typical test items that might appear

at the end of a textbook chapter introducing the ideas of extinction and endangerment.

>   1. Which of the following species of animals is now extinct?
>   a) The African Elephant
>   b) The Dinosaur
>   c) The Horse
>   d) The Gypsy Moth
>
>   2. True or False: Animals are said to be endangered if they no longer exist.

These are typical multiple-choice and true-false test items. Their function is ostensibly to monitor student learning of what is presented in the text. They are solely information-oriented.

What conclusions can be drawn from responses to these items? Not many, except whether a student can memorize discrete bits of information. But suppose we want to know more. What if we also want to know whether students understand the significance of endangerment and extinction, their causes, and ways that they can be prevented—and can apply this understanding to specific situations in the contemporary world? What sorts of test items will bring these things out?

Here are three different assessment activities that contrast with information-oriented items and have specific uses connected with these different goals:

>   1. When prairie dogs are near farms they eat farmer's crops. Because of this, farmers have killed thousands of prairie dogs. Black-footed ferrets eat prairie dogs. Explain what problem this poses for the ferrets and why this is a problem.
>
>   2. Can you think of any ways that people can save ferrets and still control prairie dogs? Explain what you might do. What would you have to make sure of in order to be sure your solution will work? Is there anything you already know that has bearing on this?
>
>   3. Suppose you were asked to observe the feeding habits of black-footed ferrets so

that you could gather some data about this problem. Describe what you would do to make sure that your observations were as accurate as possible and that you brought back data that other people could trust. Write out a plan listing all the things you would think about beforehand.

These are extended-response test items. They represent natural next steps to going beyond multiple-choice test items to expose student understanding and thinking abilities. These items call upon students to perform activities that people engage in as a natural part of doing science. Thus, the test items call for authentic performances, even though the performances are written. We highlight this type of test item to dispel one myth about performance assessment: not all performance tests involve students in doing things such as actually going out and making observations mentioned in the third test item. As long as the task requested is an authentic one, the performance can be written or oral. (Oral responses are more time-consuming to note and assess, but sometimes they are more revealing than written responses, if only because it is easier to ask for clarification and elaboration.)

Note how these assessments are constructed. They contain one or both of the following: open-ended questions or task-specific directions. Both questions and directions are constructed to prompt students to engage in natural scientific tasks. In the case of these test items, the tasks are thinking and communication tasks.

WHY USE EXTENDED RESPONSE PROMPTS?

There is a vast difference between multiple-choice questions and the open-ended extended response items described above. What can student responses to the latter tell us? What specific understandings, skills, and processes do they assess? And how can different student responses be interpreted?

The three extended-response items were designed to provide information about three different kinds of processes:

- Constructing a conceptual understanding of a phenomenon.
- Using information to solve problems and make decisions.
- Using a critical thinking skill (in this case, assessing the accuracy of an observation).

Active Understanding

Typically, understanding in traditional science instruction involves knowing a simple definition. *Active* understanding involves students in:

1. Constructing the concepts and relationships that stand behind simple definitions.
2. Applying this understanding to new situations.
3. Drawing out the implications of the presence of these relationships in such situations.

These are active processes in which students use relevant information they already know in science rather than processes that merely involve remembering words that make up a definition. The elementary grades are not too early to begin to help students develop this deep understanding of the notions of endangerment and extinction.

How can we interpret student answers? Consider one answer to the first question:

> If there aren't enough prairie dogs for the ferrets to eat many of them will starve to death. That's because prairie dogs are their main food. If the farmers kill most or all of the prairie dogs, this will be a big problem because most of the ferrets might die. This would mean that their population would become very low. This would mean that they could become an endangered species. And if they all died they would become extinct. Then there would never be any other ferrets. And maybe this would not just be a problem for the ferrets. If other animals depended on the ferrets for their food, they could become extinct too.

What does this show us about this student's understanding of the concepts of endangered species

and extinction? Most striking is an active application of a number of different ideas connected with food chains and population to develop the notion that ferrets could become endangered and even extinct (e.g., "That's because prairie dogs are their main food." "If other animals depended on the ferrets for their food, they could become extinct too."). Notice also that the student affirms the relationship between endangerment and the possibility of extinction ("And if they all died they would become extinct."). In addition, this response shows an appreciation for the potential disaster that would result ("Then there would never be any other ferrets.").

This student not only seems to understand what endangerment and extinction involve and the relationship between them but can actively apply these concepts to a new situation and draw out implications. Notice how important it is to ask students why they think what they do.

Instruction for active understanding challenges and guides students to make the appropriate connection between ideas that yield a basic understanding of a key concept like that of endangered species. This can be accomplished by using a case-study method to present a variety of examples, each of which students study in enough depth so they are able to draw out the implications of applying the new concept to these examples. The examples can be contrasted to cases in which the concept does not apply. Prompting by teachers who ask challenging questions to guide these processes is typical in classrooms geared toward active understanding. Such activities can be hands-on, accompanied by readings, or a combination of both.

Let's look at three other examples of test items that are structured for the purpose of assessing active understanding. Figure 8.2 is a 4th grade example assessing the depth of active understanding students have of the concept of an ecosystem.

The best student responses distinguish between those ingredients necessary for the survival and development of the fish in the tank and those that are incidental to this purpose, though perhaps of interest to humans looking at the tank (like the castle). This reveals students' grasp of the concept of an ecosystem. Such responses show that students can apply the concept constructively to a new situation and explain its implications. This is how their understanding of a key scientific concept is demonstrated. Notice how, like the example of the prairie dogs and ferrets, students are not given the term "ecosystem" in the example (Massachusetts Department of Education 1989).

Here's another example for the 4th grade that tests students' active understanding of the key concept of conductivity in physical science. (It is adapted from an item described in Massachusetts Department of Education 1989.)

> Objects are often made of more than one material for a variety of reasons. Suppose you were asked to make a frying pan out of two different materials. What materials would you use? Why do you select these materials?
> Material 1: Why?
> Material 2: Why?

Students express their understanding of conductivity by explaining why metal is a good substance for the main body of the frying pan while wood or plastic is good for the handle. Such explanations should make explicit the connection between these substances and the transmission of heat.

A more challenging example for 6th grade students relates to the more specialized process of photosynthesis (Massachusetts Department of Education 1989):

> A small tree is planted in a meadow. After 20 years it has grown into a big tree, weighing 250 Kg more than when it was planted. Write a passage that might go into a science textbook explaining where the extra 250 Kg come from.

To summarize, each of these test items accomplishes the following:

- Gives students new examples to which they can apply a basic science.

- Asks them to display this new application by explaining why they emphasize what they do in answering the question.
- Prompts student responses by asking appropriate questions without mentioning these concepts directly.

For your own practice, you may want to construct an open-ended performance assessment item at your own grade level that will yield similar revelations about your students' understanding of one of the following basic concepts: food chains, gravity, convection, plate tectonics, galaxies, predator, heat exchange, antibodies, symbiosis, change of state, or biological system.

Problem Solving and Decision Making

Let's return to assessing students' grasp of endangerment and extinction. Ideally, we want them to understand more than just the implications of endangerment and extinction for a species. We also want them to understand that noting that a species is endangered gives us both a warning and an opportunity to try to do things that will ward off extinction and bring the species back to a flourishing existence. This should be accompanied by a sense of why it might be desir-

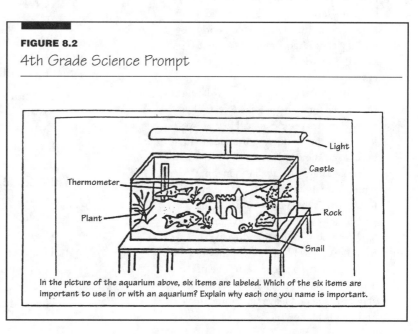

FIGURE 8.2

4th Grade Science Prompt

In the picture of the aquarium above, six items are labeled. Which of the six items are important to use in or with an aquarium? Explain why each one you name is important.

able to prevent species from becoming extinct and how accommodation for human needs may be achieved without threatening animal and plant species with extinction. The second test item on ferrets prompts students to do some problem solving about how this might be achieved.

In problem solving in science, we want students to use what they know to construct possible solutions to problems and to determine whether they will work. In so doing, students should think carefully before they judge which solution is best. Predicting the consequences of proposed solutions based on reliable information is crucial in doing this well. Imagining these constructive and weeding-out processes in action as students think through a problem can give us a clue about how to produce an item like the second test item on ferrets. Let's consider a student response to that item. What does it show about this student's problem solving skills?

> I suppose they could move all the ferrets away and feed them something different, while they keep on killing prairie dogs. Or they could protect the ferrets from the animals that kill them so that more of them would survive and they would eat more and more of the prairie dogs. This would solve the farmers' problems for them and they wouldn't have to kill the prairie dogs. Or they could find some other way to keep the prairie dogs from eating the crops.
>
> I'm not sure any of these will work. Maybe the ferrets won't like to eat other things besides prairie dogs. How do we know that they will? And if there are more ferrets and they eat more and more prairie dogs, that may save the farmers for a while, but what then? If there are more ferrets won't the ferrets eat up all the prairie dogs and then not have any food left? And how can prairie dogs be kept from the crops? I learned that they burrow in the ground, so a fence won't help. They'd just go under. Maybe the farmers should move and leave the prairie dogs and ferrets alone.

It is easy to spot this answer as one in which good problem-solving strategies are present. Here are some of the important things we can detect:

- The student *makes use of* information she already knows about ferrets, prairie dogs, and animals in general;
- The student uses this information to construct some possible *solutions*; and
- The student raises significant questions about the effectiveness *of these possible solutions.*

You may wish to note exactly where in this response these important features are displayed as we did in analyzing the student response to the first assessment item. Instruction in skillful problem solving (and decision making) involves explicitly helping students pay attention to these points in their problem solving, prompting them to reflect metacognitively on how they do this, and providing sufficient opportunities to deliberately practice this way of solving problems using interesting examples. The challenge for the science teacher is to construct interesting problems and create an open classroom environment in which students can grapple with them guided by this organizational strategy (Swartz and Perkins 1990, Swartz and Parks 1994).

The same challenge exists in constructing examples that can be used to assess the level at which students actively engage with problems. Good problem situations for this purpose:

- should not have a simple solution, or a solution that the students can derive by using a simple algorithm; should be authentic problems similar to those we face in the real world and for which we need scientific insight to solve well;
- should call for students to use information they already have;
- should call for students to explore a number of possible solutions; and
- should encourage students to raise important questions about the feasibility of some of these solutions, if not endorse or reject some because of what they already know.

Notice how the strategies used in the second ferret test item accomplish each of these. Students are asked what they might do in order to prompt explicit consideration of possible solutions. They are then asked what they will have to make sure of in order to help them pick the best solution. This prompts them to raise important questions about the feasibility of their solutions. Finally, they are asked whether there is anything they already know that has bearing on how well these solutions will work. This is a direct prompt to get at their sense of the relevance of information they have learned about prairie dogs and ferrets. Finally, this is obviously an authentic problem, yet clearly not a problem with a simple solution.

For your own practice, you might want to construct a prompt that requires students to use this problem-solving strategy around one of the following topics: moving things using simple machines, pollution, exercising for a purpose, colonizing another planet, protection from severe weather, ocean farming, setting up a working ecosystem, or traveling to a distant place to get there by a certain time.

Critical Thinking Skills

A crucial feature of solving problems and making decision in science lies in making critical judgments about the adequacy of possible solutions and the viability of options. This requires the use of a variety of critical thinking skills. These skills are as important in thinking about saving ferrets as they are in setting up a laboratory experiment or constructing a working aquarium. Some of these skills—like being able to make good judgments about the consequences of our options (prediction)—are generic and have broad application outside of science. Others are specific to science content and the procedures used in science, like understanding how to control variables. These skills fall into three basic categories: data collection, analysis of information, and inference.

Prediction is a matter of inference, for example. To teach students to do it well, we should help them base their predictions on good evidence. Classifying things is a matter of analysis. To teach students to do it well, we should help them base their classifications on

important similarities and differences among the things classified. The assessment item about feeding habits of black-footed ferrets aims at assessing the skill of data collection and, in particular, determining the reliability and accuracy of an observation. There are, of course, other skills that fall into these categories. For a more comprehensive list see Swartz and Perkins (1990), Swartz and Parks (1994), and Schraer and Stolze (1988).

One of the most important things we want to teach students in science is to gather information from their own observations with care and thoughtfulness. Just giving practice in observation is not sufficient. Students should also learn to discriminate between accurate and reliable observations and those that are not. This key critical thinking skill is generic; it is also useful in assessing eyewitness reports in history, for examples. So when we imagine a student thinking about an observation in order to determine whether it is reliable or unreliable, we want the student to be thinking about things like the following:

- the observation conditions, the use of observation-enhancing instruments, the knowledge that the observer has of what he or she is looking at, and
- the observer's expectations as well as a number of other factors that can influence the accuracy of an observation report.

The third assessment item about ferret feeding habits is a natural way to try to bring out students' understanding of what influences the accuracy of an observation. The performance here is developing and articulating a plan for bringing back accurate observation reports. The following is a response to that item from a student who has learned how to do this well.

> I wouldn't just go and look around. I would make sure that I was close enough to the ferrets to see what they were eating (I might bring binoculars), and I would also make sure that I had looked at some pictures of the different animals around so that I could identify correctly the ones the ferrets were eating. Maybe I should also write down what I saw when I was seeing it instead of waiting 'til later when I might

forget. That means I'd have to bring a pencil and paper along. And someone else should come too so that we can compare what we are seeing. Then if I tell people that that's what I did they will think that my observations are pretty good ones.

It's very easy to see this is a first-rate response. On the other hand, a student who said simply, "I would go there and look at things," wouldn't be doing very well at this skill.

Instruction in this critical thinking skill involves helping students develop an understanding of what to look for that makes observations reliable by having them work through challenging examples and develop a checklist based on their own collective judgments (Swartz and Perkins 1990, Swartz and Parks 1994). This is not a hard skill to teach, but it does require enough explicit practice to sensitize students to these standards of good judgment about observation reports. (These standards are the basis for any scoring rubric a teacher may develop to fine-tune her assessment of students' mastery of this skill.)

Similar test items can be constructed that reveal how students think about the reliability of written material as a source of accurate information, another generic critical thinking skill. Here's one adapted from an instructional activity connected with library research (Barman et al. 1989):

Randy was interested in the ocean floor and was thinking about how he could get accurate information about it. He went to the library and got a lot of things that were listed under "oceans." Here are some of them:

1. "Man's New Frontier" by Luis Marden, from the *National Geographic Magazine*, April 1987.

2. "Mysteries of the Ocean" by Patrick Harrington, from the *Magazine for Children*, January 1988.

3. "Monsters Under the Sea" in *Great Science Fiction Stories*, 1955.

4. "Incredible World of Deep Sea Oases" by Robert Ballard and J. Frederick Grassie, from the *National Geographic Magazine*, November 1979.

Suppose you found out that one of these authors was an explorer who went to the bottom of the ocean in a submarine. What would that indicate about whether he was a good source of information? Why?

Is there anything about these works that would make you choose some of them as more reliable than the others? What?

What other questions would you want to ask about these sources to try to decide whether they were reliable?

Here's another example of an open-ended item designed for 5th graders that can help us determine whether students have mastered skills related to the need to control variables in making comparative judgments in science, a content-specific critical thinking skill (Massachusetts Department of Education 1989):

A person wants to determine which of two spot removers is more effective. Describe in detail an experiment the person might perform in order to find out which spot remover is better for removing stains from fabrics.

We would like students to provide responses like these:

- We should keep the quantity of the spot removers the same.
- We should make sure the fabric is the same.
- The two spots should be as similar as possible (same kind of stain).

Controlling variables is not a difficult concept for students to grasp, but some don't. A similar example can be constructed using well known laundry detergent commercials. What would you want to find out about the circumstances of the experiment to be able to say that the second detergent really does make clothes whiter? Answers we want students to be able to give include: use of the same washing machine, the same speed of wash, the same water temperature, and the same quantity of detergent.

For your own practice, you might want to construct examples that can be used to assess your students on the following critical thinking skills and topics:

- **Accuracy of observation:** reports of laboratory results, of results of an exercise program, or of results of an earthquake.
- **Reliability of secondary sources:** information from old texts, newspapers, or science magazines.

These, then, are three types of verbal performance items that help us assess students' active understanding of basic concepts in science, their ability to use information in problem situations, and their ability to make discriminating critical judgments that are necessary in solving problems well. Analyzing them, as I

have done, can enrich our understanding of the deeper processes that are important to teach science.

References

Barman, C., et al. (1989). *Addison Wesley Science.* Menlo Park, Calif.: Addison *Wesley.*

Massachusetts Department of Education. (1989). *On Their Own: Student Response to Open-Ended Tests in Science.* Quincy: Massachusetts Department of Education.

Schraer, R., and J. Stolze. (1988). "Critical and Creative Thinking." In *Biology: The Study of Life. Teacher's Resource Book.* Newton, Mass.: Allyn and Bacon.

Swartz, R., and S. Parks. (1994). *Infusing Critical and Creative Thinking into Content Instruction: A Lesson Design Handbook for the Elementary Grades.* Pacific Grove, Calif.: Critical Thinking Press and Software.

Swartz, R., and D.N. Perkins. (1990). *Teaching Thinking: Issues and Approaches,* rev. ed. Pacific Grove, Calif.: Critical Thinking Press and Software.

9 Whither Standardized Assessment?

CHARLOTTE DANIELSON

Talk of assessment fills the air. Most serious discussion of educational reform—whether improvement of classroom learning or more sophisticated approaches to accountability—includes a recognition of the significance of reliable assessment. Yet in all this discussion, few educators seriously argue the merits and demerits of standardized tests. Indeed, much energy is expended on various forms of "alternative assessment," "authentic assessment," and "performance assessment," which are all assumed to be superior to standardized tests. But in order to speak of superiority, one must be clear about purposes. Superior for what? Only when we understand our reasons for administering any form of assessment can we determine the best type. As this chapter will demonstrate, of the various purposes for assessing students, standardized tests are suitable for only a few.

First, what are "standardized tests"? As typically used, the term refers to tests that are administered to large numbers of students, usually through multiple-choice questions and machine-scorable response sheets. Even performance tests, of course, may be "standardized" in the sense that all students complete the same tasks. But for the purposes of this chapter, "standardized tests" will refer to norm-referenced, multiple-choice tests produced by testing companies.

It is important to remember that standardized tests are relatively new on the educational scene. Particularly with the advent of computer technology, standardized, multiple-choice tests made possible the assessment of huge numbers of students at low cost. The availability of inexpensive achievement data enabled educators and policy makers alike to rank students; to place them in special programs; and to compare schools, districts, and states.

Even defenders of standardized tests acknowledge that the results have been used for purposes for which they were never intended and are poorly suited.

This brings us again to the question of purposes. Until we are clear on those, we cannot determine whether standardized tests have a role in schools of the future. And as we consider purposes, we must ask ourselves what information is sought, who will use the information, and to what end.

PURPOSES OF ASSESSMENT

Assessment is a legitimate activity in schools. Indeed, many educational reformers argue that school improvement at all levels is and must be assessment driven. But assessments are not conducted for their own sake; rather, they must be administered for some legitimate purpose. What are those purposes, and which are the most suitable forms of assessment for each?

Instructional Decision Making

Every teacher from kindergarten through graduate school knows the value of good assessment. As teachers work with students every day and as they determine which students need additional help with certain concepts or skills, they require information about children's learning. Naturally, such information must be timely, and it must be aligned with instructional goals. That is, it does not help a teacher to discover in May that her students did not learn a concept that she taught last November, nor to know that her students did—or did not—learn a concept or skill that was not part of the curriculum at all. Thus, for the purposes of instructional decision making, assessments must be aligned with the instructional goals, and they must be administered (and the results known) in a timely fashion.

It is evident that standardized tests are poorly suited to this purpose. Their content is determined through surveys of widely used texts and curriculum guides. However, any particular school or district may or may not have a curriculum that matches what is assumed to be typical and is included on the standardized test. Moreover, any standardized test at a given level almost always includes concepts and skills that are typically taught either before or after that level.

For example, a 3rd grade math test will include items that are usually taught in the 1st and 2nd grades as well as some from a typical 4th or 5th grade curriculum. In this way, the tests can generate a "spread" across the full range of the test and can report that a certain percentage of students, for example, are "performing at the 5th grade level."

In addition, since most standardized tests have a machine-scorable, multiple-choice format, they are clearly only suitable for content that can be assessed in that manner. Thus, such tests may be adequate for assessing students' knowledge of facts and possibly of procedures. But they are completely inadequate to assess students' generative capabilities. That is, these test are inadequate for assessing students' skills in:

- expressing themselves orally or in writing,
- organizing and analyzing an abundance of data,
- devising an experiment to answer an interesting question, or
- working collaboratively with others.

Therefore, to the extent that educators want their students to perform well on norm-referenced, standardized tests, their curriculum becomes that which can be assessed on such tests: primarily low-level knowledge and skills. And while all curriculums include some such content, it is well recognized that citizens of the future will require far more from their schools.

Determining Program Eligibility

As educators strive to maximize the learning of all students by offering them both success and challenges in a high-level curriculum, they recognize that some students require either additional support in that curriculum or challenge that goes beyond the rigor offered. But in order to provide such support or challenge, they must know which students need them. In making their daily instructional decisions, teachers must know which students are learning well in the curriculum and which need more assistance.

To fully meet students' needs and to ensure that the right students are receiving additional assistance or challenge, teachers require the same quality of assessment as for their own teaching: tests aligned to the curriculum that can be used on a frequent basis. To determine that individual students either require additional assistance or can handle additional challenge, teachers must be able to determine which aspects of the curriculum they are learning well and which less well.

Again, standardized tests are poorly suited to this purpose. For one reason, they are not timely. They are administered at most once per year and usually only once every several years. Secondly, they are not aligned. Any student in the school is potentially in need of special assistance at some point. And any student is potentially eligible for additional challenge. But unless teachers have the capability to frequently assess students on the curriculum, they have no way of knowing which are which. So some students fall farther and farther behind until they are far enough behind their peers to qualify for special education services. Likewise, other students who either learn the content quickly or who entered the door understanding it must endure repetition and slow pace. Many of them find other ways to amuse themselves.

Of course, few schools and districts have a clearly defined curriculum with aligned assessments. And the richer the curriculum—the more thinking skills and social skills it includes—the less likely the school is to have developed techniques to assess student learning. For many schools, then, the first step in a comprehensive reform effort to improve the quality of learning for all students is to specify curriculum outcomes and the techniques to be used to assess student performance. Precisely what is the learning, and how will teachers know that students have been successful?

Assessing Course Goals

To ensure success and challenge for each student, educators must also know, on an annual basis, that students have learned the content of the curriculum. This is particularly important when the outcomes of one course are prerequisite for successful learning in another. For example, it is hard for students to learn physics successfully without an understanding of algebra; they can't write a successful paragraph without knowledge of how to construct a sentence. Many schools now require students to demonstrate their proficiency on prerequisite knowledge and skills before

declaring them eligible to enroll in a course. This is not punitive; such educators are concerned that students not be set up for failure. If students lack prerequisite knowledge or skills, the assessment makes clear what has yet to be learned.

In addition, many schools use assessment of course goals for more than the certification of prerequisites. These professionals recognize the consequences for student learning of preparing for good course assessments. When students prepare for a final exam, they must revisit the content of the course, often at a higher cognitive level. They can compare one work of literature with another in English, or one cooking technique with another in Family Life. This encourages students to synthesize and consolidate their understanding and to think more deeply about the content.

Such an approach to the course final illustrates the importance of coordination among different educators within a school or district. If three teachers all teach Algebra I, it is important that students from all three teachers be equally prepared to be successful in, for example, Physics or Geometry. This is not to argue that the courses must be identical. But, given the goal of successful learning for every student, all must be adequately prepared to build on that learning in future study. And those who teach Geometry or Physics must be able to count on the knowledge and skills of those students who enter their classes.

For the purposes of assessing student learning in courses, standardized tests are poorly suited, particularly at the secondary level. Not all students elect to study Physics or Auto Mechanics or Family Life. Any of those courses can and should be intellectually rigorous, and that rigor should be reflected in both the instructional approaches and the assessments used. But a generic test for high school juniors will not yield the information educators need to ascertain the degree to which students have successfully learned Physics or Auto Mechanics or Family Life.

Assessing Program Goals

Educators in most schools and districts with a clearly defined curriculum have prepared program goals for each major area of the curriculum. That is, they have determined what all students in the district will learn as a result of studying Social Studies or Language Arts. Such program goals typically include broad statements such as "understand major historical trends" or "communicate effectively in speaking and writing." But in order for educators and the public to know the extent to which students have achieved those goals, they must be able to assess them. Planning for such assessment involves several steps, including identifying indicators of each goal and setting standards. For example, what does it mean for students to be able to communicate effectively? What can they do? How well?

Therefore, no discussion of assessment is complete without also addressing standards. It can even be argued that setting performance standards in the curriculum is the single most important activity in designing assessments. But setting standards should not be confused with the administration of a standardized test. A district or a school or a single teacher can set standards for student performance. What is needed is a clear articulation of the curriculum and a thoughtful approach to indicators. The standards embodied in a standardized test may or may not be those desired by particular educators.

Many schools and districts use standardized tests to provide information on student performance in a particular program. That is, when determining whether their math or science curriculum needs revision, educators analyze student performance on the math or science portion of a standardized test. As a result of such analysis, they might conclude that students could use improvement in computation or science vocabulary. Such information is useful. However, it is also limited, since it is based on the implicit assumption that the curriculum reflected in the test is that which is valued by the school or district. And since we know that standardized tests are most suitable for assessing low-level knowledge and skills, such information will be over-represented in the results.

Therefore, educators using standardized test results to structure curriculum planning are working with incomplete information. Their students may perform poorly in evaluating the reasonableness of results in math computation or designing science experiments.

But since such skills are not assessed on the standardized test, the educators will never know it.

Assessing Exit Outcomes

Increasing numbers of schools and districts are preparing "exit outcomes," that is, statements of the knowledge and skills their students will possess after completing schooling. In writing such outcome statements, educators and the communities they serve answer the questions, "Why do we have schools? When students leave us, what do they know? What can they do?" Statements of exit outcomes are typically very broad and include such things as "critical and creative thinking" or "the skills of lifelong learning."

Most schools do not attempt to assess exit outcomes directly. Instead, they use them to guide further efforts in curriculum planning and as a tool for curriculum audits. Thus, if a district has an exit outcome relating to critical and creative thinking, those educators might examine their curriculum to ensure that the science program does not rely solely on the memorization of facts and the performance of "cookbook" labs.

In some schools, however, students are being asked to demonstrate proficiency on the exit outcomes themselves and such exhibitions are, in addition to course requirements, a condition of graduation. In these schools, all students are required to demonstrate their ability to think critically and creatively. Such demonstrations may be in any discipline and might consist of an original garment design, a creative solution to a situation in auto mechanics, or a unique approach to a problem in trigonometry. In these schools, students assemble their own portfolios and defend them before a committee of teachers, community or business leaders, and other students.

It is unlikely that any standardized test could enable a school or district to assess student performance on exit outcomes. It depends, of course, on what the outcomes are. If a school's exit outcomes consist of the types of learning that may be assessed on a standardized test, then they might be suitable for that purpose. However, most statements of exit outcomes include competencies that do not lend themselves to the multiple-choice format.

External Curriculum Audit

Occasionally, a district wants to look beyond its own boundaries and answer the questions, "How well are we doing? Even if we know that our students are performing well on our curriculum, how good is that curriculum compared with others?" These are reasonable questions that school boards, for example, have every right to ask and expect an answer to.

District-prepared assessments, no matter how well designed, cannot answer such questions. What is needed is a system by which students from all over the state, or the nation, are assessed using the same procedures and techniques and the results shared.

That is, of course, precisely the purpose of a standardized test. It is intended to enable educators and citizens of an area to compare their schools with others. And if the test were capable of assessing the full range of the curriculum, all the types of knowledge and skills that educators and the community considered important, few would object. The problem with standardized tests, therefore, is not that teachers "teach to the test," but that they are not tests worth teaching to. While few educators maintain that the knowledge and skills assessed on most standardized tests are not worth teaching, many do maintain that they do not represent all that is worth teaching and that they neglect many of the most important outcomes of schooling.

Moreover, increasing numbers of educators also reject the premise that success on such "basic" skills and knowledge represented by the tests is prerequisite to more advanced work. That is, they know that for many students engagement in higher-level thinking—such as imagining themselves as soldiers in the Battle of Gettysburg and writing a letter home—is itself an incentive to learn the more basic skills.

So while the use of standardized tests is appropriate for a curriculum audit, the actual tests used must reflect the entire range of the curriculum deemed important by educators and the community. Otherwise, the information that results from such a test will be skewed in the same way the test itself was skewed.

ASSESSMENT ISSUES

Above we considered the different educational purposes for which educators assess student learning. Each is legitimate and suggests different techniques. For only one of them, however—that of an external curriculum audit—are standardized tests even remotely suited. But there are still several other major issues to consider when looking at assessment.

Different Audience, Different Stakes

Assessment can be either high or low stake. That is, the results of assessments can have more or less serious consequences for students, teachers, or their schools. Classroom assessments designed and administered by teachers, reflecting the curriculum, and for the purpose of feedback to students and guiding instructional decisions are typically low stake. That is, students are not adversely affected if they perform poorly. Because such assessments are typically formative in nature, the consequences for students and teachers are to focus the attention of both on the knowledge and skills that have not yet been learned.

End-of-course finals, on the other hand, normally carry higher stakes for students, since some large proportion of their course grade might depend on it. College admissions tests such as the SAT or the ACT are high-stakes assessments for students because admission to colleges and universities is affected by these scores. Statewide assessments, or in some cases standardized tests, are typically high-stakes assessments for teachers, schools, or districts but not students. In some communities, the average scores of different schools within the district or different districts within the state are published in the newspaper, which can influence real estate values within the communities. Needless to say, administrators and teachers in those schools want their students to perform well.

When educators design assessments, they must determine whether the assessments will be high or low stake and for whom. There are advantages and disadvantages of each.

If assessments are low or no stake, neither students nor teachers will invest much energy in them. Students won't study and teachers won't ensure that students have the opportunity to learn the content. If teachers and students do invest energy in no-stakes tests, it is because they themselves believe the content is important, not because of the test.

On the other hand, if tests are very high stakes for either students or teachers, one or both of them will be tempted to cheat in some manner. Education is full of stories about schools that exclude low-achieving students from a standardized test because including them would depress their average score and cause them to lose face (or worse) in the comparison game. Other stories tell of teachers who unfairly coach their students on the test items or provide unauthorized assistance during the actual assessment. Such practices are more widespread when teachers believe that the test is not aligned to their own curriculum and when they don't believe that the outcomes it assess are of value.

Advantages of Sampling

In most assessments, all students are tested. And for many situations, that is appropriate. But once again, depending on the purposes of the assessment, universal testing may not be necessary, and it increases costs significantly.

For the purposes of instructional decision making, every student must be assessed. That is, in order for teachers to determine which students need more assistance in learning the curriculum, they must ascertain the knowledge and skill of all students. Similarly, if final examinations are given for the purpose of encouraging students to synthesize their understanding and to award final grades, all students must be assessed. And if students are eligible for graduation only after demonstrating proficiency on exit outcomes, they must all be assessed on those outcomes.

But if a school assesses students on its exit outcomes, or even on its program goals, solely for the purpose of learning where to strengthen the curriculum, there is no need to assess every student. And since most schools' exit outcomes do not lend themselves to

paper-and-pencil assessment, sampling for such assessment is especially appealing. Since an unfortunate characteristic of more authentic or performance assessments is that they are far more costly than paper-and-pencil, machine-scorable, multiple-choice tests, one way that many schools can afford to assess their exit outcomes is to assess them in only a relatively small sample of students.

The same reasoning can be used for state-level performance assessments administered for the purposes of school or district accountability. Many states have now enacted high-level exit outcomes and are preparing to assess these outcomes using a variety of formats, including portfolios and observations of performance. These assessments are standardized in that all students are subject to the same exercises. They are high stakes, since a school or district's accreditation often depends on the outcome. But since such assessments are very costly, some states are concluding that they may have to revert to cheaper but less authentic multiple-choice formats. However, there is no need for every student to be assessed. The results of such assessments would never be used to make instructional decisions about individual students; the individual assessments only contribute to calculations of average performance. Thus, a state's interests are better served by spending limited funds on better assessments of fewer students than by limited assessments of more students.

There is nothing inherently wrong with standardized tests. They are unparalleled for certain purposes such as the large-scale, cost-effective assessment of large numbers of students on low-level cognitive objectives. For other purposes, however, other types of assessments are better suited. Why, then, have standardized assessments become so widely used in America's schools?

We can only speculate, of course. One answer almost certainly relates to the fact that standardized tests provide data, and when schools and districts don't have a well-defined curriculum with aligned assessments, some data is better than none. So while standardized tests are acknowledged by most educators as being inadequate for most of the purposes of assessments, they are better than nothing. And in the political school environment, school board members and administrators welcome the seemingly objective appearance of numbers.

The danger in this situation is that as we strive to improve our schools, educators recognize the importance of assessments. And as assessment plays an increasingly important role in the reform process, we must be sure that the assessments we use reflect the breadth and depth of the curriculum we want for our students. Otherwise, our curriculums will revert to that which is assessable using the standardized tests we have, namely low-level cognitive skills. Our children, and our teachers, need more than that.

10

Creating a Cadre for Performance-Based Assessment: A Process Approach for Connecting the Pieces Through Staff Development

ANN JOHNSON AND KATHRYN SCHLADWEILER

Too often in education, staff development is a "talking heads" experience that does little to address what we all know about learners—that they learn best by doing and experiencing. The typical staff development design is expedient, but it offers little in the way of developing the conceptual understandings that performance-based assessment requires. A process-oriented staff development experience is a far more productive and meaningful introduction to performance-based assessment.

In order to assist teachers in north central Iowa who were interested in implementing authentic assessment, we organized and formalized a process we call Cadre Training in Authentic Assessment. The workshop comprises approximately 60 hours of training in authentic assessment and staff development processes that provide the training design and support structure necessary to sustain any innovations. Following the initial intensive training session, we meet approxi-

mately every four to six weeks to provide follow-up training.

ELEMENTS OF TRAINING

The complexity of transforming assessment is overwhelming when we consider the implications for curriculum, instruction, and the system itself. Because of this complexity, staff development plays a critical role in supporting and sustaining the initiative. In working with building leadership teams to implement authentic assessment, we have incorporated the model by Bruce Joyce and Beverly Showers (1988). We have combined this structured staff development process with the Peer Helper Model, which we have found to be very successful in providing the social technology necessary for creating a sense of community. The skills emphasized in the Peer Helper Model—such as active listening, questioning, clarifying, paraphrasing, and listening with both the head and heart—provide the foundation for developing a sense of community that makes people more receptive to dealing with complex change.

Feedback from participants tells us that certain elements in the delivery and organization of our workshops are critical:

- We always co-facilitate.
- We include time for processing the learning.
- We use multiple strategies such as modeling, cooperative learning, and inductive teaching.
- We encourage participants to come in teams that include an administrator.
- We emphasize the follow-up support structure that needs to be addressed in order to sustain an innovation.
- We ask teams to make a commitment to continue the study groups back in their own school districts in order to maintain the support structure.

Overwhelmingly, the most positive feedback always centers on the fact that participants have the chance to work together. It is clear to us that teachers are hungry for opportunities to talk to one another professionally. Their feedback also reaffirms the power of team participation and the collective wisdom that can come from group interactions. Another aspect that keeps coming through in feedback is the power and practicality of having a staff development experience that is task oriented. Hands-on learning activities allow participants to interact with the ideas and focus on a meaningful product connected to essential learning. Through this approach, participants connect the pieces of and practice the design of assessment elements.

A SENSE OF COMMUNITY

Because of our belief in the importance of community building to establish a climate that allows educators to take risks, we spend a significant amount of time with a variety of strategies for group dynamics that will create a sense of community for the workshop participants and also engage them as learners. The "Special Child" is one strategy we use to create a sharing experience that connects participants to one anoth-

er. It also introduces the idea of focusing on what's really important in terms of learning.

We ask participants, "What's more important than the content we teach or test?" Plainly, children are far more dear to us than any content, and they are our hook for getting workshop participants centered. We begin by asking them to make personal connections among learning, assessing, and children.

> Close your eyes and picture a child who's special to you. It can be a child of your own, a grandchild, a niece, a nephew, or a child in your neighborhood. Perhaps it's that child who always sits alone in the lunchroom, tugging at your heartstrings. What are your hopes and dreams for that child? What do you want that child to be able to do, to be like, once he or she is launched into the world? Keep very focused on that child as we proceed with this activity.

We have note cards on each table, and we ask everyone to write his or her name in the center of the card. We also ask them to write at the bottom of the card something they believe is essential for that special child to be able to demonstrate in order to be successful later in life. Sometimes we have participants share at their tables, and sometimes we have them get up and move around the room to share with several people they don't know or don't work with routinely.

After a brief time for sharing, we refocus the whole group by recording on chart paper some of the outcomes they all identified for that special child. We return to this list in every stage of the workshop. Not surprisingly, the outcomes are very similar from place to place, and discrete content issues are seldom mentioned. Instead, educators want children to be self-directed, confident, competent, caring, communicators, responsible, and learners. Why do we spend time like this at the beginning of a staff development on assessment? We want the participants to always keep two things in mind: Assessment is about children. Assessment that's disconnected from essential learning is not helpful or meaningful for children. The special child is a point of reference we use throughout the workshop to keep participants centered on the who, not the what, at the heart of learning.

THE CREATION OF TASKS

Prior to working on assessment tasks, we introduce participants to the idea of planning backwards, a four-step design that models beginning with the end in mind as a means of planning for assessments and instruction. This beginning with the end in mind is definitely a reversal of the planning strategies that teachers have typically used. We keep participants focused on the outcomes they generated for their special child, then we give them a task to work on in teams.

> You are members of a task force from your school that has been asked to draft the significant learnings you believe are essential for all children to demonstrate before they leave your educational program. Please prepare a draft of the significant learnings and be ready to share them at your next faculty meeting.

By modeling the use of an authentic task, we create a context for their learning and stimulate them to generate a list of outcomes that will be a focal point for all of the subsequent learning experiences in the workshop. We ask them to reach consensus at their table on the most important outcome and report out in their group. The outcome that is selected most often becomes the focus of our next steps in the staff development experience. (Frequently, this outcome is "effective communicator.")

> What evidence would you accept that your child or any child has successfully demonstrated this outcome? What would a quality performance of the outcome look like?

Now we brainstorm a list of criteria for the outcome that provides us with a context for introducing "task" and serves as a point of reference later in the workshop when we are ready to introduce criteria.

Rather than define "tasks" for the participants, we distribute a packet of tasks that we have collected.

Participants scrutinize these carefully, looking for the attributes that are consistent among them. Then participants discuss their observations in their small groups. As the groups report out, we compile the list of attributes they have observed. By engaging the participants through the use of inductive teaching, it takes very little direct instruction on our part to flesh out the definitions of task for participants.

To reinforce their learning, we next put participants through a two-step development process. We refocus the group on the significant learnings they identified earlier in the workshop and on the lists of criteria for those outcomes. Generally we select three or four of the criteria from the brainstormed list, and then we ask participants to work in teams. Their job is to design a task that would be an acceptable demonstration of the outcome and includes the three or four performance criteria we isolated. Each team is also asked to record their task product on chart paper so it can be shared with everyone in the workshop.

After about 20 minutes in design dialogue, we ask the groups to share their tasks. As participants share, we invite the others to think about the attributes that we talked about and to put themselves in the role of students. Can the task be clearly understood? Have the designers included the attributes of a worthwhile task?

This activity provides guided, collaborative practice with task development that builds participants' confidence in their understanding of task and its attributes. It also connects the concept of task to what Wiggins calls "the big ideas" within the content (1989). Consequently, we find the tasks that are developed to be amazingly rich. Tasks developed at a recent workshop included:

> **For high school economics:** You are a high school student who has decided to purchase an automobile. You have $500 in savings and a part-time job yielding $75 weekly income. You need to follow the total car-buying process from shopping to financing to insuring and obtaining a title and license. Your task is to choose a car you can afford with your income and pre-

sent your choice and your rationale to the class.

For high school science: You are working for the Department of Natural Resources and have been asked to test the river conditions near a local business. This business, which employs 1,500 people, has been dumping waste into the river for years. Based on your data, develop a list of possible solutions and present your results and recommendations to the appropriate local and state agency.

For 4th grade: The Oregon Trail immigrants are arriving in town tomorrow morning. You have been assigned to go meet the travelers and get all the facts about life along this trail. After you have learned all you can about their experiences, you are to present your findings. Your audience must be a group found in that time period.

Most participants leave the workshop eager to refine this assessment "start" and try it with their own students. In the design step we always encourage participants to connect the task activity to a unit they currently teach so they have a product that is linked to their world when they complete the workshop.

After this activity, it is more comfortable to talk about criteria for evaluation and scoring standards because teachers have their own task to which they can connect the concepts. Processing the activity is a critical dimension of the group dynamics in the training.

CONNECTING THE PIECES

Our final activities introduce the concepts of criteria and performance standards for evaluation. We invite team members to look back at their tasks and to begin to determine the attributes of a quality performance of that task. Focusing on questions regarding the difference between an exemplary performance versus just an acceptable performance versus one that still needs help leads to all sorts of questions. To model the

process, we usually select a task one of the teams has developed and work through criteria and performance descriptors with the whole group before having them make some attempts with their own tasks. The process is simplified because we have previously isolated three to four of the criteria to be used in the task design.

The time we spend on processing and connecting the pieces involved in authentic assessment is well spent. By beginning with an activity that focuses their discussion on significant learning, we attempt to have participants experience the concepts essential to performance-based assessment and to practice developing the components in the backwards planning approach that "beginning with the end in mind" implies.

We have just briefly described aspects of an initial training that involves three days. Through this type of an interactive structure, we offer experiences that ground participants in the theory relevant to authentic assessment and enable then to connect the theory to their own practice through a hands-on approach. Beyond that we encourage them to continue their development and understanding by continuing to function as a study group back in their own districts so that they can have ongoing support.

As we have assisted schools in planning staff development programs for implementing authentic assessment, we have attempted to integrate all that we have learned regarding best practices for staff development, change theory, and adult learning. Some of the ideas have worked better than others, but we have continually adjusted our format and our materials based on participants' feedback, our own observations, and the ever-broadening pool of information regarding authentic assessment.

Since our first staff development effort, we have trained teaching teams from a variety of school districts. We have learned that teachers and administrators develop an understanding of performance-based assessment best when they are immersed in learning-by-doing experiences. Through a process approach, our participants connect assessment to significant learning outcomes and practice designing assessment elements collaboratively and independently. Strategies that help build community are integrated into the staff development model.

After the training we invite participants to continue the study groups back in their own building, and we suggest a number of ways that would be appropriate. We give them several articles to use as a way of building their awareness and helping them discuss different assessment development philosophies. We also encourage them to begin to test the waters by experimenting and developing ideas together in study group settings. We encourage them to keep study group logs to use in the reflection process. We model the use of logs in our training in order to gain valuable data essential to making adjustments to our program. The logs also give participants the opportunity to respond and to give us feedback about their own particular needs. This kind of feedback has helped us make training more effective and meaningful.

Although this process approach to staff development requires an extensive commitment of time by a district or school, our experiences with assessment cadres have reinforced our belief that it is time well spent. Groups we have worked with in this process have indicated high degrees of success with the innovation of performance assessment, primarily because they have learned some strategies for sustaining one another during the implementation period. It is tempting to short circuit the process for the sake of saving time, but expedience in staff development often offers little in the way of developing conceptual understanding. A process-oriented staff development such as we have described offers a productive and meaningful introduction to performance assessment.

References

Joyce, B.R., and B. Showers. (1988). *Student Achievement Through Staff Development.* New York: Longman, Inc.

Wiggins, G. (1989). "A True Test: Toward Authentic and Equitable Assessment." *Phi Delta Kappan* 70, 9: 703-713.

PART IV
....

Shared Vision

Shared Vision

ARTHUR L. COSTA AND BENA KALLICK

> The future is not a result of choice among alternative paths offered by the present, but a place that is created—created first in mind and will, created next in activity.
>
> The future is not some place we are going to but one we are creating. The paths are not to be found, but made, and the activity of making them *changes* both the maker and the destination.
>
> —JOHN SCHAAR

Rapid changes in society are requiring rapid changes in educational organizations. Yet, we also need to regularly revisit our missions to be certain that we have not lost the end in pursuing the means. At the same time that we revisit our purposes, we must continually re-envision what our organization will look like and be dedicated to in order to fulfill the mission. This vision is, as is suggested by Schaar, created first in the mind and will.

Peter Senge (1990) suggests that leadership for creating a shared vision—one that will capture the collective mind and will—begins with creative tension. He describes how creative tension emerges from seeing clearly where we want to be (the vision) and describing truthfully where we are now (the current reality). The gap between the two generates creative tension (Figure IV.1).

This principle of creative tension has long been recognized by leaders such as Martin Luther King Jr., who stated, "Just as Socrates felt that it was necessary to create a tension in the mind, so that individuals could rise from the bondage of myths and half truths . . . so must we create the kind of tension in society that will help men rise from the dark depths of prejudice and racism." Or, as Steven Jobs observed, "If you are working on something exciting that you really care about, you don't have to be pushed. The vision pulls you."

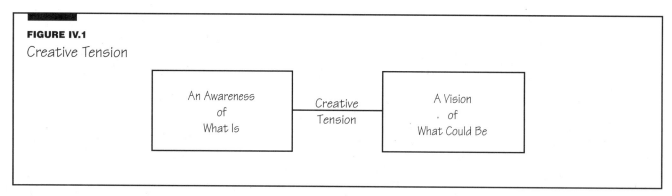

FIGURE IV.1
Creative Tension

An Awareness of What Is — Creative Tension — A Vision of What Could Be

This tension, according to Senge (1990), can be resolved in two ways: by raising current reality toward the vision or by lowering the vision toward current reality. We suggest that it is an individual's or organization's continual assessment that provides a mirror for reflection about the relationship between vision and reality. Assessment is what drives the feedback spiral and provides the creative tension between what is and the best we can imagine.

Effective leaders know how to cause creative organizational tension and how to harness the energy and intellectual stimulation it produces. They create for themselves and facilitate for others the process of developing visions of what could be, images of desired states, valued aspirations, and scenarios of more appropriate futures. Educational leaders bring together the stakeholders—community, staff, and students—to form visions of what a desirable education and school organization could be. They also set in motion a process to assess the alignment with and progress toward achieving that vision. They instill the value of assessment—an assessment frame of mind—that pervades all levels of the organization. The vision will be shared and valued only when a process of assessment is in place to provide feedback about the degree to which the vision is being achieved.

When we consider shared vision, we recognize that an entire organization consists of many parts. Our conception is an unintentional relationship between parts and whole. We cannot expect more of our students than we do of ourselves. The entire organization must be guided by a set of principles.

In Part I we refer to this as an holonomous learning organization where there is a congruence within the organization and, at the same time, any one part of the organization provides a lens into the whole organization. For example, many natural systems possess a fractal quality; that is, they share similar details on many different scales and levels (Briggs 1992). Consider the endless duplication of the patterns of a cauliflower or the repetitions in the shape of a fern. Focusing on any part of the system reveals a reproduction of the system itself.

We contend that assessment creates a fractal quality that reproduces the values of goal setting and clarification, actions to achieve the goals, assessment and feedback, reflection, and further action (the feedback spiral). Only as these attributes spread throughout the entire organization will the vision be shared.

SEARCH FOR INTEGRITY

Although leadership is important in recognizing the need for shared vision, the alignment process is not a simple one. At the center of any vision is a core set of beliefs or a world view. People are actors within their world view, but they do not always examine what guides their actions. The work of shared vision requires a deeper understanding of not just the rhetoric of what we believe but how our actions must be changed to be congruent with the organization's beliefs as well as with the self.

Fullan (1993) points out that sharing a vision does not mean adopting someone else's vision. Reliance on someone else's vision perpetuates cultures of dependence and conformity. Visions die prematurely when they are merely hollow statements developed by leadership teams and when they attempt to impose false consensus that suppresses rather than enables personal visions to flourish.

Fullan goes on to state that deep ownership and sharing of vision comes through the learning that arises from full engagement in solving problems. He states: "The development of authentic shared vision builds on the skills of change agentry: personal vision building through moral purpose, inquiry, mastery, and collaboration. Collective vision building is a deepening, reinforcing process of increasing clarity, enthusiasm, communication and commitment. As people talk, try things out, inquire, re-try—all of this jointly—people become more skilled, ideas become clearer, shared commitment gets stronger."

Fullan supports the "ready, fire, aim" sequence of reform. While there needs to be some notion of direction at the "ready" stage, it is through action and inquiry where skills, clarity, and learning are fostered at the "fire" stage. "Aim" is a crystallization of new beliefs, formulating mission and vision statements, and commitment building. Vision comes later at step three, not at step one. The process of continuous assessment—of constantly monitoring the results of actions, comparing them with the emergence of values, and making personal and organizational meaning through reflection—is what builds shared vision.

Figures IV.2 and IV.3 describe how individuals and organizations employ assessment to search for integrity and congruence between practice and vision. At the center of each diagram is a core set of beliefs. And at the heart of change is the question about how congruent individual beliefs are with the system's set of beliefs, parents' beliefs, and the community's beliefs. The process of shared vision is an alignment process. A learning organization is prepared to work on alignment as an ongoing process to guide its actions.

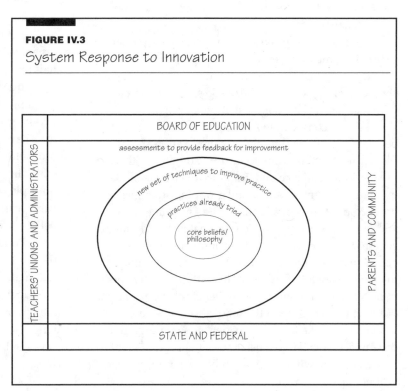

FIGURE IV.2
Individual Response to Innovation

assessments to provide feedback for improvement
new set of techniques to improve practice
practices already tried
core beliefs/ philosophy

FIGURE IV.3
System Response to Innovation

BOARD OF EDUCATION
TEACHERS' UNIONS AND ADMINISTRATORS
PARENTS AND COMMUNITY
assessments to provide feedback for improvement
new set of techniques to improve practice
practices already tried
core beliefs/ philosophy
STATE AND FEDERAL

Let us examine two levels of alignment, individual and system.

Figure IV.2 illustrates how an individual's belief system responds to innovation or change. Say, for example, this center represents a teacher's core set of beliefs about group process as a tool for developing higher-order thinking. The teacher believes firmly that students should be able to work in groups as a way of constructing knowledge. She perceives the need for students to have powerful conversations about subject matter and would like the students to develop more autonomy and authority in their thinking.

The next ring suggests the existing practices that the teacher has used to take action on those beliefs. She has attempted to have the students work in small groups but has found that students do not stay task focused and that the work does not lead to higher-order thinking. She tries to focus her discussions, but she finds that they always seem to be dominated by a few students. After many attempts, she returns to more traditional practices in frustration. She uses traditional management strategies and keeps a tight control over the classroom. She is disappointed with the level of discussion and thinking in the class, but she sees no way to change this.

The next ring provides for the teacher's participation in some experience that suggests a new way of dealing with this question: a staff development workshop or training course, a book she's read, a conference with a coach, a classroom visitation, or attendance at a professional convention. Although she has appeared to be a fairly traditional teacher, the innovation she tries fits her now latent desire to nurture students with greater independence and authority over their thinking. She learns more successful grouping strategies, how to structure more complex and engaging tasks, and how to develop a curriculum that is more student centered. The only way that this innovation becomes a chosen way of practice rather than another technique to use occasionally is when it fits with the center core of beliefs or if the center core of beliefs changes in light of her engagement with the innovation. In other words, unless the teacher experiences some cognitive dissonance or creative tension with the present mental model, change will take place only on the surface and will not last.

The frame for this organizer is assessment. When it is not seen as punitive or intimidating, assessment can frame the opportunity to stabilize the change. When the teacher agrees to collect evidence of students' process and product regarding higher-order thinking, the evidence will provide a lens through which she can re-examine her assumptions about teaching and learning. For example, the teacher may try one of the group strategies that she learned. She may ask students to solve a complex problem and focus on the level of thinking that takes place as they work. The evidence she collects might include scripting one group, videotaping group work, developing criteria regarding successful thinking in group work, and using a self-assessment tool for students.

The key point is that the teacher will be prepared to frame her assessment in light of the core beliefs as well as the instructional strategies. She may need to list her assumptions about learning in groups as a way to assist her as she determines what evidence to collect. This process, as we have described in the feedback spiral, provides a frame for what Phil Jackson refers to as the 1,300 decisions a teacher makes while teaching (1968).

Figure IV.3 illustrates how holonomous learning organizations seek congruence among all the individuals and groups that work within the system. As individual teachers examine their core beliefs about teaching and learning, so do parents, administrators, and boards of education. So, for example, a system may have established in its core beliefs that higher-order thinking and self-directed learning are important. They may have established that learning from multiple perspectives is a significant strength of a diverse learning community. The next ring around those beliefs is, once again, the actions that have been taken.

Perhaps the superintendent says, "I believe that these attributes are important, and I hope that teachers will make them happen in the classroom." Or perhaps the superintendent says, "I believe that these attributes are important, and I will make certain that my behaviors reflect the significance of these attributes." If she says the latter, she is working toward alignment. If she says the former, alignment will be less likely.

The ring around the core beliefs represents how the superintendent has tried to realize these beliefs through her work but has had difficulty. She tried shared decision making, but it led to system paralysis. She tried to engage teachers in conversations about their practice, but it didn't lead to higher-order thinking. She is frustrated and, under pressure, falls back to the tradition of making decisions on her own. She has fewer meetings and says there is no time for shared decision making and thinking.

The next ring brings her to some new strategies and innovations. She now has learned something about how to facilitate a group discussion with administrators that will lead to higher-order thinking. She is able to facilitate more thoughtful group work in schools for shared decision making. She is learning how to use new techniques that are compatible with or change her beliefs.

Once again, the assessment frame serves as a catalyst for either creating or dealing with her cognitive dissonance. She not only learns new ways of dealing with groups, but she examines her purposes more closely. She is able to collect evidence in relationship to questions that have disturbed her about group work. For example, her impression is that group work led to paralysis. How can she collect evidence about that impression? As she tries the new strategies, how will she define success for the group? What would she look for that would tell her that meaningful decisions are being made? How might the group build practices that require them to self-assess their work?

The significance of these maps is in examining how well they are aligned. If a system finds that there is a high degree of alignment between individual and group in terms of core beliefs and continuous examination of actions on behalf of those beliefs, it is a learning organization—there is integrity and congruence. If there is a great deal of misalignment and incongruence, the organization is at odds with itself and it is likely that individuals, who are extremely sensitive to the subtle cues of organizational integrity, will retreat to safety rather than commit to system change.

Systems can have conflicting forces pulling them from many different external sources in many different directions. For example, as Figure IV.3 illustrates, there might be pressures from the board of education, the community, parents, the teachers' union, the state department of education, federal education acts, and administrators. Each of these groups may have a different perspective to bring to the task of establishing a core set of beliefs. However, the challenge of a democratic nation is bringing multiple perspectives together and finding enough agreement to move forward in the best interest of society. Since the purpose of schools is to prepare students for participation in a democracy, its practice at all levels of the school system becomes essential to the significance of that purpose.

ACHIEVING THE SHARED VISION

In an interview on National Public Radio, former New York governor Mario Cuomo was asked how he could explain the fact that he described in very articulate and visionary terms what he thought needed to be done in the best interest of the people of his state and yet was unable to deliver on that vision. A paraphrase of his response was, "A leader needs to be a visionary. A leader has to remind people of the best possible circumstances toward which we must strive. A leader must be able to do this in spite of the fact that he will probably be unable to reach that ideal during his leadership." Cuomo is espousing the philosophy of shared visioning.

Our premise for re-examining schools is that it will take agreement from the entire community before schools will really be able to make the necessary changes to meet the needs of our diverse society. Nothing short of a commitment to continuous improvement toward common purposes that will take place over time will achieve change. We are faced with the need to modify our linear way of thinking and accept that to provide a better education for each of our children, we will be navigating dynamic, responsive, and ever-changing waters. Our journey will feel more like whitewater rafting than an easy cruise across the ocean.

To begin this journey, we will need to revisit what we consider to be the purpose of school in our democratic nation. We suggest that the schools have a threefold mission:

- To educate people so that they can live productively in our economy.
- To educate people so they can fully accept the responsibility of citizenship in our democracy.
- To educate people so they can make the best use of their leisure time through the arts and personal well-being.

These have always been the mission of schools in our society. We need to have continuing dialogue that reminds us of this mission as we develop aims, goals, and expected outcomes for students. Those conversations will eventually lead to agreement about what it is we expect students to know and be able to do when they leave our schools. However, in an holonomous learning organization, we must be certain that we do not expect more from our students than we expect of ourselves. Our shared vision must include all members of the community, not just the children. As long as we expect the vision to be for the future, we allow ourselves to behave as if the achievement of that vision is the responsibility of the next generation.

Outcomes, on the other hand, are what we all should live by and expect of ourselves in our own performance. For example, if we want students to be able to think and communicate critically and analytically, do we find attributes of critical and analytical communication in ourselves, in our classrooms, in our schools, in our district, and in our community?

Schools across the country are struggling through a process of developing their missions, describing outcomes, deriving goals, setting standards, and identifying performance indicators. Let us examine one typical set of outcomes or results from one community and ask whether they make sense not only for the students but also for the other members of the school community.

In the first district, staff members, students, and community members met regularly, over time, to describe student outcomes. After much consideration, they described the following:

- Responsible, caring citizens.
- Lifelong learners.
- Responsible citizens in a diverse and global society.

- People with a sense of well-being and healthy self-esteem.
- Caretakers of the earth.
- Appreciate the arts.
- Enthusiasm in academic pursuits.

Consider these outcomes in light of four criteria for the holonomous learning organization:

- The outcomes transcend all subject matter and grade levels—all staff members can commit to them.
- Cumulative evidence along a developmental continuum may be gathered regarding the increasingly complex performance of these outcomes over time.
- Evidence of these results may be observed by the time our students complete their schooling.
- These outcomes are lifelong pursuits, as appropriate for the adults as they are for students. We see similar evidence of increased learning among the adults in the school community.

By these standards, are this first district's outcomes worthy of assessment? Notice some of the problematic words when you consider demonstrations: responsible, sense of, caretakers, appreciate, enthusiastic. Each of these statements represents a vision of what would be good to see but would be difficult to demonstrate.

There seems to be some confusion between what is meant by a shared vision and outcomes. We are confused about what we consider to be a vision and have difficulty distinguishing the sense of direction a vision offers us from the small and concrete steps we take to get there. We share a vision that all students in our society will have an equal opportunity to be educated. We now need to examine the small, concrete steps that we take to get there. We refer to those steps as outcomes and we need to constantly ask ourselves, "Do the outcomes we have described help us to arrive at our shared vision?" When we look at the above outcomes, we question whether they are measurable, concrete steps. Many of them might be better stated as a shared vision for the future.

In a second school district, after considerable dialogue with community, the following outcomes were stated:

- Students will demonstrate competence in academic areas as measured by a set of standards.
- Students will know how to use technology to acquire information and solve problems.
- Students will be able to think and communicate critically and analytically.
- Students will be able to work cooperatively in order to accomplish more thoughtful work.
- Students will be able to see patterns and trends in raw data.
- Students will know the rigors of experimental inquiry.

This set of outcomes appears to be more demonstrable for students, staff, and community. We see the potential for each of these outcomes to be assessed. They were derived from a shared vision about the purpose of schools. Note, however, that the first outcome—all academic areas—is the only outcome that refers to measurement because it is the only one for which we presently have accepted systems for measuring. The implication of this set of outcomes is that only one will be put to a test of accountability. The others appear to be valued, but there is no assurance that they will be valued enough to be assessed.

The present challenge we face in education as we name the more important and more valued outcomes for students is that we will need to create ways to assess whether students demonstrate evidence that they are showing progress in these areas. Our present pencil-and-paper testing system is too limited to provide evidence in areas such as critical thinking, finding patterns in raw data, and knowing how to and being able to perform rigorously when faced with a problem not seen before. These goals need to drive new curriculum alignment in thoughtful schools of the future. The delivery system—curriculum materials, instructional strategies, school organization, and the curriculum alignment decision-making processes—needs to embody these goals not only for students but for all of the school's inhabitants.

Likewise, our methods of assessment must be transformed to become more consistent with our new goals. We cannot employ product-oriented assessment techniques to assess the achievement of these new,

process-oriented educational outcomes (Costa and Kallick 1992). If a school or district values these outcomes, it will assess students' demonstrations of and proficiency in these more process-oriented outcomes.

THE ASSESSMENT MATRIX

"Look here," said the proud superintendent. "Here is our completed statement of our mission, our vision, our outcomes, and our goals for the school district. It's taken a long time, and we worked hard. We've involved the community and staff, parents, and even the students in hammering out this document. Our job, however, is far from complete. We must now decide on strategies to assess our progress toward and achievement of our outcomes. We must set in motion a mechanism for informing us about how are we doing in aligning our practices with our philosophy."

Many school boards adopt lofty and valuable goals, outcomes, mission statements, vision statements, and other philosophical creeds. While these may be inspirational, many staff and community members may see them as yet more "these too shall pass" documents to fulfill a public relations responsibility and to demonstrate the district's innovative stance by participation in a current educational trend. Such statements may end up gathering dust in the archives. Do they really make a difference?

We suggest that the addition of assessment is the signal to the staff and community that this is something different. We've had years of innovations in education that have made little difference. One reason the innovations failed to be adopted widely and fell short of their desired ends was that they were not assessed adequately or they were assessed for the wrong reasons. (For example, does a program for enhancing self-esteem affect increased scores on standardized reading tests?)

Unfortunately, school environments, cultures, and traditions send mixed signals to teachers, support staff, parents, students, and the community, leading to confusion in practice.

- We want students to think, but they must improve their scores on low-level cognitive standardized tests.

Figure IV.4

Assessment: A Planning Matrix

STANDARDIZED ACHIEVEMENT Subtests								
MATRIX SAMPLING (NAEP/STATE TESTS)								
TEACHER–MADE CRITERION– REFERENCED TESTS								
TEACHER OBSERVATION								
JOURNALS AND WRITING SAMPLES								
CHECKLISTS								
INTERVIEWS								
EXHIBITIONS								
INVENTORIES								
PORTFOLIOS OF STUDENT WORK								
CHILD/STUDY ANECDOTAL RECORDS								
EXTENDED PROJECTS								
CRITICAL INCIDENTS								
OTHER								

- We say we value creativity, but students are given multiple-choice tests.
- We want students to learn to work in cooperative groups, but when they are tested, they must quietly work individually and not look at others' papers.
- We want students to take the time to explore issues in depth, consider consequences, and identify assumptions, but tests are timed and the curriculum must be covered in preparation for graduation, the test or college entrance exam, or passing to the next grade level.
- We value student thinking, but school awards are given for athletic performance, attendance, grades, and citizenship.
- Teachers are admonished to teach for thinking, but they are evaluated on their performance of a limited range of instructional behaviors that have been correlated with high test scores.

Thus, while using energy to further define and elaborate critical thinking, teachers are more influenced by the cues from their environment and school culture as to what is important to teach and assess (Frymier 1987). Traditionally structured schools, classrooms, testing procedures, and curriculum may send confusing and complicating signals to the staff, students, and community about what is truly valued and rewarded in school. The addition of congruent assessment of all that is valued as outcomes of schooling is the key to sharing the vision.

The matrix in Figure IV.4 can serve as a tool to ensure that we take into consideration all of our outcomes and find appropriate measures for them, and do not overload the system with one particular way of looking at student performance but develop complementary systems for assessing.

The purpose of this organizer is to assist district planning teams in making sure all their valued outcomes are assessed in a suitable fashion. The intent is to enter the outcomes in the spaces across the top and then select from the array of assessment strategies in the left-hand column those that will best disclose data about achievement of that particular outcome. For example: Students may demonstrate "competence in academic areas" as measured by standardized achievement tests. These same tests, however, may not be the best way for students to demonstrate their "ability to think and communicate critically and analytically." Perhaps performances or journals would be more appropriate. Students' demonstrations of their "ability to work cooperatively to accomplish more thoughtful work" may best be assessed through extended projects and teacher observation.

While all the assessment tools listed in the left column have their individual merits, no single form of assessment will prove adequate in providing information about all the goals. Each goal or outcome will necessitate one or more forms of assessment uniquely designed to disclose desired information in a form that will be meaningful to the audience for which it is intended: students, community, school board, teachers, or parents.

Our priorities are another signal of what is valued. Through the use of the matrix there can be a more systematic, complete, and balanced assessment of all the district's cherished outcomes. It is not intended that all outcomes will be assessed using all the assessment tools every year. Outcomes should be prioritized and rotated over the years. Some may be assessed yearly—academic areas, for example. The outcomes of "use of technology" or "working cooperatively" or "communicating critically and analytically" may be assessed periodically.

As we consider the discipline required for coming to a shared vision, we must also differentiate the outcomes or results we expect to see as we move toward that vision from the more idealistic vision itself. If we truly value our outcomes, we'll devote our resources to assessing them.

> Anytime a change takes place in the future, it starts as a vision in someone's mind. The person draws other people into that vision, and when enough people are drawn into share that vision, it explodes into activity.
>
> —NANCY HATHAWAY, TEACHER
> ADRIAN, MICH.

References

Briggs, J. (1992). *Fractals: The Patterns of Chaos.* New York: A Touchstone Book.

Costa, A., and B. Kallick. (1992). "Reassessing Assessment." In *If Minds Matter*, edited by J. Bellanca, R. Fogarty, and A.Costa. Palatine, Ill.: Skylight Publishing.

Frymier, J. (September 1987). "Bureaucracy and the Neutering of Teachers." *Phi Delta Kappan* 69, 1: 9-14.

Fullan, M. (1993). *Change Forces: Probing the Depths of Educational Reform.* New York: The Falmer Press.

Jackson, P. (1968). *Life in Classrooms.* New York: Holt, Rinehart, and Winston.

Senge, P. (Fall 1990). "The Leader's New Work: Building Learning Organizations." *Sloan Management Review*, pp. 7-21

From Paradigm to Practice IV: Shared Vision

One of the frustrations many educators experience in school change is how to make certain that, once a vision is developed, everyone in the school feels accountable to work toward it. In the work of Chris Louth, we see a classroom teacher's struggle to draw upon the shared vision from the Coalition of Essential Schools in her work with students. Marcia Knoll, Susan Kreisman, and Timothy Melchior discuss the strategies they used to try to bring coherence to classroom practices as they strive toward a shared vision for students.

11   The Dirty Hands of a Visionary

Chris Louth

We hear a great deal about vision these days. Schools embarking on reform are cautioned to spend time thinking through and articulating a vision. While this work is not to be taken lightly, it does raise a dilemma. How we can we be sure the vision does what it's intended to do? How can we be sure a vision guides faculty in their practice instead of gathering dust on a shelf? Historically, the latter has been the reality, not the former.

Michael Fullan (1992) reminds us of "the importance of reculturing, and not just restructuring." In fact, Fullan argues that action to solve problems precedes clear articulation of a vision since "people need to get their hands dirty before they can articulate their vision, make it more focused, then use it as a guide." Fullan's point is verified in my work as a classroom teacher and as a National Faculty Member of the Coalition of Essential Schools. I work with other schools in their struggle to shape a vision and use it to build schools where all kids can learn. I have seen just what it means for people to "get their hands dirty."

BEGINNINGS OF A VISION

An initiative in my district called The Writing Workshop brought K–12 teachers, administrators, and board members together for a dozen release days a year to explore language and learning theory across the curriculum and to reflect on their own practice in the classroom. The facilitators of that program clearly worked within the frame of a vision, and they modeled for us what it meant to be reflective practitioners. They were colleagues who did not try to disguise problems behind classroom doors but acknowledged the need to collaborate in order to provide long-term learning opportunities for kids.

As a group, we wrote together and recommended to the district a language policy. For most of us, this policy represented the first time we had worked on articulating a vision that might have a life beyond the unread pages of a school policy manual. The policy read in part:

> Students at all grade levels and in all subject areas need to talk in order to share new information, to organize ideas, and to ask their own questions. They need opportunities to use informal writing to summarize, question, and explore answers. Students must become active participants in their own learning. The learning process is short circuited when students have the impression that there is always one right answer to a question.

It was about this time that I first read Nancie Atwell's *In the Middle* (1987). It helped shape a vision with my colleagues that I was also trying to enact in my classroom. I wanted my classroom to be a place where kids could participate in reading and writing workshops that reflected the same sort of intellectual engagement typical of skilled readers and writers in the "real world."

Struggling with the many problems that arise when a vision in a teacher's head intersects with the day-to-day realities of diverse students, I had the luxury of sharing my work with peers—many of them veterans of The Writing Workshop—who were undergoing similar struggles of their own. We commiserated with each other, but we also provided the beginnings of a new kind of accountability—to ourselves and each other. We continually asked, "Is what happened in my classroom today (or this week or this unit) in accordance with what I believe about teaching and learning?"

Enter Sherry King, our new our high school principal, who suggested our school explore membership in The Coalition of Essential Schools, which holds that a vision, not a blueprint, is requisite for schools to structure themselves so that all students can "use their minds well." Based on the work of Ted Sizer's research

in the early 1980s, the Coalition's vision is encapsulated in the "9 Common Principles" and fully articulated in *Horace's Compromise* and *Horace's School*. Those of us in the high school who had participated in The Writing Workshop found an immediate sense of connection with Sizer's work, and his vision provided a forum for the entire faculty to explore—and argue about—what learning really was.

Most readily accepted were the ideas that all students should be actively engaged in their work, that mastery should be required of them, and that a maximum class load of 80 to 1 was necessary to connect with students. More contentious elements of the vision included the ideas that teachers should be coaches rather than deliverers of a commodity called knowledge; that less could be more (teaching everything results in mastering nothing); that teachers should be generalists who coach students in integrated, not discipline-based, courses; and that an environment of trust, decency, and unanxious expectations should be the hallmark of the school. After school visits, faculty workshops, and attendance at Coalition conferences, we voted as a faculty to affiliate with the Coalition. What followed was a more whole-school effort to bring a vision to life.

A TIME OF CHANGE

The list of changes over the last four years that resulted from this commitment are numerous. Interdisciplinary classes were piloted, and teachers began to enhance their previously informal collaboration by team teaching. Previously "self-contained" students were mainstreamed into heterogeneous classes, a student-faculty congress was formed, and advisory groups were started for students—all in order to build a sense of community in a school and live up to the idea that all kids can learn. The daily schedule was revised twice in order to provide longer blocks of time for students to do focused work and for teachers to work together.

A senior options program emerged, which seemed to be a first step toward students graduating by exhibition rather than by accumulating Carnegie units. Teachers began developing local authentic assessments to replace state exams. All of these changes provided opportunities for teachers to collaborate around building a program reflective of a shared vision. They were, in fact, "getting their hands dirty," and their mental image of a school vision reformulated with each of these changes. It would be false, however, to indicate that this has been a comfortable process.

ON THE FAULT LINE

Recently, Ted Sizer has begun speaking of this kind of work in schools as being on "the fault line of educational reform"—the place where practice and theory meet and inform each other. While we all know that the products of fault lines eventually can be whole new landscapes, we also are reminded by recent earthquakes in California that devastation can result as well. Change in my high school reflects that paradox. Students have blossomed when given the chance to develop portfolios of writing based on their own experience and their own reflections about learning. Students who were not inspired to write a classic research paper on Tiananmen Square astounded an audience of peers and adults by producing a series of interior monologues about that conflict. A class of students impressed a visitor recently with their knowledge about India, most of which was developed via collaborative research.

I can also attest to the power of team teaching and planning with colleagues. It's good to have someone else to reflect with about the same experience, and we model for students collaboration in action. Yet my teaching teammates and I have experienced the tremors—and sometimes quakes—that erupt at fault lines. They occur in the classroom when innovative assignments don't inspire kids to explore and connect or when we know that there are still too many kids that we have to prod to work toward high levels or who would prefer to take a multiple-choice test to show their learning. Pressures build just from the sheer exhaustion of trying to collaborate with others in designing curriculum and assessment along with participating actively in "whole-school change" and also from long-term pressures of the reculturing of a school.

Even as more and more faculty take advantage of professional development opportunities and advanced course work provided by The Coalition and similar initiatives, other educators continue to question whether our decision to join the Coalition was a valid one and whether the changes we've made really have prompted students to use their minds well. These questions and concerns are rightfully raised, and while they have provided for difficult faculty meetings on more than one occasion, they are also imperative if we are to forge a culture atypical in the American school: one that supports the open and difficult dialogue necessary for teachers to construct a school where everyone works toward a common vision. The attendant danger in such a dialogue, if not conducted within clear norms where colleagues work together toward continuous improvement, is a degeneration into win/lose arguments not conducive to fine-tuning a vision. The dilemma then becomes how to get one's hands dirty without continually feeling as though everything about the work is "mud."

This dilemma is not idiosyncratic to the high school where I teach but is typical in light of my experiences as a Critical Friend to other schools. My journey toward enacting a vision included a decision to become a member of The National Faculty of the Coalition. This included intensive professional development focused on reflective classroom practice and facilitation of work with colleagues in my own and other Coalition schools. Much of my work in other schools and with other teachers has aimed at building capacity for reflective practice and peer coaching. While specific issues within faculties are different, the varying levels of staff support for enacting a vision are typical, as are the various interpretations of what that vision would mean for the school if enacted.

Observing classes and planning sessions, and then facilitating sessions where teachers help each other analyze the data that classrooms provide, illustrates a vision of a school where peer coaching for continuous improvement became the norm. Learning would become more coherent for kids, because teachers would be much more able to build on work in other classes and grades. Arguments among the faculty might be more likely to center on how to solve problems rather than clashes in values that can't seem to be solved (at least in the short term). Each teacher's ability to reflect and explore various possibilities for their own practice would increase. One of the greatest beneficiaries of observing another class is the observer, because observation fosters reflection on the spot, something that can't happen while one is teaching.

Difficulties emerge in most schools, however, because part of the regular, ongoing work of the school is not structured around examining "the dirt on the hands." Time is not regularly set aside for teachers to carefully examine their work, nor to clearly identify problems and then use appropriate strategies (as opposed to knee-jerk reactions) to solve them. It cannot be ignored that while teachers attest to the power of collaboration with each other, they also acknowledge that it exacts a toll. Teachers who have been schooled by years of experience to be isolated must endure "unlearning" old patterns even as they learn new ones. This is hardly a comfortable task, and it is further complicated by the fact that being new to collaboration increases the time it takes, a commodity not significantly provided even in restructured (and ostensibly rescheduled) schools. Also, simply providing time won't do the trick; faculty members need additional skills in order to do this sort of work well.

According to ethnographers Patrick McQuillan and Donna Muncey, Coalition schools that have more successfully weathered the difficulties of change "have created opportunities . . . to help faculty and administrators develop the skills needed to implement Coalition philosophy and realize their desired outcomes. These include not only skills to improve collaboration with colleagues, make parental interactions more productive, and cope with teachers' expanded roles as student advisors. Other skills of concern to Essential school teachers include: team teaching; shared leadership (management and administrative techniques); interdisciplinary planning; developing curricula driven by essential questions; devising appropriate performance-based assessments; and creating long-term goals and a vision for their schools" (p. 7).

And so, for the moment, it sometimes seems we are in the mud, mired in the momentous task of fundamentally changing not just individual classrooms but whole school cultures. I once believed that changing my classroom was enough; but I now realize that belief just reinforces the ingrained culture of "close the door and do what you want." Despite serious disagreements, we are moving toward a much more articulated vision of what we would expect from a graduate, and the need to use student work as the data to help us find that vision. Elsewhere, I continue to meet an ever-growing group of professionals who realize that they may have to play different roles and relate differently with their colleagues in order to "move" a school. At the risk of sounding complacent, however, there are some discoveries that have been made along the way that might make the work less anxiety producing and, most important, more likely to reculture schools in the long run:

- An official awareness of the time necessary—for educators on a day-to-day basis and for schools over a period of time—to enact visions that are worth sharing. This must be supported via national, state, and district policies, but it will also require that teachers rethink their own roles as professionals.
- Support from school districts, states, and national reform groups to provide long-term, intensive professional development for faculty and an environment that both encourages and demands that a vision be lived up to.
- A personal commitment to lifelong learning from all involved. If teachers are not continuing to learn, neither will their students. Teachers cannot possibly model what they do not do themselves. This will entail ongoing reflective practice and a supportive structure. No more closed doors for administrators, teachers, or students.
- A commitment by teachers and schools to seek a Critical Friend—"an outside pair of eyes"—not in an evaluative sense but in order to provide schools the ethnographic data necessary to fine-tune a vision.

While all this talk of earthquakes and mud is hardly inspiring, it grounds us in the realities we need to acknowledge. And that combination of reaching for a lofty vision with muddy hands may strike just the right balance if we are indeed to build schools that embody visions worth enacting.

References

Atwell, N. (1987). *In the Middle: Writing, Reading, and Learning with Adolescents.* Portsmouth, N.H.: Boynton/Cook Publishers.

Fullan, M.G. (1992). "Change: A Guide for the Perplexed." Excerpt of keynote address to the 1992 Annual Symposium, NEA Center for Innovation.

McQuillan, P., and D. Muncey. "Change Takes Time: A Look at the Growth and Development of the Coalition of Essential Schools." *The School Ethnography Project, No. 10.* Providence, R.I.: Coalition of Essential Schools, Brown University.

Sizer, T.R. (1984). *Horace's Compromise: The Dilemma of the American High School.* Boston: Houghton-Mifflin.

Sizer, T.R. (1992). *Horace's School: Redesigning the American High School.* Boston: Houghton-Mifflin.

12 Toward More Authentic Assessment

Susan Kreisman, Marcia Knoll, and Timothy Melchior

Authentic assessment was a very appealing prospect for the Valley Stream Central High School District. For many years we have been committed to teaching thinking with an information-processing approach that prizes and targets students' abilities to use information in critical and analytical ways. Although our efforts in this area span a decade, a five-year staff development program specifically targeting information processing began in 1990-91.

Using ASCD's Dimensions of Learning program and Edward deBono's CoRT thinking program as a framework, the staff has been immersed in learning about and using information-processing skills such as problem solving, decision making, comparison, and CoRT tools that will enable students to process concepts and information in meaningful ways. It became increasingly critical, then, to find a means of assessing how well these information-processing tools were being used by students.

A steering committee was formed in the spring of 1991 to explore how we might assess students' abilities to use course information in meaningful ways that would demonstrate their thoughtful application of the content. The steering committee represented all four schools in the district and was composed of interested administrators, counselors, and teachers. It was our intent to have a systemic impact across all disciplines.

The sharing and discussion of information about authentic assessment continued for several months as the committee labored to define authentic assessment. The following definition resulted: Authentic assessment actively involves students in a process that joins what is taught, how it is taught, and how it is evaluated. The definition, its graphic representation, and an advance organizer were produced as a means of more clearly guiding those who chose to become involved (Figures 12.1 and 12.2).

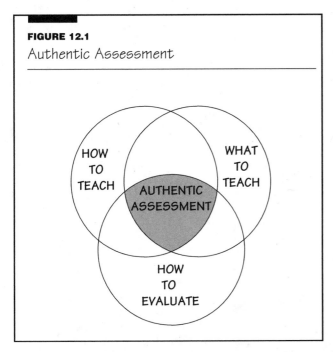

FIGURE 12.1
Authentic Assessment

HOW TO TEACH

WHAT TO TEACH

AUTHENTIC ASSESSMENT

HOW TO EVALUATE

The district's Executive Council (composed of the superintendent, district administrators, and principals) reviewed the steering committee's work. There was unanimous agreement with both the concept and the product. The Executive Council's support was further demonstrated by their agreement to suspend traditional local finals for courses in which an authentic assessment would be conducted. The next step was to encourage teachers to participate in a pilot program that would employ authentic assessment strategies.

Steering committee representatives encouraged teachers within each school to become involved in the pilot program. Fourteen proposals were submitted by teachers of English, social studies, mathematics, and home economics, representing all of the district's schools.

Several staff development activities were conducted to support these teachers' work as well as develop some knowledge and skills for other interested teachers. The first efforts targeted a building support system so that all teachers involved in the pilot program would have others at their site with whom to talk, solve problems, and explore. This informal network was made visible to other members of the building staff and interest was aroused.

Additional efforts were designed to support teachers in the pilot program and to entice teachers to find out about this new process of authentically assessing students' abilities to think about and use course content. The district's authentic assessment coach offered a Board of Cooperative Educational Services course for inservice credit, and many teachers participated. The course simulated authentic assessment by requiring the participants to learn by actually proposing and conducting an authentic assessment with one of their courses.

Two other district staff-development strategies contributed to the support and information objectives. First is an Options Program, which provided district teachers with one day in which to pursue a professional activity. Second is a Teacher Study Group Program, which awards one inservice credit toward salary improvement for any group of teachers who meet together for 15 hours to work on a professional topic. Teachers in the district are currently engaged in both of these strategies on the topic of authentic assessment.

As a part of the evaluation of the 14 pilots conducted during the 1991-92 school year, teachers and students in the pilot were asked to reflect on the following questions:

- How was my involvement in the authentic assessment different from what I expected it to be?
- Was there a difference between the depth of knowledge represented by student products and that which might have been achieved through traditional testing?
- How did students react to authentic assessment?
- How would you change the assessment you designed for future use?
- What recommendations would you make to a colleague interested in authentic assessment?

The responses from teachers and students were very positive. Teachers said that the actual experience lived up to and exceeded their expectations. Many teachers reflected on how limiting the former practice of relying on the textbook had been. In general, teachers said that the knowledge gained by the students was more relevant to them and would probably be of more lasting value. Teachers noted that their students'

FIGURE 12.2

Authentic Assessment Worksheet

Authentic assessment actively involves students in a process that joins what is taught, how it is taught, and how it is evaluated.

SUBJECT:

What major and critical concepts, knowledge, skills, and understandings will be addressed?	
What is the task through which students will demonstrate their understandings?	
What instructional strategies may be used to teach the concepts?	
How will students be involved in reflective activities with the teacher and peers so that they will be able to explain and discuss their ongoing progress?	
How will the authentic assessment be evaluated?	

reactions to authentic assessment evolved. At first, students were reticent and fearful. After they understood and made connections, they became amazed, which led to involvement with and commitment to excellence. Teachers had many ideas about how to change the design they had created and used for the pilot. These included refining the grading process; enlarging the scope of alternatives offered to students to include opportunities involving the larger community; and detailed and early communication of specifics to students. Pilot teachers also offered the following recommendations to their colleagues: create a framework for the entire process and communicate it to all staff members and establish the criteria for the assessment and the accountability measures of the program.

Students said that the actual experience was pleasurable, interesting, and more related to real knowledge and resulted in greater understanding. They stated that the experience produced greater knowledge because of the need to really understand so that you could apply what you learned to an actual product or task. At first, students' reactions to authentic assessment was apprehensive, but later the feelings became positive and they were motivated. Students suggested that the guidelines and specifics should be given at the beginning of the course to prepare students. They urged their classmates to try their best consistently and conscientiously because it is a wonderful experience.

THE WHY, HOW, AND WHAT OF AUTHENTIC ASSESSMENT

What is perhaps of greatest interest is the process that teachers went through as they worked to first appreciate, then understand, and finally create a design for authentic assessment of the course they were teaching. Teachers met over a period of months to study Authentic Assessment and share their experiences as they struggled to apply it in their classrooms. As their "feel" for Authentic Assessment and all its implications grew, they found themselves recognizing the necessity of defining clearly in their minds three aspects of their teaching tasks: what is taught, how it is taught, and how it is evaluated (Figure 12.3).

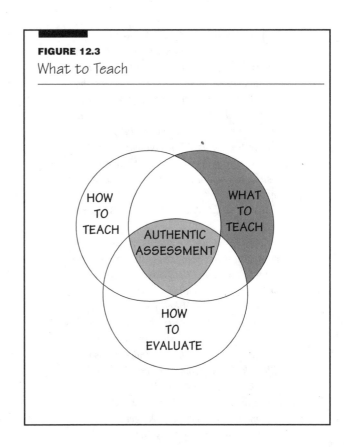

FIGURE 12.3
What to Teach

The members of our study group were attracted to Authentic Assessment for various reasons:

Whoever coined the phrase ". . . we test what is easily tested" is unimportant. What matters is that I have been guilty of the practice and authentic assessment tasks have forced me to rethink this practice and restructure the delivery of all concepts in every course I teach.
EVA DEMYEN

The one thing that attracted me more than any other to authentic assessment was the element of personalization. I believe that the "personalization factor" is the hook that helps focus and internalize each student's "stake" in the assessment. If the assessment can relate to the student's own personal life and if the student understands that this activity may benefit him/her, then the opportunity for success is quite great and, more importantly, enjoyable.
DAN SAITTA

I was attracted to Authentic Assessment because my subject area (Earth Science) is exciting and fascinating. Generally, Regents questions in Earth Science are dull and boring. Authentic Assessment seemed like a way to get my students fired up about Earth Science, and to be creative in the process. Furthermore, most tests are graded based on what students don't know. I believe it is more effective and positive to grade students on what they do know.

CAROL SCHAEFER

What attracted me to Authentic Assessment was that it was a change from the way we normally test in math. Math is not a typical or natural process and although students, people, may use it, it is not always pointed out where or why. Authentic Assessment helps me, as a teacher, to pick out those wheres and whys and give math a meaning for the students. Also, although there are some partial-credit type problems I have to ask myself if it is fair to have any no partial-credit problems. Although it is important in some cases to get an exact answer, is that what is being tested?

DONNA TASSA

It was a natural for me. I teach conceptually. My students discover knowledge independently and in cooperative groups in class. But my tests rarely reflected their processes. Authentic Assessment tasks provide me with a way of crediting students for their ongoing work, not just their performance on a given day.

RICHIE ADAMS

Like any class, we came together as a collection of "students of instruction." Our specific objectives varied, our disciplines were diverse. For as many reasons as there were members, this "thing" called Authentic Assessment intrigued us. Common to each of us was the understanding that building authentic assessments is as complex as building meaningful instruction. Building assessments would cause us to address and answer many of the same questions we address when we design instruction. The assessments we would build would be integral to the instructional program—not end products.

We understood too that while specific assessments would vary, all would require the completion of a clearly understood task over a period of time that would:

- focus on the critical concepts, skills, and core questions relevant to the course or unit of study;
- approximate the complexity and ambiguity of a real-world task;
- require students to integrate information, skills, and processes, and to display higher-level thinking and effective habits of mind and work in order to produce a response, product, or performance;
- integrate more fully teaching, learning, and assessment by engaging students frequently with the teacher and others in the activities of reflecting, revising, justifying, metacognating; and
- have a scoring system that presents clear criteria and standards and is understood at the outset of the task.

So we began at the end by asking ourselves, "What will the successful student in Sociology, Earth Science, Math 2, or Spanish 4 understand and be able to do?" We also reviewed specific units of study within a course, reducing each to its critical concepts.

This was not an easy task. It caused each of us to brutally examine content and excise particulars not at the heart of the course. Some of those particulars were personally dear, yet were viewed concept by concept, reducing each to its critical attributes unclouded by personal preference. We found ourselves questioning some long held absolutes: "Why must students be able to name the conflicting factions in the Puritan Revolution?"

Some of our thinking and focus on critical objectives is reflected in Figures 12.4 thru 12.9. Perhaps you would like to build the major critical concepts, knowledge, skills, and understandings of your own assessment with us. On page 122, you'll find a blank "What to Teach" form that you can photocopy for use in your own work (Figure 12.10).

FIGURE 12.4

What to Teach: Advanced Placement Calculus   EVA DEMYEN

At first I thought of calculus as a compilation of the following: functions and graphing, limits and continuity, derivative formulae, theorems about derivatives, applications of derivatives, techniques of integration, applications of antiderivatives, the definite integral, theorems on the definite integral, properties of the definite integral, theorems on the definite integral, applications of the definite integral.

Then I stepped back and got the "big picture," which contains two major concepts encompassing all, not some, of the above:

What major and critical concepts, knowledge, skills, and understandings will be addressed?

- Differentiation
- Antidifferentiation

FIGURE 12.5

What to Teach: Sociology   RICHIE ADAMS

What was extremely difficult when I first began was the thought of covering all of the concepts in sociology through one authentic assessment task developed by students and worked on throughout the course. My original list of concepts looked, in part, like this:

sociology as a study	deviance	socialization
approach to research	labeling theory	culture
norms	mores	values
status	roles	social mobility
open social systems	closed social system	courtship
divorce	reinforcement theory	stereotypes
peer groups	urban ecology	crime
alienation	functionalist theory	subsystem

This list could go on. Then I asked myself, "What is it that a sociologist does?" and I was able to achieve my goal. I found myself teaching more--but always teaching to the task.

What major and critical concepts, knowledge, skills, and understandings will be addressed?

- identifying social problems
- formulating a hypothesis
- gathering data
- analyzing data
- defending findings

FIGURE 12.6

What to Teach: Spanish 4   DAN SAITTA

What major and critical concepts, knowledge, skills, and understandings will be addressed?

- Vocabulary relating to specific age groups, i.e. adult: likes/dislikes, needs, hobbies, etc.
- Vocabulary related to running a house, i.e. heat, taxes, insurance
- Food vocabulary
- Unstructured problem solving
- Decision making
- Comparison

FIGURE 12.7

What to Teach: Liberal Arts Mathematics   DONNA TASSA

What major and critical concepts, knowledge, skills, and understandings will be addressed?

- averages—mean, median, mode
- range
- standard deviation
- normal distribution
- Z scores
- percentiles

FIGURE 12.8

What to Teach: Regents Biology   LYNDA HUEBSCH

What major and critical concepts, knowledge, skills, and understandings will be addressed?

Unity and diversity of life functions among the five representative organisms.

Comparing life functions among organisms from simple to complex:
- amoeba
- paramecium
- hydra
- earthworm
- grasshopper

FIGURE 12.9

What to Teach: Regents Chemistry   LARRY GREENBERG

What major and critical concepts, knowledge, skills, and understandings will be addressed?

- Relationship between pressure and volume for a gas (Boyle's Law)
- Relationship between volume and temperature for a gas (Charles' Law)
- Relationship among pressure, volume, and temperature for a gas (Combined Gas Laws)

FIGURE 12.10

What to Teach: _____

What major and critical concepts, knowledge, skills, and understandings will be addressed?

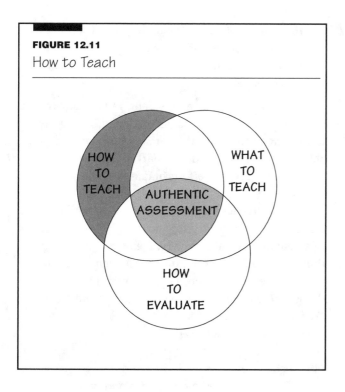

FIGURE 12.11
How to Teach

When I plan the task before beginning a unit, it forces me to think about the central things students will need to know. Prior to Authentic Assessment I used to plan to teach in increments and then test whatever I had managed to teach. The instructional strategies I choose now have greater validity and justification in my own mind since I must continually look at the entire picture or unit.

MARIA CARNESI

Authentic Assessment, in my opinion, is incorrectly labeled, named. "A.A." should actually be named Authentic Teaching. It more closely evaluates what you teach and how you have taught it than any previous evaluation/assessment methods practiced in the field of education. However, if you teach like you test (i.e. lecture and multiple choice, true/false) then you should stay away from A.A. Authentic Assessment evaluates better teaching better.

RICHIE ADAMS

How to Teach

The cart must not always follow the horse! I have always formed the plan of a unit by teaching the basic skills first and then pulling them together with an application problem. Why not reverse this process and start with presenting the assessment first? I am an up-front person, so why not be so in the classroom? Start each new concept to be taught with a "real life" problem and then discuss the skills and strategies that will be needed to tackle it.

EVA DEMYEN

By looking at, or for, real-life applications you are giving value and credence to your subject matter. Trying to find these applications gets rid of the fluff that bogs down and confuses our teaching.

CHARLIE VARADIAN

Our second charge was to begin to build the tasks through which students would demonstrate their knowledge, skills, and habits of mind and work. In trying to visualize what those tasks might look like, we found ourselves remembering Bloom's taxonomy, especially application and synthesis, those two levels that embraced more complex and less easily categorized activities.

We concluded that authentic assessments will mirror the attributes of application and synthesis activities. Authentic assessments call upon youngsters to engage in tasks that simulate challenges facing professionals in that field of study or mirror the complexities of real-life problems and challenges. These challenges require the application and/or synthesis of knowledge.

We further determined that the task design should drive teaching decisions. We would use instructional strategies that model and directly teach those processes we expected students to use as they engaged in the assessment. During authentic assessments, teaching and testing are often the same activity. For example, any one of us engaged in a dialogue with a student regarding the student's current thinking regarding a project might simultaneously provide support by helping the student to think more complexly or assess the quality of that thinking.

Students engaged in authentic assessments are engaged in large measure in extended guided practices, although the specifics of the practice may be unique to each student. As is consistent with guided practice, we found ourselves truly becoming coaches—reteaching as necessary, assisting, questioning, and asking clarifying questions. Because authentic assessments by their nature extend over time, and because they require discourses over time between the teacher/coach and the student/performer, our classrooms more frequently have a "workshop look" (guided practice) than a "lecture look."

Among the benefits of placing the task in front of students at the outset and allowing students and the task to drive instructional decisions is the freedom to work with diverse abilities within the classroom. We found ourselves able to attend more readily to learning styles and varying abilities. Where students began with a comfortable experience base, they were able to "dig in" to the task at hand and seek assistance when they needed it. Where the knowledge base of a group of students or particular students was limited, we sought not to simplify the task but to provide scaffolding. We sought to engage students in a meaningful, complex task while providing them with just enough support (information, structure, direction) to enable them to succeed without "spoon-feeding" them. Some of the tasks we put before students are offered in the figures that follow (Figures 12.12 thru 12.18). On page 130, you'll find a blank "How to Teach" that you may photocopy for use in your own work (Figure 12.19).

If some of these tasks seem somehow reminiscent of the kinds of activities good teachers routinely offer their students, they should. Remember, we continue to find ourselves building tasks that incorporate the elements of application and synthesis. What has been new, for each of us, has been:

- the point at which the task is placed in front of students,

- the making of instructional decisions based on the task and the student needs that arise, and
- an increased emphasis on process and student reflection.

Because authentic assessments tend to be organic, they are perpetually in progress. All of life's tasks tend to be organic and ongoing: parenting, teaching, citizenship, even recreation. All are marked by an ongoing need to reflect on our efforts and seek greater effectiveness.

Reflectiveness embraces all those self-monitoring, self-evaluating, self-directing activities in which effective people frequently engage. We want students to think about what they are doing. We want students to pursue excellence rather than meet minimum standards, and we want to encourage review and revision. We want to provide opportunities for learning within the process—experiences rich with opportunities for consultation and introspection to promote the activities of reflecting, revising, justifying, and metacognating.

This represented a breach in standard operating procedure for most students whose academic experiences have been punctuated by cycles of remembering what is taught, being tested periodically at specific points of time, and receiving a single hard grade. We recognized that we were asking students to engage in extended assessment processes unlike anything they had experienced. The habits of mind so central to authentic assessments had to be taught and nurtured. Likewise, techniques of cooperative learning and discourse had to be taught and nurtured.

To acclimate students to a process that acknowledges and credits process, encourages risk taking, and may celebrate the imperfect product if the process has caused the student to learn, we needed to break "psychological contracts" that only required students to behave (be passive) and listen. When we required more of them, they objected. Therefore it was necessary to take the time to provide a rationale for change, teach them how to do it, and encourage them in their efforts.

Classroom opportunities for students to reflect on their progress may be provided in a number of ways: a written reflection log shared periodically with the teacher, individual consultations with the teacher, and peer consultation. Once students have become familiar with the evaluation criteria and have begun to see how those apply to their own work, they may become excellent consultants to each other.

> Each of my students has a "research group" of 3-5 fellow sociologists. They come together to review each other's work and progress informally and formally at each"checkpoint" (problem selection, hypothesis generation, research design, data analysis and defense of conclusions).
>
> RICHIE ADAMS

> I am getting ready to try this with my statistics unit—to extend student thinking I will pair students. Each will use the other's data to try to argue the opposite conclusion. I believe this will cause students to stretch and really wrestle with data.
>
> DONNA TASSA

> In my French class, students assess each other in a practice stage and come up by themselves with the critical elements of the rubric for grading a final presentation. For example, after letting kids hear tapes of other kids' doctor office skits they came up with the critical elements of a good skit—clarity, pace, use of high level vocabulary, feeling and inflection so as to convey meaning. They then reviewed their own work against their criteria.
>
> CHARLIE VARADIAN

Most of us have found peer consultations to be an effective way to encourage reflectiveness. In most cases, students review,probe, and suggest enhancements before consultation with the teacher using some guide or organizer. One of our members encourages students to view this role seriously by having students rate their consultant (Figure 12.20 on page 131).

FIGURE 12.12

How to Teach: French   CHARLIE VARADIAN

The "time machine" metaphor allows students to go ahead into the future to see exactly what the test/performance will be like and have them design a plan of action for that expected outcome backwards.

Here's the task: What do you need to know? How do you want to learn it? How should I teach it?

For example, my French students were given this task:

What is the task through which students will demonstrate their understandings?	You are ill in France and you need to find a doctor, get through the nurse's questions about your medical history, explain to the doctor what ails you, and be able to follow his advice.
What instructional strategies may be used to teach the concepts?	In groups of three and four you will work to answer the following questions: (1) What do you need to know to be able to complete this task? (2) How do you want to get this information? (3) How do you want to show me that you are able to complete the task?

Based on their answers, I was able to scaffold instruction, providing information and skills to students as they needed it. Their demonstrations--including skits, audiotapes, videotapes, and spontaneous dialogues-- capped the process.

FIGURE 12.13

How to Teach: Advanced Placement Calculus   EVA DEMYEN

What is the task through which students will demonstrate their understandings?

What instructional strategies may be used to teach the concepts?

Through our work thus far, we have come to agree that calculus can be boiled down to two major concepts. You are now ready to view an aspect of real life "mathematically." Mathematicians have a peculiar way of seeing issues and problems from a mathematical point of view. You are the mathematician.

1. Recall the mini-tasks that we have engaged in--the "Box" problem, the "maximizing profit" problem, etc.

2. Locate and identify a key area we have studied with which you feel most comfortable and then summarize and cite subconcepts contained within it.

3. Select an area of interest to you in the "real world" and illustrate the use of the concept selected including a detailed solution to the problem that the area faces that needs resolution. You will probably find yourselves drawing conclusions from the data you have collected during your research of the problem.

4. Depending on the area that you have selected and the problem you address, you may propose solutions or advice, you may design a new plan of attack for the company or industry.

5. You must support your solutions with strong mathematical evidence.

• Some mini-tasks preceding this assignment include:
  • Starting a business
    – determining profit margins (maximum profit)
    – designing gift boxes (maximum volume)
    – depreciation of machinery
    – increasing production
  • Show how the AIDS virus is growing exponentially and make predictions about the future.
  • The dynamics involved in throwing an object:
    – initial force
    – total distance traveled
    – velocity
    – acceleration
  • Why do dams leak? (discovery force problem--fluid and liquid pressure)
  • You manage a property development company and manage a senior citizen development where each unit rents for c dollars. When you rent x units and $c =$ _____, how many apartments must be rented before the marginal revenue is zero?

FIGURE 12.14

How to Teach: *Sociology*   RICHIE ADAMS

What is the task through which students will demonstrate their understandings?	You are a sociologist. Like other sociologists, you will choose to examine in depth some area of society that interests you, and you will conduct your own study of some problem in that area and present and defend your finding. Specifically you will:

What is the task through which students will demonstrate their understandings?

What instructional strategies may be used to teach the concepts?

You are a sociologist. Like other sociologists, you will choose to examine in depth some area of society that interests you, and you will conduct your own study of some problem in that area and present and defend your finding. Specifically you will:

- Identify a social problem (a topic you wish to research).
- Formulate a hypothesis (a research proposal).
- Gather data (surveys, interviews, etc.).
- Analyze data (tables, etc.).
- Draw conclusions.
- Present findings (paper, oral defense).

FIGURE 12.15

How to Teach: *Spanish 4*   DAN SAITTA

What is the task through which students will demonstrate their understandings?

What instructional strategies may be used to teach the concepts?

You are about to become a member of a family. As a family unit, your group will explore its finances. You will:

- Determine what each family member believes he/she will require for the year and determine what the total cost will be.
- Determine those costs necessary for generally running a household.
- Compare your projected expenses to the total family income I will give you.
- Come to a consensus regarding how you will budget in order not to be in debt at the end of the year.
- Compose your budget for the next year.

Before giving students the task, I broke them into families of four to five family members. Each group contained a mix of all ability levels. Families were generally not what we might consider typical. For example:

- Father--50 years old--carpenter
- Grandmother--73 years old--retired
- Son--16 years old--student
- Son--19 years old--college student
- Daughter--20 years old--college student

Each student's role in the family is very important as it relates to family finances and the potential for controversy in attempting to reach consensus on an annual budget. The entire unit is conducted in the target language.

FIGURE 12.16

How to Teach: Liberal Arts Mathematics   DONNA TASSA

What is the task through which students will demonstrate their understandings?

What instructional strategies may be used to teach the concepts?

You have before you two sets of data--one for the results of a recently administered SAT exam, the other the results of an ACT. You are going to use these data, which I know look like gobbledy-gook now, to help someone decide which exam would be better to take.

As a class we considered what we might need to know in order to complete the task. We produced the following key questions.

- Who is taking the exam?
  (yourself, a friend, males, females)
- Who are you trying to convince?
  (yourself, counselor, parents, friends)
- What is meant by statistical analysis?
  (How do we use this data?)
- Which tests and which grades do you look at? (verbal only, combined scale, math only)

FIGURE 12.17

How to Teach: Regents Biology   LYNDA HUEBSCH

What is the task through which students will demonstrate their understandings?

What instructional strategies may be used to teach the concepts?

Task: Invent an Organism

You have the distinct pleasure of being a genetic engineer. You have been given the task of looking at a selection of organisms, taking the best of the life functions from the amoeba, paramecium, hydra, earthworm, and grasshopper and creating a brand new organism for any place on Earth.

You may decide to create this organism in any way that you like. You may place it in any environment as long as you can convince me and your critics that your organism can survive where you have placed it. You may present this to me in any way. It can be: (1) a written report, (2) an audiocassette, (3) a videotape, (4) a drawing, (5) a model, or (6) any other way that you first clear with me.

As a part of your work, you must keep a research notebook with all pertinent information about the five organisms and your organism as it develops (for example, questions, ideas, thoughts, sketches as you begin to create).

Also, as part of this creation process you will have the chance to be reviewed by your peers and to become a peer critic. This is very important to you because it gives you the chance to rethink your ideas before your work gets turned in. Plus, being a critic lets you help your classmates and helps you really see how much you are learning.

FIGURE 12.18

How to Teach: Regents Chemistry   LARRY GREENBERG

What is the task through which students will demonstrate their understandings?

What instructional strategies may be used to teach the concepts?

Congratulations! Your research team has been selected to redesign the lunar space suit for the recently built Moon Base Gamma. Management at NASA has some immediate questions and concerns for your team to answer. Please provide your team's assessment of the questions and their solutions to the Program Director (your teacher), Moon Base Gamma Division, NASA, as soon as possible.

Related Information:
- Atmospheric pressure on the Moon = 0.1 atmospheres (Earth)
- Temperature on the dark side of the Moon = -15 degrees C
- Temperature on the light side of the Moon = +100 degrees C
- Volume of the lunar space suit on the light side of the Moon = 150 liters

Any additional information needed is available from the Program Director's office.

Question 1: The pressure inside the lunar space suit is to be maintained at 1 atmosphere (Earth). As a lunar geologist crosses from the light side of the moon to the dark side of the moon, what change in volume would occur if compensation for temperature variations were not present?

Question 2: What design(s) has your team incorporated into the lunar space suit to compensate for this change in volume as well as for the change in temperature?

Question 3: While on the dark side of the moon, a micro-meteorite punctures the geologist's lunar space suit. What happens to the volume of the lunar space suit? What would occur to the geologist inside the lunar space suit?

Question 4: What design safeguards has your team incorporated into the lunar space suit to ensure the inhabitant's survival after a micrometeorite puncture?

FIGURE 12.19

How to Teach: _____

What is the task through which students will demonstrate their understandings?

_____

What instructional strategies may be used to teach the concepts?

‖ | | | | | | | | | | | | | | | | | | ‖

FIGURE 12.20

How to Teach: Regents Biology   LYNDA HUEBSCH

INVENT AN ORGANISM

Critique By: _____

For: _____

1. They have chosen _____ as the environment for their organism.
2. Some special considerations for life functions in that environment are:
   a.
   b.
3. The _____ type of _____ has been chosen.
4. Can explain the process of _____.
   NO   SOME   YES
5. Can explain the _____'s type of _____.
   NO   SOME   YES
6. Can convince you why this type of _____ will work for their organism in the environment.
   NO   SOME   YES
7. Anything else that could help them think more about their organism?

Critic's Rating Sheet

Critic's Name: _____
Rater's Name: _____

1. Critic made me explain my choices.
          NO   SOME   FULLY
2. Critic asked me questions other than those on the critique sheet.
          NO   ONE   SOME
3. Critic asked me questions that made me think more about or change my ideas.
          NO   ONE   SOME
4. Critic thought only his/her ideas were correct.
          NO   ONE   SOME
5. Anything else about this critic that made him/her especially good/bad?
6. Would you choose this person as a critic again?
          YES   NO
                              If NO, why?_____
                              If YES, why?_____

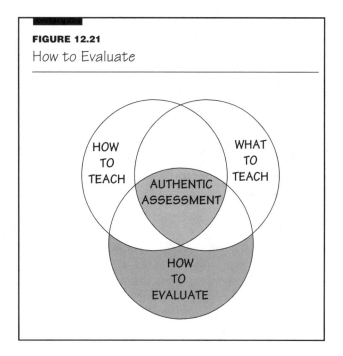

FIGURE 12.21
How to Evaluate

How to Evaluate

I think probably the most initially disconcerting part of Authentic Assessment was student response. I know we had talked about not expecting students to respond enthusiastically to being invited to take responsibility for their own learning, but I guess I believed my students would immediately rise to the occasion. Not so. In a nutshell, their first response was, "It's your job to tell us stuff and see if we know it." It took time and effort to get them to buy in and become engaged—time spent valuing and crediting their thinking and processing. In the end, they decided this authentic assessment was "better than regular class."

RICHIE ADAMS

An important point in grading an assessment task is giving credit for imperfection. This is extremely important. Many tests contain questions that are marked right or wrong with no credit for the process or thinking involved in the solution of the problem. If we want to encourage students to think we must credit

that thinking, that processing—sometimes we learn more from evaluating where we went wrong and considering what we would do next time than by guessing correctly.

EVA DEMYEN

I began by basing evaluations only on the critical competencies (key concepts) to be demonstrated. Over time, I have incorporated such reflective processes as justification of task selected, anticipation of opposing arguments, etc.

MARIA CARNESI

My students and I built the scoring rubric for our sewing assessment together. They had already completed a mini-task so they were able to tell me the major stages in any sewing project. We then considered what it would take to complete each stage perfectly and out of that grew our scoring rubric.

LORRAINE SCHLOSS

For each Authentic Assessment, a detailed rubric will be created, explaining exactly what is required for each individual grade. The clearer and more thorough the rubric is the better students can determine exactly what they need to do in order to achieve a specific grade.

CAROL SCHAEFER

We understood that authentic assessment recognizes that knowledge and conceptual understanding are necessary but not sufficient for the attainment of our most important educational objectives. Only when students understand the usefulness of the knowledge and can demonstrate the ability to apply it have we begun to achieve our objectives.

Therefore, the manner in which we would evaluate how well we and each of our students have achieved became more complex. We wanted our evaluations to be marked by:

- the use of models of excellence as benchmarks, not listings of correct answers;
- a focus on process as well as product (the crediting of "good" thinking and effort regardless of end product);

- the provision of a scoring system with clear criteria and standards "up front" when the task is set forth; and
- understanding by students that how they reached a final result is as or more important than the final result. (Sometimes our best efforts fail while our worst efforts fortuitously succeed.)

Therefore, we tried to develop rubrics for scoring, providing standards of acceptability in such a manner that each student would understand:

- What outstanding looks like.
- What satisfactory looks like.
- What minimally acceptable looks like.
- What unacceptable looks like.

Because each student's work is unique, this becomes a critical and challenging task.

No single aspect of our authentic assessment will contribute more to its success than the establishment of standards. These standards are shared with and understood by students at the outset. For some of us, the rubric for grading is an elaborate piece. For others, it is a more simple statement of a scoring system. We continue to grapple with how explicit the system should be, at what point it might discourage some creativity, and how to avoid overcrediting glitz and undercrediting plain vanilla competence. Because we are neophytes, we do not, as yet, have models of excellence to put before youngsters. We believe that these examples of outstanding work will grow, over time, out of the work of students (Figures 12.22-12.28). On page 137, you'll find a "How to Evaluate" form that you may photocopy for your own use (Figure 12.28).

FIGURE 12.22

How to Evaluate: Advanced Placement Calculus

How will the authentic assessment be evaluated?

- 50 points--collection of data, reference materials, and statement of application of concept
- 15 points--solution of application model
- 15 points--written work, graphs, or models
- 20 points--presentation

FIGURE 12.23

How to Evaluate: Sociology

How will the authentic assessment be evaluated?

- Identifying the social problem--total 20% (5% per conference)
- Stated hypothesis--20%
- Method outline--10%
- Gathering and analyzing data--50%

Models are provided. No perfect models.

FIGURE 12.24

How to Evaluate: Spanish 4   DAN SAITTA

How will the authentic
assessment be evaluated?

I haven't used a formal rubric yet for grading. I have used a
two-part system. First, each student earns a daily grade for
each day's work. This way I can credit process in a way that is
tangible for each student. The second part involves a student's self-evaluation at the conclusion of the assessment. The
students receive a self-evaluation sheet at the beginning of the
assessment. It helps them to focus and to reach for individual
goals. When the task is completed, the students rate their
work. I read their comments and finalize a grade. (I have not
found it necessary to change many self-evaluation grades.)

Self-Evaluation
With your budget complete, I would like you to reflect on your
product. Please answer all questions in Spanish in complete
sentences.

1. Ha hecho Ud. Un trabajo bueno? Por que?
(Have you done a good job? Why?)
2. Cuales son las cosas que Ud. puede usar del presupuesto
en la vida diaria? En el futuro? Por que?
(What are the things that you can use in the budget in your
daily life? In the future?)
3. Es dificil planear un presupuesto? Por que?
(Why is it difficult to plan a budget?)
4. Cual es la cosa mas importante sobre el presupuesto?
(What is the most important thing about your budget?)
5. Please do a PMI about any aspect of this task.

PLUS   MINUS   INTERESTING POINTS

〡〢〥

FIGURE 12.25

How to Evaluate: Liberal Arts Mathematics   DONNA TASSA

How will the authentic assessment be evaluated?

- Statement of the problem—15%
- Description of data selected for use and justification—20%
- Analysis of selected data—30%
- Construction of a well-supported argument—25%
- Use of peer's data to argue opposite point of view—10%

FIGURE 12.26

How to Evaluate: Regents Biology   LYNDA HUEBSCH

How will the authentic assessment be evaluated?

You are in control of your grade on this task. Please take this time to read and become familiar with the grading chart. This is how I will grade your work. AIM HIGH--You can do it!

Presentation	Excellent	Good	Barely acceptable	Unacceptable
	Has all the life functions and can survive in its environment.	Has all the life functions and can survive in its environment.	Has all the life functions but cannot survive.	Missing some functions.
Justification	Justify all your choices of life functions for your creation.	Justify at least 5 choices of life functions.	No justification of choices of life function.	No justification.
Critique	At least 30 critic points.	20-30 critic points.	10-20 critic points.	Less than 10.
Notebook	Organized notebook, complete with life function information on all model organisms and notes about the development of your organism and all critic notes.	Organized notebook but missing some life function on all model organisms about the development of your organisms and critic notes.	Organized notebook but missing half of life function on model organism and about the development of your organism and critic notes.	Unorganized or missing.

FIGURE 12.27

How to Evaluate: Regents Chemistry   Larry Greenberg

How will the authentic assessment be evaluated?

Grading Criteria. Four possible grades are available for this exercise:

Exceptional Work. You have answered all four questions fully in complete, well-written sentences. Your answers contain written information relevant to each question, and you have justified your solutions. In addition, answers to questions 1 and 3 have mathematical as well as written explanations. Questions 2 and 4 have multiple answers or suggestions. The work is clear and carried out with unusual precision and skill. It has demonstrated an in-depth understanding and analysis of both the content studied and the challenge itself. The work is presented in an original and creative manner that communicated either new insight or intriguing perspectives. Numerical equivalent—100.

Satisfactory Work. You have answered all four questions in complete, well-constructed sentences. Your answers contain written information relevant to the question, and you have justified your solution. In addition, one of the questions (1 or 3) has a mathematical explanation as well as a written one. The work is complete and has no significant errors. The work demonstrates a relatively thorough grasp of the content studied and an above average understanding of the challenge itself. The work is attractive, well thought out, and demonstrates a thorough treatment of the ideas presented. Numerical equivalent—85.

Minimally Acceptable. You have answered 3 of the 4 questions fully in complete, well-constructed sentences. Your answers contain written information relevant to the question, and you have justified your solution. The work reflects slight confusion or lack of understanding of the key concepts studied. The work provides the audience with only a surface treatment of the topic. The work is acceptable, but revision is recommended. Numerical equivalent—75.

Unacceptable Work. The work is incomplete and has failed to meet the basic requirements of the challenge. It lacks clarity and is carried out with little commitment to precision and excellence. The work reflects either misconceived or erroneous content knowledge. Revision is required. Numerical equivalent—55.

||||||||||||||||||||||||

FIGURE 12.28

How to Evaluate: _____

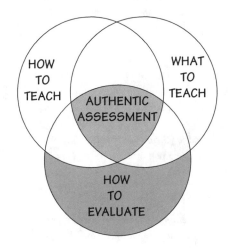

Now build your rubric or system of standards of acceptability.

How will the authentic assessment be evaluated?

As an ongoing process in her authentic classroom, one of our colleagues has students keep a journal called "Secrets of_____'s Kitchen." In it, students compile those techniques, tricks of the trade, short cuts, and unique solutions they have discovered. Since we know how much each of us has grown because of our work with each other, we thought we would "steal" that title and leave you with some of our collected "Secrets of an Authentic Classroom."

Try it! It's more work than you think in the planning, but you will see how much more students have learned and you may begin to see your objectives more clearly.
Long term assessments need time for careful monitoring, feedback and evaluation. Build this process into your classroom through journals and other activities. Finding time for reflecting has to be built into the course.
LORRAINE SCHLOSS

Frequent "check points" are a must. They also provide opportunities for students who are stuck to get help and redirection from the teacher and each other. (Some kids hate this—they'd like to be finished, right or wrong. This forces them to reflect.)
DONNA TASSA

Take the time to assure yourself that every student understands the task.
LYNDA HUEBSCH

I think the best thing to do before an authentic assessment (before presenting it to students) is to do it yourself. I've worked out every assessment beforehand, trying to anticipate problems, questions, needed information, etc. This also gives students a model—a quick and easy reference.
DAN SAITTA

In working with learning-impaired students, Authentic Assessment can serve as a low-stress, highly motivating practice, which allows students to express themselves in ways that are good for them as opposed to conventional, that solely require them to employ a weak area.
LISA MESSINA

Both the student and the teacher may experience some uneasy feelings since the order of thinking and planning has changed. But it has been my experience that students who many times do not excel on conventional tests shine on authentic assessments. That was definitely a reinforcement for me as to the worth and potential of authentic assessment.
MARIA CARNESI

There is one big secret to the Authentic Assessment classroom. It can be done! A serious skeptic at first, I have realized that time devoted to Authentic Assessment is well spent and can have exciting results. Of course each student only gets what he or she puts into it, but that applies to most life situations. It is a challenge to be involved in creating an atmosphere of curiosity and achievement, and allowing students to demonstrate their knowledge and talents.
CAROL SCHAEFER

PART V

Teams Build
Assessment—and
Assessment Builds
Teams

Teams Build Assessment— and Assessment Builds Teams

ARTHUR L. COSTA AND BENA KALLICK

A prerequisite for employing feedback spirals as continual learning designs is that the evidence gathered during the implementation phase must be examined, analyzed, interpreted, and evaluated so that actions can be modified based upon the new knowledge. This implies that individuals or organizations engaged in feedback spirals must face, be open to, and own the data.

One of the psychological hurdles that adult learners have to overcome, however, is the fear of failure. Children learn by trial and error, but by the time we're adults we're supposed to know how to perform. Our competence is challenged when we "make mistakes." We especially dislike making errors in public, and we become defensive when we fear that others will judge us.

Most people consider criticism to be negative and try to avoid it at all costs. As one person said, "I never share my work with my colleagues because it feels like I have put a target up for everyone to take shots at." How different that is from Thomas Edison's philosophy: "I've never made a mistake. I've only learned from experience."

Individuals must honestly confront and own assessment data about student achievement and about how the community perceives their schools if they hope to grow into a synergistic team and develop interdependence, a sense of community, and a feeling of interconnectedness with a shared vision. More importantly, they will need to discover how to learn about themselves as professionals and their development as a team. They themselves must confront the data from the feedback spirals. Feedback spirals can only be implemented effectively, therefore, under conditions of trust.

BUILDING TRUST THROUGHOUT THE LEARNING ORGANIZATION

> Trust is the lubrication that makes it possible for organizations to work.
> —Bennis and Nanus 1985

In a trusting environment, humans inquire, experiment, generate data, speculate, construct meanings, self-evaluate, and self-prescribe. This can only happen in a relationship without external judgments and with permission to challenge and stimulate deeper thinking and probe greater understanding.

To trust is to place confidence in, rely on, or believe in the honesty, justice, integrity, friendship, or other sound principles of another person or organization. A trusting environment allows us to act without fear of negative consequences. It permits us to expose our thoughts, feelings, and behaviors to another without apprehension. When a trust relationship exists, people laugh more, admit mistakes, ask for help, are more productive, and are more open to change.

Numerous authors, management theorists, organizational development specialists, and sociologists have illuminated the value of trust in the workplace. For example, Bennis and Nanus (1985) in their extensive study of exceptional leaders summarize: "Trust is the emotional glue that binds followers and leaders together." Trust implies accountability, predictability, and reliability.

When interpersonal trust is present, there is greater likelihood of trust in the environment. When teachers trust the principal, they also tend to trust each other and district administrators. During the mid-1980s, research was conducted at Rutgers University (Kupersmith and Hoy 1989) to learn teachers' perspectives on what made principals trustworthy. Three major characteristics emerged:

• **Principals took responsibility for their own behaviors.** They admitted mistakes, and they did not blame "upstairs." Trusted principals would not say "The school board is making us use this test," or "The superintendent says we have to evaluate basic skills." Instead, the principal might say, "As I understand the intention behind this direction, it is to accomplish X, and our job is to figure out how to get it done."

• **Principals were perceived as a person first and a role second.** Trusted principals revealed personal information about themselves so they were known as a person rather than merely a position.

• **Teachers perceived the principal to be nonmanipulative.** Principals influenced but they influenced directly, not covertly. They operated without hidden agendas.

Additionally, linkages were found in this research between interpersonal trust and trust in the environment. They found that when teachers trusted the principal, they also tended to trust each other and trust central office personnel. Assessment teams, therefore, will nurture truthfulness, openness, responsibility, long- and short-term planning, connectedness, and communication (Costa and Garmston 1994).

We need to create conditions that encourage cooperation, collegiality, and collaboration. This requires at least three levels of trust: trust in self, trust in the relationship with others, and trust in the organization. As teams regularly meet across subject-matter disciplines and grade levels to develop a systematic approach to assessment, each level becomes the focus of the feedback spiral of ongoing assessment.

Certain key dimensions should be monitored and assessed: communication, openness to diverse perspectives, ability to reach consensus, and capacity to resolve conflicts from a win-win perspective. Feedback spirals provide a model for a recursive process that continuously asks individuals, teams, and organizations to know their purposes, assess their progress across these key dimensions, examine the content of their work, and strive toward continual improvement.

Since trust is so fundamental to the work of teams, the three levels of trust referred to above can serve as indicators for assessment:

- Trust in yourself.
- Trust in the relationship with others.
- Trust in the organization.

It should be the expectation of all learning organizations that teams will practice and assess the behaviors and conditions of trust throughout the organization.

Trust in Yourself

Trusting yourself basically means being conscious of yourself, personal efficacy, and self-management. As Leo Buscaglia observes, "To do good things in the world, first you must know who you are and what gives meaning to your life."

When we know ourselves and manage ourselves, we communicate integrity, which in turn generates trust in others and ultimately trust in the environment. So, trust with another begins with trusting yourself. To know your values and act on them, to "talk the talk *and* walk the walk," engages not only a personal feedback spiral of continuous growth and self-improvement, but trust in your own capacity for self-management and self-esteem.

According to Michael Fullan (1993), the best educators are those who are clear about their values and beliefs. For example, the most effective principals know and articulate their own philosophical, pedagogical, and spiritual values. These values inform us about our motivation, what it means to learn, the purpose of schools, the attributes of an educated person, where decision-making power should lie, a leader's responsibilities, and potentials that are envisioned for the school and community.

Furthermore, if you are to be considered trustworthy, you must strive for consistency. Consistency comes from being inner-directed and taking actions in matters small and large that repeatedly are self-referencing, reflecting your inner core.

Personal consciousness means being aware of the ways we process and make meaning out of our experiences. This includes knowledge of our own cognitive styles, modality strengths, intelligences, personal history, and current emotional conditions. Self-knowledge in each of these areas is a prerequisite to employing personal feedback spirals. At each step in the feedback spiral we are aware of our values, our repertoire of data-generating strategies, how we process data, our repertoire of implementation strategies, and the biases with which we interpret data and explore alternative next steps.

Personal consciousness of one modality strength means being conscious of how we intake, process, and represent our experience through visual, kinesthetic, and auditory channels.

Knowing yourself also involves knowing your special intelligences. Howard Gardner (1983) of Harvard University postulates that there are many forms of intelligence. He proposes a schema of seven intelligences and suggests that there are probably many yet to be discovered. He labels them: verbal/linguistic, logical/mathematical, visual/spatial, bodily/kinesthetic, musical/rhythmic, interpersonal, and intrapersonal, which involves knowledge of the self.

Knowledge of our own cognitive styles, modalities, and intelligences is critical when working with others who have different attitudes, perceptions, and styles. Knowing how to network; how to draw on the diverse resources of others; and how to value each person's expertise, diverse views, perceptions, and knowledge base is increasingly essential to survival. We might view this as a new form of interlocking intelligences: collaboratively melding the perceptions, modalities, skills, capacities, and expertise into a unified whole that is more efficient than any one of its parts.

Another way of knowing yourself is to be aware of the many perceptions born of your personal history. Gender, culture, race, religion, geographical region, childhood experiences, and family history predispose us to draw certain inferences, attend to certain stimuli, and block out others.

Finally, consciousness of our current spiritual and emotional condition affects our processing of information, decisions, and behavior. None of us leaves our emotions on the doorstep when we enter the work environment. At times we functional at less than 100 percent for a variety of reasons. We must respect the fact that we are all subject to emotional shifts, illnesses, and external problems that distract our attention and consume our intellectual and emotional resources.

Personal efficacy also means taking charge of our own life—having an internal rather than an external locus of control. Locus of control refers to the location where the responsibility for the achievement of outcomes is placed. We can either assume responsibility for our own actions or we can place the blame on others or external forces: parents, genetics, other teachers, and weather conditions. To face the data of assessment, we need to develop an internal locus of control. In the classroom, for example, external locus of control means misplacing the responsibility for achievement of objectives on situations or persons beyond the teacher's control:

- "What do you expect from these kids? Look at the home background they come from."
- "Of course they can't learn long division. The teacher last year didn't prepare them properly."

Seligman (1991) suggests that persons develop "explanatory styles" with which they unconsciously form internal hypotheses or rationalizations to explain to themselves good and bad events in their environment. Explanatory style is the way you "explain to yourself" why an event is happening. It's more comforting to attribute increases in achievement to ourselves but attribute decreases in achievement to the environment.

Efficacious individuals who seem to have an internal locus of control assume responsibility for their own successes or failures:

- "Those kids were confused today because my directions were garbled. I've got to make my directions clearer."
- "John still isn't getting long division. I've got to do something special to help him."

Sometimes external locus of control is also demonstrated through denial of self-efficacy. We display an external locus when we deflect or deny credit for success:

- "It was my lucky day."
- "Jupiter is in my house this month."

People with an internal locus of control take credit for their accomplishments:

- "I know how to get kids to think at higher levels—I know how to pose questions that engage the intellect!"

People who are insecure, pessimistic, or have low self-esteem may allow such explanatory biases to enter their interpretations of the feedback data. Those who possess a positive self-image are more likely to hold

themselves responsible for their outcomes—whether successful or not. They can confront, accept, and act upon the assessment data generated through feedback spirals.

Assessment of our own consciousness, personal efficacy, and self-management can take many forms. Reflecting on personal or group journal entries over time is a powerful way of standing back and observing ourselves. Making a journal entry in problematic and stressful situations as well as joyful ones helps us understand how we react and how we can improve in the future.

Seeking and receiving feedback from coaches, mentors, and critical friends is yet another powerful means of nurturing self-awareness. Inviting them to keep a "How Am I Doing Checklist" for themselves while participating in meetings provides feedback and assists in building trust (Figure V.1).

Trust in the Relationship with Others

What creates trusting relationships? Some indicators of trusting relationships are that people maintain confidentiality, are visible and accessible, are consistent in their behaviors, keep commitments, share personal information about their out-of-school lives, reveal their feelings, express personal interest in the other person, are nonjudgmental, critique in a constructive way, listen reflectively, admit mistakes, and work to continually develop their own professional knowledge and skills (Costa and Garmston 1994).

These descriptors illustrate that trust is a product of behaviors in a relationship and that certain behaviors invite certain responses that we characterize as trusting. These behaviors and the reactions they produce form a feedback spiral of deepening regard and confidence.

To build trust, we must learn to listen to and empathize with others. To move beyond an egocentric perspective and see things from another person's point of view is essential to any healthy relationship. Empathy—seeking to understand—is one of the most important trust builders because it communicates that you value the other person. To effectively face assessment data, teams will need to meet together regularly

FIGURE V.1

"How Am I Doing?" Checklist

DIMENSION: Communication	OFTEN	SOME-TIMES	NOT YET
Verbal Restates/paraphrases a person's idea before offering personal opinion.			
Clarifies a person's ideas, concepts, or terminology.			
Expresses empathy for others' feelings/emotions.			
Poses questions intended to engage thinking and reflection.			
Expresses personal regard and interest.			
Nonverbal Faces the person who is speaking.			
Establishes eye contact if appropriate.			
Nods head.			
Uses facial expressions congruent with speaker's emotional message.			
Mirrors gestures.			
Mirrors posture.			

over time and across subject matter disciplines and grade levels to practice their empathic skills.

We can seek to understand others' sense of personal identity—what is important to them—through their values, goals, ideals, interests, passions, and hobbies. We can also seek to understand the way they process information—the person's cognitive styles, modality preferences, personal history, and educational beliefs. And by listening empathically, we can seek to understand their moment-to-moment reflections, concerns, thoughts, and feelings.

On average, adults find more meaning in nonverbal cues than in verbal ones. A recent summary of communication literature supports the theory that nearly two-thirds of meaning in any social situation is derived from nonverbal cues. At the Boston University School of Medicine, William Condon (1975) studied films of many sets of two people talking. Not only were the bodies of the speakers matched, but a "very startling phenomenon" was observed: entrainment existed between the speaker's words and the listener's movements. As one person spoke, the second person would make tiny corresponding movements.

As Condon (1975) expressed it, "Listeners were observed to move in precise shared synchrony with the speaker's speech. . . . It also appears to be a universal characteristic of human communication, and perhaps characterizes much of animal behavior in general."

Some examples of nonverbal trust-building behaviors include:

- Establishing eye contact (if culturally appropriate).
- Displaying facial expressions that are congruent with the speakers emotional message.
- Mirroring the speaker's gestures and posture.

Thus, communication is like a dance with each person engaged in intricate and shared movements across many subtle dimensions, yet each is strangely oblivious to those actions.

While nonverbal communications may convey much of the meaning in an exchange, the words we choose—and how we state them—also have a strong effect. Teams must seek a nonjudgmental environment where members feel safe to experiment, to risk, and to be honest with data.

We have identified seven nonjudgmental verbal indicators that contribute to interpersonal trust:

- Structuring
- Posing open-ended questions
- Silence
- Accepting nonjudgmentally, including paraphrasing and empathizing
- Expressing personal regard
- Clarifying
- Providing data.

Assessment teams will want to learn more about, practice, critique, and assess their use of these behaviors as well as assess the effects these behaviors have on the team's growth in trust building and cooperative relationships.

1. Structuring. A safe, trusting relationship exists when you know what others expect of you and what you expect of them. Structuring is defined as the many ways we communicate expectations about purposes and the use of such environmental resources as time, space, and materials. Clear, conscious, and deliberate structuring generates a common understanding of the purposes for a meeting or task, the roles various members should play, time allotments, ground rules, outcomes, criteria for achievement, and seating arrangements. Clear expectations about the purposes and procedures for learning, assessment, and evaluation also contribute to environmental trust. When the expectations are unclear, energy and mental resources are consumed reading and interpreting cues about what the other person wants—detecting if there is a "hidden agenda."

When expectations are not clear and shared, simple misunderstandings are compounded and can turn into communication meltdowns. Many—if not most—relationship difficulties are rooted in conflicting or ambiguous expectations about roles and goals. Whether we are dealing with the question of who does what at work or what form of decision-making process is being used in a meeting, we can be certain that unclear expectations will lead to misunderstanding and disappointment, which detract from trust.

Examples of verbal structuring behavior include:

- *In a classroom observation:* "Since you want me to observe the students' on-task behavior, I'll need to sit in a place in the room where I can see them all. Where would that be?"
- *In a team meeting:* "It will take about 15 minutes for us to generate and adopt an agenda. You should give us a signal when that time is up."
- *In a parent conference:* "Before we begin our conference, I'll be asking you to share with me your observation of Danielle's desire to learn. By what indicators do you know your child is continuing to learn?"

2. Open-ended Questioning. Open questions signal there are no preconceived "right" answers. Effective questions invite others to state impressions, recall data, make inferences, develop cause-effect relationships, metacogitate, evaluate, predict and self-prescribe. Some examples include:

- "How did you feel about the meeting?"
- "How did you decide what to do next?"
- "What do you think might have contributed to the success of our meeting?"
- "What would happen if we derived the performance criteria and scoring rubrics with our students ahead of time?"

Well-intentioned but poorly formed questions can send judgmental signals that weaken trust in you and the process. For example, the question "What two things went well?" implies that someone has made a judgment that only two things went well, and it allows a lingering possibility that some things did not go well. (Strategies of open-ended questioning are elaborated in Peg Luiden's contribution in Chapter 15.)

3. Silence. It may seem nothing is happening unless someone is talking, but silence is actually an indicator of productive meetings. Periods of silence communicate respect for others' reflection and processing time along with faith in their ability to perform a complex cognitive task.

When I ask a question and then wait for an answer, I demonstrate that I not only expect an answer but also that I have faith in the other person's ability to perform the complex cognitive task. If I ask a question, wait only a short time, and then answer myself or give

hints, I subconsciously communicate that the other person is inadequate and really can't reason the question through to an appropriate answer (Good and Brophy 1973).

Sometimes, periods of silence seem interminably long. Some people may wait only one or two seconds after having asked a question before asking another question or giving an answer to the question themselves. But if trust is the goal, team members must have the opportunity to do their own thinking and problem solving.

When we wait after hearing an answer, we allow people to continue thinking about the task or question (Rowe 1974). Furthermore, when we wait after the person asks a question or gives an answer, we model for them the same thoughtfulness, reflectiveness, and restraint of impulsivity that are desirable behaviors to use in the classrooms with students.

4. Nonjudgmental Accepting Responses. Acknowledgment simply indicates that a person has been heard. Examples of this type of response are:

- *Verbal:* "Um-hmm," "That's one possibility," "Okay,""Could be," or "I understand."
- *Nonverbal:* Nodding the head or recording without altering a participant's statement.

Paraphrasing is possibly the most powerful of all the nonjudgmental verbal responses because it communicates "I am trying to understand you and I value you." To be paraphrased is an incredibly validating experience and is far more encouraging than praising. By rephrasing, recasting, translating, summarizing, or giving an example of what the person said, the listener strives to maintain the intent and accurate meaning of the person's idea, even while using different words and phrases.

Nonjudgmental acceptance of others' ideas provides a psychologically safe and secure climate where they can take risks and where they can honestly own the data accrued in the implementation stage of the feedback spiral. It communicates that they are entrusted with the responsibility of making decisions for themselves and can explore the consequences of their own actions. Nonjudgmental acceptance provides conditions in which others are encouraged to examine and compare their own data, values, ideas, criteria, and feelings with those of others.

Here are some examples of paraphrasing:

- "So your explanation for Catherine's behavior today is that she profits more when directions for her are given in a step-by-step sequence, rather than giving the directions all at once."
- "I understand. Your idea is that we should all write our legislators rather than send them one letter from the group."
- "An example of what you mean was when you had your students arrange the rock collection according to several different classification systems."

5. Expressing Personal Regard. Little courtesies and kindnesses in action or conversation contribute to trust and team building. Small discourtesies, little unkindnesses, and little forms of disrespect soon accumulate into major trust inhibitors. This is true in all relationships.

We can express our regard for others by asking questions or making statements related to their personal interests or experiences, complimenting appearances, using phrases of courtesy, and simply spending personal time in nontask-oriented time. Sometimes staff members get so busy and so task-oriented, the little personal connections are abandoned and the day-to-day workplace of the school becomes an emotional wasteland.

A teacher we know, Rick, bought a new truck. To his colleagues, the truck was unimportant. But to him it was temporarily the most important focus in his life. During this period, building trust with Rick involved listening enthusiastically and learning (probably more than desired) about trucks, hauling capacity, curb weight, mileage, maintenance, and costs. Friends building trust with Rick spent time being interested in what was important to Rick. What is important to another person must be as important to you as the other person is to you.

6. Empathizing. This response accepts feelings and emotional states as well as related thoughts. Such responses communicate that we not only "hear" the person's idea but also the underlying emotions.

Empathizing does not mean that the we agree with the emotions or behaviors being expressed; rather, the feelings that give rise to those behaviors are understood. Some examples of empathizing are:

- "You're confused. Those directions are unclear to me, too."
- "You're frustrated because the students are not doing their homework when you assign it."
- "You're discouraged with the results of your experiment. Did you expect more?"

As Carl Rogers (1961) stated: "The way of being with another person which is termed empathic . . . means temporarily living in their life, moving about in it delicately, without making judgments. . . . [To] be with another in this way means that for the time being you lay aside the views and values you hold for yourself in order to enter the other's world without prejudice . . . a complex, demanding, strong yet subtle and gentle way of being."

7. Clarifying. This is similar to accepting in that both behaviors reflect the concern for fully understanding the other person's idea. While paraphrasing may demonstrate that you are attempting to understand, or that you *do* understand, clarifying means that you *do not* understand what the other person is saying and, therefore, need more information.

When a person uses unfamiliar terminology, expresses an unusual concept or idea, or asks a question you do not understand, you may clarify both the content of that idea and/or the process by which that idea was derived. You may invite the person to become more specific by requesting elaboration, rephrasing, or a description of the thinking processes behind the production of that idea.

Clarifying is often stated in the form of an interrogative, but it could also be a statement inviting further illumination. For example:

- "Could you explain what you mean by 'appreciate the music?' I'm not sure I understand."
- "What you are saying is that you'd rather have students work by themselves individually rather than in a group. Is that correct?"
- "You say we should study the situation. Tell us what specifically we should do to study it."

- "Would you describe to me the specific thought processes you used to arrive at that decision so that I can understand your thinking?"

By clarifying, we show that the other person's ideas are worthy of exploration and consideration; the full meaning, however, is not yet understood. Furthermore, when we encourage others to elaborate and clarify, it produces more purposefulness and greater accuracy in their thinking and behaving. Causing others to metacogitate by talking aloud about their thinking processes and strategies during and after problem solving enhances their ability to think. Evidently, thinking and talking about thinking begets even more thinking.

As Covey (1989) points out, trust in verbal communication is supported by a simple principle of sequence in communication. Seek first to understand, then to be understood.

Trust in the Organization

One of the major steps in the feedback spiral is processing the data by comparing, inferring, or drawing causal relationships. Data, therefore, must be richly and readily available for students, teachers, a group, or an organization. Providing data nonjudgmentally means that it is possible to acquire or produce the data needed to draw these relationships. One of the main objectives of team building is to nurture the team's capacities for processing information by comparing, inferring, or drawing causal relationships. Data, therefore, must gathered and made available for the individuals and the team to process.

Keeping a "How Am I Doing Checklist" such as Figure V.1 during meetings, when solving problems, and after interacting with others can provide valuable feedback on which to self-reflect and plan for enhancing skills and learnings.

A staff meeting might start with a facilitator drawing from the group these criteria as indicators of one or more of the key dimensions of trust building: communication, openness to diverse perspectives, ability to reach consensus, or capacity to resolve conflicts from a win-win perspective. Group members are in-

vited to be conscious of their own and others' behaviors and to make a commitment to employ those behaviors that contribute to team trust building. The leader invites the team to identify what information is desired, when it should be collected, and in what format the data will be recorded: "Tell us what should be recorded about our participation that will help us continue to improve our working together.

A process observer volunteers to record for the group. The process observer solicits from the group and clarifies descriptions of behaviors that would be indicators of those dimensions, how the data should be collected, and in what form it will be collected so it can provide the most meaningful feedback to the group. The "How Are We Doing Checklist" in Figure V.2 is an example of such a data collection device and provides only a sampling of the type of observable behaviors that are indicative of that dimension. Team leaders or meeting facilitators will want to derive the indicators about which data should be collected from the team: "So my job will be to keep a tally on this checklist of which team members paraphrase what was previously said before they offer their own interpretation."

During a team meeting, the process observer may use whatever technique or instrument was agreed upon to gather information: a video or audio recording, a seating chart, interaction matrix, or verbatim transcripts, for example.

Before the end of the meeting, the facilitator asks the group to reflect on the meeting and to describe how the criteria were or were not met. Feelings are explored and indicators of how the team is working together more synergistically are expressed. The observer shares the data with the group. This information should be presented to the group in a nonjudgmental, nonconfrontational fashion:

- "You asked three questions within the first five minutes of meeting."
- "Eric spoke four times, Theresa spoke two times, Shaun spoke once, and the remaining team members not at all."

The data are examined, analyzed, and interpreted by the team. The data-gathering mechanisms are discussed and analyzed, and ways of improving are

FIGURE V.2

"How Are We Doing?" Checklist

DIMENSION: Openness to Diverse Perspectives	OFTEN	SOME-TIMES	NOT YET
Restates/paraphrases a person's idea before offering personal opinion.			
Clarifies a person's ideas, concepts, or terminology.			
Expresses empathy for others' feelings/emotions.			
Takes an allocentric point of view: "If I were in your position . . . "			
Changes mind with addition of new information.			

described. Plans for next steps of how to better exhibit those behaviors are explored by each member and commitments are made to become more aware of these behaviors at future meetings.

Increasingly, as teams work together in a non-threatening relationship, they realize the intent of this process is to grow intellectually, to learn more about learning, and to mutually increase their capacity for self-improvement. They realize that the process is not another evaluative one in which the "superior" judges the "inferior"; rather, it is a self-evaluative one in which they are dedicated professionals striving to solve problems and improve their own learning while in turn working together to improve learning for their students.

Two response behaviors tend to shut down trust and terminate analysis of the feedback spiral: criticism and praise. Criticizing and other put-downs may be defined as negative value judgments. On the other hand, when conditions and indicators for criticism are agreed upon by the group, criticism can be received constructively as feedback. When negative and unsolicited, criticism can terminate the individual's or group's thinking about the feedback.

Negative responses can sometimes be subtle, such as "You're *almost right*," or "Can you give a *better* answer?" or "You're getting *close*."

Other times they include intonation that sounds sarcastic and may involve negative inflections: "Why would you want to do it *that* way?" or "Where on earth did you get *that* idea?"

The use of criticism is not helpful in promoting learning or trust and, not surprisingly, it produces negative attitudes. Criticism, therefore, is obviously not an appropriate way to respond since it leaves others with feelings of failure, cognitive inadequacy, and poor self-concept.

Praising may be defined as the opposite of criticism in that it employs the use of positive value judgments such as good, excellent, great, and so on. Following are some examples of responses that use praise:

- "That was an *outstanding* teaching strategy you used today, Linda."

- "Your lesson was *excellent*."
- "You're doing a *great* job, Leo."
- "Yours was the *best* lesson plan that anybody shared."
- "Your students are progressing *well* and certainly did a *good* job today."

Believing that praise is beneficial and that we should do more of it, some teacher evaluation or staff-development strategies advocate the use of praise in attempts to reinforce behaviors, to enhance self-worth, and to increase motivation. Unfortunately, these strategies ignore the research on praise, which indicates that the opposite is more often the case. While most of us enjoy rewarding and praising others, Brophy (1991) found that the one person for whom praise has the most beneficial effect is the praise giver. It is understandable, therefore, that research studies showing the detrimental effects of rewards are met with resistance.

Mary Budd Rowe (1974) found that when verbal rewarding is reduced there is an increase in comparative and speculative thinking leading to experimentation. When praise and rewards are given, experimentation tends to be inhibited.

Alfie Kohn (1993) finds that praise builds conformity. It is negatively associated with learning and is negatively associated with a trustful climate. Using rewards and praise as motivators of learning increases students' dependency on others for their learning; it does not help them view learning as inherently satisfying. Learners tend to acquire or exercise the skills the praise giver values rather than the skills they themselves value (Lepper and Greene 1978).

In the team-building process, conflicts and differences will abound. Congratulations! Conflict, chaos, and diversity of opinion are signs of growth. Trust is the single most important factor in conflict resolution. To determine the effectiveness of the conflict resolution process, individuals and teams are encouraged to assess the degree to which disputes are resolved: how much time, energy, and frustration was spent resolving the conflict? To what extent do team members feel fairly treated? Do the various participants have a more positive attitude toward each other and the conflict resolution process that will help resolve future dis-

ı ı ı ı ı ı ı ı ı ı ı ı ı ı ı ı ı

putes? And to what extent have participants developed new skills for preventing or resolving future disputes in schools and in other settings?

Thus, teams will learn to assess their own skills in dealing with diversity so they can function effectively in facing the data of assessment. As teams build assessment strategies, so too do they learn more about their own functioning as a team. They assess growth in their own communication skills, the enhanced levels of trust, their greater ability to deal with divergent points of view, their ability to achieve consensus, and their increased capacity to resolve conflicts with dignity. They employ feedback spirals as they learn how to effectively assess continual learning.

> People are not willing to take risks when they feel afraid or threatened. But if you manage people by love—that is, if you show them respect and trust—they start to perform up to their real capabilities.
> —JAN CARLSON

References

Bennis, W., and B. Nanus. (1985). *Leaders: The Strategies for Taking Charge*. New York: Harper and Row.

Brophy, J.E. (1991). "Teacher Praise: A Functional Analysis." Occasional Paper No. 28. East Lansing: Michigan State University.

Buscaglia, L. (1992). *Born for Love: Reflections on Loving*. Thorofare, N.J.: SLACK distributed by Random House.

Condon, W.S. (1975). "Multiple Response to Sound in Dysfunctional Children." *Journal of Autism and Childhood Schizophrenia* 5,1: 43.

Costa, A., and R. Garmston. (1994). *Cognitive Coaching: A Foundation for Renaissance Schools*. Norwood, Mass.: Christopher Gordon Publishers.

Covey, S. (1989). *The 7 Habits of Highly Effective People: Powerful Lessons in Personal Change*. New York: Simon and Schuster, Inc.

Fullan, M. (1993). *Change Forces: Probing the Depth of Educational Reform*. New York: Falmer Press.

Gardner, H. (1983). *Frames of Mind: The Theory of Multiple Intelligences*. New York: Basic Books.

Good, T.L., and J. Brophy. (1973). *Looking in Classrooms*. New York: Harper and Row.

Kohn, A. (1993). *Punished by Rewards: The Trouble with Gold Stars, Incentive Plans, A's, Praise, and Other Bribes*. Boston: Houghton Mifflin.

Kupersmith, W., and W. Hoy. (1989). "The Concept of Trust: An Empirical Assessment." Presentation at the annual meeting of the American Educational Research Association, New Orleans, La.

Lepper, M., and D. Greene. (1978). *The Hidden Cost of Reward: New Perspectives on the Psychology of Human Motivation*. Hillsdale, N.J.: Lawrence Erlbaum.

Rogers, C. (1961). *On Becoming a Person*. Boston: Houghton Mifflin.

Rowe, M.B. (1974). "Wait Time and Rewards as Instructional Variables: Their Influence on Language, Logic and Fate Control." *Journal of Research in Science Teaching*, volume II: 81-94.

Seligman, M. (1991). *Learned Optimism*. New York: Alfred A. Knopf, Inc.

ı ı

From Paradigm to Practice VI: Personal Mastery

The Developmental Continuum

An intriguing question we have raised in our chapter on Critical Friends is how we are able to be, at the same time, critical of one another's work and an advocate for its success. Sherry King describes the experience of building trust with her board of education to the point of becoming Critical Friends. She seeks and respects the critique from her board and has designed a system whereby they will respond to her work with both support and critical distance. Peggy Luidens' work demonstrates the power of how a teacher can be a Critical Friend to students as well as show how students can be Critical Friends to one another with the advocacy for all students to do their best work possible. She incorporates not only nonjudgmental trust-building behaviors but also the posing of carefully designed, open-ended questions intended to engage self-analysis, self-reflection, and self-evaluation.

13 Through the Lens of a Critical Friend

ARTHUR L. COSTA AND BENA KALLICK

Every function in . . . cultural development appears twice: first, on the social
level, and later, on the individual level;
first between people (interpsychological),
and then inside (intrapsychological). This
applies equally to voluntary attention, to
logical memory, and to the formation of
concepts. *All the higher functions originate as
actual relationships between individuals.*
— LEV VYGOTSKY

She was waiting for the ophthalmologist to bring
her to his office. The routine was a familiar one. Sit
in the chair. Place your eyes in the machine that
imitates glasses, and tell whether the letters on the
wall could be seen better or worse as the focusing lens
changed.

We believe that such an eye exam can be an analogy for assessment. It is only when you change the
lens through which you view student learning that you
find a new focus. If you never change the lens, you
limit your vision.

Sometimes your frustration mounts and you ask,
"Why do I have to say which lens is better or worse?
Can't you just tell me the right prescription?" Furthermore, you need another person to continually change
your focus, to guide you to look through multiple
lenses in order to find that "just right" fit. And it is not
entirely a matter of science. It requires a subjective perspective: "Which looks better or worse to *you*?"

As we work to restructure schools, we become
increasingly aware of asking the right questions and
collecting appropriate evidence. We are in the business
of constantly reframing our work. This suggests that
no single perspective on student learning will be suffi-

cient to truly focus on what we know about that student's capabilities and performances. It also suggests that, in the final analysis, assessment feedback should provide as clear a vision as possible about the learning performance in the eyes of the learner. And it requires someone who will be willing to provide new lenses through which learners can refocus on their work—a Critical Friend.

THE ROLE OF CRITICAL FRIENDS

The role of Critical Friend has been introduced in many school systems as a way to provide someone who will help others "change the lenses." These school systems think of their organizations as learning organizations (Senge 1990) and know that learning requires assessment feedback. A Critical Friend, as the name suggests, is a trusted person who asks provocative questions, provides a different perspective on data to be examined, and offers a critique as a friend to the person's work. A Critical Friend is prepared to take the time to fully understand the context of the work and the outcomes that a colleague is working toward. A Critical Friend is also an advocate for the success of that work.

Since the concept of critique often carries negative baggage, a Critical Friendship requires formal discipline. Many people associate critique with judgment. And when someone offers criticism, a learner braces for comments about what is wrong with the work. We often forget that Bloom refers to critique as a part of evaluation, the highest order of thinking.

Critical Friendships begin through building trust. The learner or group needs to feel assured that the Friend will:

- Be clear about the nature of the relationship, establishing that it is not for the purpose of evaluation or judgment.
- Be a good listener, working to clarify ideas, encourage specificity, and take the time to fully understand what is being presented.
- Only offer value judgments upon request from the presenter.
- Respond to work with integrity and advocacy for the success of that work.

The art of criticism is often overlooked in school life. Good critics in theater, literature, and dance serve a significant function in maintaining and elevating the standards of performance. Performing artists are accustomed to the dialogue that ensues after making work public. In fact, most performing artists have an outside editor built into their work. As they work, they often hear the voice of these editors and have sufficiently internalized criticism so that they are able to become more sharply self-evaluative (Perkins 1991).

A PROCESS FOR CRITICAL FRIENDS

We have found that once trust is established, the following process facilitates useful conversation with a Critical Friend:

1. The learner describes a practice for which he desires feedback. For example, a teacher might describe a new problem-solving technique she used with her students, or a student might describe a project he is considering.

2. The Critical Friend asks any questions that help her understand the practice described. This is an opportunity to clarify the context in which the practice takes place. For example, the Critical Friend may ask, "How much time did you allow for the students to do the problem solving?" or "When you do the project, what do you hope other people will learn from it?"

3. The learner sets desired outcomes from this conference. This is an opportunity for the learner to be in control of the feedback.

4. After observation, the **Critical Friend** offers interpretations about what she sees as significant about the practice. This is an opportunity to provide another perspective for elevating the work, not cursory praise. For example, the Critical Friend might say, "I think it's significant that you are asking students to do problem solving because it will help them become more self-directed." Or a student's Critical Friend mighty say, "I think your project will be significant because you are trying to bring a new insight into the way people have understood the changing role of women in the United States."

5. The Critical Friend raises questions and offers critique about the work, an opportunity to guide the learner to see through a different perspective. A typical query might be, "What does the evidence from your students' work indicate to you about their capacity to do problem solving?" or "When you do this project, how will you help others follow your presentation?"

6. Both participants reflect and write. The learner writes notes to himself, an opportunity to think about what has been raised by the conference. For example, will changes make this work better or worse? What have I learned from this refocusing process? The Critical Friend writes to the learner with suggestions or advice that seems appropriate to the desired outcome. This part of the process is distinguished from typical feedback situations in that the learner does not have to respond or make any decisions on the basis of the feedback. It allows the learner to reflect on and process the feedback without defending his work to the critic.

Time for this conference is flexible, though we have found it useful to limit the meeting to about 20 minutes. Once Critical Friends are accustomed to the structure, the time may be shortened.

CRITICAL FRIENDS IN PRACTICE

In the classroom, students use the Critical Friends strategy for conferencing about their writing, project work, and oral presentations. The process provides a formalized way for students to interact about the substantive quality of their work. They are readers of one another's text. They are peer editors and critics. These conferences make the role of assessor a part of the role of learner.

Many teachers guide student Critical Friends to use scoring rubrics—descriptive systems that help them know the rationale behind a rating. Because Critical Friends are advocates for your doing your best possible work, they use only the highest part of any scoring rubric. For example, if 5 is the highest score, the Critical Friend gives feedback to the learner in relationship to indicators described under the score 5. As an advocate for successful, high-quality work, the Critical Friend tries to provide feedback that will stretch the work to its best potential. This feedback session is a little different from others because it frames

the conference around performance standards set by the teacher (though the standards are often developed with the collaboration of students).

In staff development, teachers use this Critical Friends strategy to plan and reflect on their process. Instead of the usual show-and-tell kind of sharing, this strategy allows them to understand one another's work at a deeper level. The Critical Friends group can consist of as many as six people. They may meet and share practices every other week. Some teachers do this during their planning period, though there may only be time for one person to share a practice.

Administrators often find themselves too busy to reflect on their practice. In addition, they are isolated from one another. Some administrators have designed Critical Friendships as a part of their working relationships. They call upon their colleagues to provide critiques. One superintendent has called upon board of education members to be Critical Friends from time to time.

The spirit of this new role in assessment practice is to provide a context in which people can receive a response to their work that is at once critical and supportive. For example, a superintendent recently was asked to make a presentation to her board. She was warned that certain board members were difficult; they were often referred to as "bottom line." When she entered the board meeting, she said that she hoped the board would not sit as a panel of judges but as a group of Critical Friends who would help her ask the best possible evaluation questions for the proposed project. She, too, wanted to be able to identify the "bottom line" and then know how to collect data that would evaluate the project. The board, taken off guard, responded favorably. They shifted from asking her questions to helping her ask the right questions. During reflection time, each member offered concerns. As a result, in the privacy of the superintendent's own reflection, she was able to reassess her design work in light of the issues that were raised.

Organizations can also benefit from Critical Friends. In 1993, the giant but faltering blue-chip corporation IBM wooed Louis Gerstner from RJR Nabisco to turn IBM around and make it viable again. Upon assuming his new duties as CEO, Gerstner called in

IBM's major customers to determine what IBM was doing right, what it was doing wrong, and how it could better serve their needs. He was establishing feedback spirals and inviting consumers to serve as Critical Friends.

In school districts too, each level of the organization invites Critical Friends: at the individual level students and teachers provide feedback, and at the classroom level parents and teachers from other classes are invited to comment. Likewise, at the district level, school board members, parents, community members, teachers' unions and professional organizations, and community agencies are invited to ask questions and to give feedback, opinions, and comments about district practices, plans for improvement, and achievement of goals.

Introducing the role of Critical Friends into many layers of a school system builds a greater capacity for self-evaluation as well as an open-mindedness to the constructive thinking of others. As people begin to look through many lenses, they learn to ask, "Is the practice better or worse than it was previously? Are we working toward continuous improvement?" Critical Friends help us change our lenses and ask these questions.

References

Perkins, D. (1991). "What Creative Thinking Is." In *Developing Minds: A Resource Book for Teaching Thinking*, edited by A. Costa. Alexandria, Va.: Association for Supervision and Curriculum Development.

Senge, P. (1990). *The Fifth Discipline: The Art and Practice of the Learning Organization.* New York: Doubleday, Currency.

Vygotsky, L. (1978). *Society of Mind.* Cambridge, Mass.: Harvard University Press.

14   Even a Superintendent Needs Critical Friends

SHERRY KING

The superintendency is often described as a highly stressful and lonely job. In a traditional school structure, that vision might well be accurate. The superintendent sits in an office away from students and teachers, working most directly with principals who hope she will stay out of their school. The "good" superintendent manages budgets, boards of education, and local politics so the real work of education can proceed at the building level. This role definition provides limited support for systemic change because it continues to omit key stakeholders from meaningful participation—the board of education, the community beyond school, parents, and the state department of education.

If we are to truly embrace top-down support for bottom-up change, we must develop new relationships not only at the school level but in the wider community as well. A colleague recently said of her superintendent, "He doesn't have to have a vision—he should manage money, clear obstacles, and leave education to us. Keep him out unless there's a problem brewing." That vision of the superintendency is no longer valid. We know that instruction and assessment require a host of feedback loops. The superintendent cannot be an effective supporter and creator of a learning organization if data flow is one-way. The challenge is to break the assumption of the superintendent as the ultimate decision maker who wants to maintain peace at any cost. Instead, we must create contexts for Critical Friendships among the superintendent and various stakeholders.

In 1992, I became superintendent with the hope that the board of education and I could view the position differently. During my tenure as principal of the district's high school, the community saw that school change from a tired, passive institution in danger of losing many students to private education to a school visibly transforming into an exciting learning community. The board of education had been through two years of tumultuous conflict with the community over tenure decisions and a perceived lack of intellectual rigor in other schools in the district. In addition, the board wanted a radical change from the old-line managerial style of the retiring superintendent (Lester and Onore 1990), characterized by unilateral control aimed at avoiding controversy. As we embarked on the task of bringing the same renewal to the elementary and middle schools, we discovered that redefining the role of the superintendent with the board, the community, and the state in order to support systemic reform is as complex a challenge as efforts to rethink schools.

REDEFINING THE BOARD'S ROLE

Like other superintendents and boards, we began the 1992–93 school year by creating a set of goals. Chief on our list was a desire to improve communication with the community; we had a fair sampling of curricular and financial concerns as well. We also faced the immediate task of hiring an elementary principal and acclimating a new high school principal and assistant principal. It was the hiring process that brought to the surface the need to rethink the role of the board.

Although the district had always had committees of parents and teachers involved in principal selection, the groups met separately, and people believed the hiring decision really belonged to the superintendent and the board. In an effort to overcome some of the tension between the school and the parents in the aftermath of a tenure denial that split the community, we convened a joint committee with representatives of teachers, teacher assistants, secretaries, custodians, and parents to select a principal.

One candidate emerged as the clear selection of the committee, but we chose to take two candidates to the board, as was customary practice. During the interview with the board, two things happened. First, the board appointed the committee's candidate and concurred with its decision. Second, board members were torn about their place in the process, with some believing that their job was to create a participatory process and others believing that they had merely become a rubber stamp. That evening's discussion led us to rethink the topic of our Saturday work session to deal with the question of what a restructured board would look like in a restructuring district.

The conversation moved in many directions during the course of the day-long work session facilitated by a consultant who works closely with the district. We discussed what it means to set and oversee policy. Board members didn't want to micromanage the schools, but they also believed they were the one group left out of the decision-making loop in New York State's movement to more inclusive decision making. Bena Kallick, the consultant working with us for the day, helped frame the board's short- and long-term work, which included focused ways to improved feedback spirals.

IMPROVING COMMUNICATION WITH THE COMMUNITY

Communication between the board and the community generally has meant mass mailings or articles in local newspapers. A board representative and I worked with the press to enhance coverage and improve relations by opening communication. Furthermore, we increased our use of cable television and established a regular board column in the PTSA and district newsletters. As a result of our work session with Bena Kallick, we sought ways to enhance two-way communication. Our messages were going out, but we did not always know what the community had on its mind beyond PTA meetings or supermarket conversations.

In December, the board hosted a Town Meeting to inform the community about the work of the schools. We sent personal invitations to parents, senior citizens, chamber of commerce members, the mayor and village officials, pre-school directors, and every person in the community who had ever served on the board of education and in preschools. We aired the meeting on the local cable station.

At the meeting we had a panel that included the president of the board of education and representatives from the Coalition of Essential Schools, of which the high school was a member. Also on the panel was someone from the state department of education to talk about the state's restructuring initiative.

At the meeting, the board president and I defined our hopes for the district, announced that we would seek the community's input through focus groups, and assured the audience we would then work with the newly forming building and district planning councils to prepare a mission and vision statement for the district. Board members further stated that they saw themselves becoming a panel of judges of students' work to help assess how well students were meeting the district's educational goals.

The Town Meeting was enormously successful. First, it informed the community about current educational issues in the district and state. More important, creating focus groups gave concrete reality to the board's determination to expand its feedback system beyond parents' calling with individual issues or the information received from the superintendent.

In addition to focus groups, the superintendent and board scheduled a work session each month to address in depth the district's priorities. We studiously avoided the inclination to inject other work into these meetings. We also varied the format of each meeting, from having a guest who worked directly with the board on understanding the new regulations for shared decision making in the state, to curriculum reports, to meetings designed to provide community input that would inform our practice in implementing principles like All Students Can Learn. While we originally envisioned the meetings as times for the board to discuss priorities in depth, they became valuable opportunities for the board to engage in open dialogue with the public and school personnel about emerging issues and the work of the schools. In fact, they have been much better attended than the monthly meetings at which we conduct our regular business.

USING POLICY TO SUPPORT PRACTICE

This work by the superintendent and the board helped create a climate of open communication with the community, but it still left board members puzzled about the question that emerged in the principal selection process. Is the board's role to simply ascertain the pulse of the various constituencies, or is it to set policy?

Furthermore, while the board's shared commitment to the direction of the schools was positive, our consultant pointed out in the second year's goal-setting workshop that the board and superintendent were supporting each other so much that we had lost the ability to ask critical questions, anticipate issues, and use critiques to improve our work.

That insight was valuable for the board and me as superintendent. I realized that I had assumed the enormous burden of the entire responsibility for the work of the district since the board and faculties accepted our direction with very little debate. I also realized that I was the main voice supporting our work to any skeptics in the community. Those closer to the work should have been assuming more of that responsibility if the work was truly theirs. Board members felt similar relief at this recognition that they could raise difficult questions and still support the direction and work of the schools.

For example, one member of the board had been seeking more substantive "evidence" of what all of our efforts actually meant for student learning. We had discussed sharing student work, showing exemplars, and demonstrating how our restructuring efforts were holding students to standards equal to or greater than the more traditional instruction and assessment. Another member of the board wanted to see how our work was actually being informed by our affiliation with the Coalition of Essential Schools and New York State's New Compact for Learning. The entire board wanted to seize the opportunity of its consensus on the direction of our schools and the general community support for our work to set policy that would ensure that current initiatives were not simply a passing fad. As the plan for our second year emerged, all of us felt we had finally defined a process for working together as Critical Friends and using the policy-making function of the board to frame the work of curriculum, instruction, and assessment without intruding on the domains of the professionals.

The results of that work session have been twofold. First, in December 1993, we fulfilled our commitment to demonstrate what alternative assessment means in real practice for students by showing the board and community actual examples of past and present assessment tasks at each school level. Second, we have embarked on the work of creating a "systems map" on which we identify all educational initiatives in the district and align them with the principles of the New Compact for Learning and the Coalition of Essential Schools. The chart gives history where it is important, for example when mainstreaming was introduced and the various times its progress was reported to the board of education in public session. It then defines data we will gather on the effectiveness of the initiative and the implications of the data analysis on future work. Finally, it identifies the people at the school level who are responsible for the initiative. The process of creating a map of our work has included all members of the staff of our schools and has generated significant discussion about our commitment and the direction of our work. By aligning practice with principles, it has brought greater coherence to work that often feels fragmented.

Our next step will be a conversation with the board about these initiatives and what the schools need in terms of board and community support to continue their work. Because the meeting will be constructed as a dialogue, not a presentation, the staff will also be able to hear community concerns and what the board needs to fulfill its role as a panel of judges. As superintendent, the process has enabled me to disseminate and receive feedback on the work of the district in a context where no one need feel defensive.

RELATING WITH THE STATE DEPARTMENT OF EDUCATION

Creating a meaningful feedback spiral with the state is at once simpler and more complex than creating feedback spirals within a community. It is simpler because the task is to share the process and products of the work at the local level with the state. While that communication should be easy—particularly in states like New York whose New Compact for Learning empowers decision making at the local level—the many facets of the state bureaucracy make the task complex. There are those at the state level who are proponents of reform, happy to be included in the work of

a dynamic district. Others are as entrenched in traditional roles and responsibilities as some of the more resistant members of any faculty. There is enormous disparity between the possibilities of individual relationships with significant people at the state level who can help smooth the way for change and the effort to change policy and practice for all schools in the state. So while our district has had an amicable relationship with the state, our role in trying to change the process of feedback loops with the state has been more complex. Perhaps this can best be illustrated by our work connected to alternative assessment.

New York State designated Partnership Schools, schools that are in leadership positions in rethinking curriculum, instruction, and assessment, and should therefore have a special relationship with the state and help lead the way for systemic reform. We were named such a school for our educational initiatives, particularly our attempt to have more students at the high school level attain a "Regents" level education. In our efforts to raise standards for all children, we piloted a project of altering certain components of Regents exams in order to better reflect the curriculum and our knowledge of meaningful assessment practice. In working toward that end, we met with an associate commissioner, bureau chiefs in two subject areas, and a representative from the testing department along with an observer from the Education Commission of the States. We then invited teams from the New York State department of education to visit the school, meet the teachers, and see samples of student work—in short, to get to know the school. We carefully documented the testing procedures and the results. To the best of our knowledge the state was pleased to be included as partners in our work and delighted that we were forging a new direction for other schools.

In that first year, we were surprised and satisfied with the state's willingness to be flexible. In a second year, when we were ready to take bolder initiatives, we found the relationships we thought we had built had not endured. Personnel had changed, and there was no continuity in knowledge of our school or understanding that we were taking the next step in the development of our curriculum. Informal conversations have indicated that the frustrations the school personnel feel over beginning anew with the state are repeated by those charged with implementing the work at the state level. Educators there are still forced to make decisions upon variances without knowing the schools well. While our district has established a relationship with the state that allows us to negotiate our way through endless obstacles, there is deep concern among the Partnership Schools about how to implement a more open policy at the state level. For their part, representatives of the state express concern about how to affirm local control and maintain standards. Without a more effective feedback loop, local districts and the state continue to operate on a framework of distrust. In short, the state does not want to be a rubber stamp any more than the local school board does. Likewise, schools cannot proceed in the work of reform always wondering whether the state will give its seal of approval at the end of process rather than be its partner in a continual process of development, feedback, and revision.

The New York State department of education is asking serious questions about how best to receive feedback. In several instances they have sent drafts of regulations that have been altered based on responses from the field. There have been efforts to reorganize a bureaucratic structure based in Albany into regional teams that will get to know schools well. Districts like Croton-Harmon play a significant role in exploring meaningful avenues of communication with the state, which recognizes the need for new ways of achieving accountability on all sides. We are asking how to build trust, how to include each other as partners, and how to persevere in building this relationship when it would be much easier to revert to a compliance mode. The steps in this direction have been filled with gaps, but our local experience convinces us that the direction is worth pursuing.

REFLECTING ON THE CHANGES

Enhanced communication with the board, the community, and the state means a shift in the superintendent's role from a gatekeeper to a gate opener.

Rather than focusing on control and minimizing critical or questioning remarks that might get to the board, it means providing numerous and varied opportunities for shared learning and conversation about the complex issues of education. In trying to help a district rethink its work in significant ways, the superintendent's role must continue to be that of a cheerleader for the work of the schools, but the praise must be based on genuine accomplishment and must be tempered by the reality of the need for continuous improvement. The voices of parents and students provide important information about the status of our work. The superintendent's job is to help people move beyond defensiveness in order to hear a variety of perspectives in order to better inform action.

Opening and maintaining many feedback spirals does not necessarily make the superintendent's job less lonely. Therefore, it is important for a superintendent to find like-minded colleagues who can serve as Critical Friends and sounding boards. This new role definition requires exploring different collegial relationships with principals, teachers, parents, and especially the board, so all can serve as Critical Friends to each other. It means that the superintendent must let go of the notion that she can have control of an endeavor as large as a school system. Instead, she must focus on more careful selection and development of leaders within the schools and communities whose voices feed each other and the collaborative work of educating our students. The New Compact for Learning has the danger of trivializing the African proverb on which it rests: "It takes a whole village to raise a child." If we take this shift to more inclusive participation seriously, then the role of the superintendent moves from that of chief executive officer to the educational mayor of the village who knows all the players, helps build common cause, and continues to bring more voices into the conversation.

Reference

Lester, N., and C.S. Onore. (1990). *Learning Change.* Portsmouth, N.H.: Boynton/Cook Publishers.

15 The Writing Conference As a Critical Feedback Spiral

Peggy M. Luidens

A student's writing represents his or her full range of thinking at one particular moment. Although the composition may not always hold the radiant luster or the final polish a teacher hopes for, it does contain a variety of ideas to talk about and build upon. Unless the fullness of those ideas is completely elicited, the written piece may achieve only a small measure of its potential brilliance. Drawing out these inherent ideas is the overriding task of the writing conference.

The writing conference is a conversation between student and teacher or student and student. It is an essential step in the writing process. In a writing conference, a special synergism is created among the writer's thoughts, the written artifact, and the conversation with the reader. Together, the teacher and author mediate the latter's thinking beyond simple consideration and raise it to more complex reflecting and, ultimately, to more complex writing.

The writing conference honors four ingredients:

- It honors the writer as the constructor of meaning.
- It honors the role of Critical Friends who act as mediators or coaches for the writer.
- It honors the fact that authors change their minds as they refine their thinking.
- It honors the notion of collaboration. Both partners learn from each other.

Within a systems thinking model, the writing conference can be considered a feedback loop. As a feedback loop, it is a mechanism for testing the author's intentions in the written piece against the reader's perceptions of the written product. Such a feedback loop has a twofold purpose for the writer:

- It provides the writer with an opportunity to step away from the written piece and test its potential with an external audience.

| | | | | | | | | | | | | | | | | | | |

• If done accurately, the external feedback process models ways that help the writer create an internal feedback spiral within his or her own thinking and written work. (This can be referred to as self-talk.)

Among the possible elements of self-talk are these: the author asks himself or herself analytical questions about how well the written artifact matches his or her goals. In addition, the self-talking author reviews the precision and accuracy of the piece, decides if the stylistic strategies used are effective, generates formats for publication, and applies learning from this document to future writings. Authors will never outgrow the need for Critical Friends, but by being alert to these components of self-talk, authors can learn to serve as their own Critical Friends.

CONFERENCE FEEDBACK SPIRALS

The conferencing conversation, as its name implies, is a mutual exchange. It is not unidirectional from an expert teacher or student to a novice student. Instead, it is a deliberate dialogue between teacher and student or student and student. It is aimed at eliciting a clear understanding of the writer's thinking and an accurate rendering of that thinking in the writing.

The conferencing conversation takes place within a context that raises nonjudgmental questions. These questions give writers an opportunity to think aloud about their writing; they provide writers with a context to compare what's in their minds with what's on their pages. The questions are not meant to be interrogatory; rather, they are to solicit the writer's thoughts.

As I write about this questioning phase, I realize that many readers might think there is a fixed set of questions that should be raised with student authors. This is most definitely not the case. Instead, there is a wide array of potential questions reflecting the complexity of the thinking endeavor. To fully comprehend the twists and turns of a student's thought process, a teacher must be ready to follow wherever the author's thoughts lead. Careful listening and perceptive probing are essential.

When a student writes, he or she is engaged in an exercise of invention. Invention, as characterized in Bloom's Taxonomy, takes place at the "synthesis level."

This implies that the inventor or writer is drawing together formerly unattached materials (in this case ideas, insights, and perspectives) to create an entirely new entity. The very novelty of the combinations is at the heart of the inventive process—and this is the enlivening quality of writing (indeed, of all intellectual enterprises). Students are drawing together previously unrelated perceptions in order to create novel and idiosyncratic understandings. It becomes the challenge of the questioning process to plumb the depths of those understandings, especially when they are sometimes only sketchily realized in the student's writing (and thinking).

As I initiate conferencing conversations with writers, I keep in mind that the student is teaching me, so I set out to enjoy the experience. Our conversation has three objectives: to acknowledge the student as a writer, to give the student an opportunity to think in new ways about a piece, and to build a pattern of inquiry that will eventually translate into self-talk.

I find it useful to picture conferencing sessions taking one of two possible paths with parallel sets of questions—those dealing with thinking matters and those dealing with technical ones. Sometimes a conference will incorporate questions in both of these areas, but usually only some will be considered during a single setting. All will have to be considered before final publication of a written piece is accomplished.

What follows is the first draft of "My Trip," a short story written by Shelley. Imagine Shelley reading the story to us. Listen for her hidden voices. Consider what questions you would ask her. What points could be clarified? What could be expanded? After you have read this story, we will engage in an imaginary conference with Shelley.

My Trip by Shelley
On Thursday Oct. 22, Me and my class went to the Natchur Center. we wen't out on the trails. And it started to snow. But we still had to keep going till we got to the end. Before you knew it it got very cold. Then finally we got to the end. Then we got a bathroom brake. Then we got to go to the gift shop. I got som polished rocks.

FIGURE 15.1

Content Questions

Content Questions	Types of Thinking Elicited
"I really enjoyed picturing your trip to the Nature Center. You mentioned going along the trail. What kinds of discoveries did you make along the trail?"	Even though Shelley has not made any elaboration of what she saw on the trail, the question presupposes that she did see something. The hope is that she will break down the trip from summary statements to more specific subdivisions. As Shelley subdivides her narrative of the trip, she will engage in analytical thinking.

Teachers conferencing with writers must listen carefully to student responses. They may reveal that the child is not interested in pursuing a particular line of thought. This must be respected, and no further probing should take place. It is critical to the conferencing process that the author be the final arbiter of what should be included and what should be left out. On the other hand, the attentive teacher may hear a great many new facts about an issue of interest to the author. Needless to say, follow-up questions would be most important in this situation. |
The teacher restates what Shelley has just said to emphasize how well she has been heard: "You have just told me a great deal about what you saw on the trail. Is there a place to fit some of this new information into your writing piece?"	The question raises Shelley's thinking to an evaluative level. Shelley must judge the merits of adding more information. Furthermore, she must decide where to add the new material.
"Wow! It was snowing in October when you took your class trip to the Nature Center. How did your class feel about that? How did your teachers feel about the snow? Did you enjoy the snow in October?"	With this type of question, Shelley will begin to analyze her writing in terms of feelings: both her own and those of others.
"What was your favorite part of the trip? Why did you like that part so much?"	Again, Shelley's thinking is engaged in the process of evaluation. She must give her own opinion and substantiate her response.
"You mentioned buying polished rocks. How did you happen to buy those specific ones?"	Shelley must analyze her own choice. Depending on her response, a teacher may discover that Shelley knows a great deal about rocks. In such a case, follow-up questions should help Shelley expand on this issue—perhaps in her next written piece.
"Shelley, you seem to know a great deal about rocks. What do you think about doing a writing piece just about the variety of rocks there are?"	Shelley will begin to assess the potential of this new topic as a future writing theme. In this way Shelley will learn that writing is a building process and that she can apply her past discoveries to her future writing pieces.
"We've talked about different parts of your story. What do you think you will add and where might you add it? Do you need suggestions about how to fit in additional information without rewriting your whole story?"	This question presupposes that Shelley will add more information. As suggested above, she will have to evaluate what to add and where to place it. Of special importance, Shelley is reminded that the conference is a dialogue and that the teacher is willing to join in by suggesting possible changes to the piece.

(continued)

FIGURE 15.1

Content Questions (continued)

Content Questions	Types of Thinking Elicited
"I enjoyed listening to your story, but I got a little confused when you talked about the trail you walked on. Help me out. What did the trail look like?"	The reader is genuinely confused about some aspects of Shelley's narrative. Clarification is requested from Shelley, the only authority on the subject.
"It was exciting hearing your writing piece. Now that you've finished this conference, how do you feel about your draft?"	This "fluffy" question gets Shelley to evaluate the overall experience. Again, she is the only legitimate authority on how she feels. If she answers "I liked it," the teacher has the opportunity to probe further about particularly meaningful content areas: "What did you like about it?" However, if Shelley answers "I hated it," the teacher can again focus on meaningful content: "What parts were hard?" Or the teacher may elect to move on to the next project: "You've written your first piece, now. I enjoyed hearing it. What's the next topic on your list? How about that piece on rocks?"

Now that we have "listened" to Shelley, we have an opportunity to engage her in thinking about her piece and about the curiosity she has inspired in us, her Critical Friends. The collaborative feedback loop has been initiated. As indicated, a conference with Shelley might take one of two paths: focusing on thinking issues or on technical ones. Thinking issues deal with the ideas that inform the writing process. Conferences that focus on thinking matters ask questions about content, composition, and design. Conferences that focus on technical issues raise questions about the mechanics of the writing process: spelling, punctuation, and grammar. These latter issues will not be expanded upon in the following discussion, although they must be part of the prepublication review of every written piece.

Keeping in mind that there are no standard questions that must be used in every conferencing conversation, the model in Figure 15.1 suggests some of the thinking (content, composing process, and design) questions that might be raised with Shelley. The model also indicates the types of thinking that are elicited in conjunction with the questions. These samples provide a glimpse into the metacognitive thinking a Critical Friend might exercise in the process of a conferencing conversation.

AN IMAGINARY CONFERENCE

Content questions invite the author to consider the types of information that are being transmitted in the written piece. Of particular concern is the completeness and clarity of the information. The author may be invited to consider additional information that should be included but has been inadvertently omitted (Figure 15.1).

Composing strategy questions are intended to have the author consider the processes involved in the composition of the written piece. In various ways, the author is pressed to think through the steps she or he has taken in putting together the current piece and to determine what might be useful in future writing. Processing composing strategies enables the writer to strengthen his or her metacognitive thinking about the writing experience more generally (Figure 15.2).

Design questions come in two varieties: external

FIGURE 15.2

Composing Questions

Composing Questions	Types of Thinking Elicited
"How did you go about your writing? Did you dream up the idea at the beginning and then compose as you went along? Or did you make up your ideas as you wrote?"	Shelley is invited to engage in analytical thinking about the composing process. She is led to realize that the writing process is not a "natural" thing but rather a deliberate, step-by-step engagement.
"I notice that sometimes you move words around and sometimes you change words. How do you decide what words you'll use?"	Shelley is asked to evaluate the decisions she made along the way.
"You have so many pieces in your writing portfolio. My guess is that you have learned a lot about yourself as a writer. What's one thing you have learned about yourself that you want to remember the next time you write a piece?"	Shelley is being challenged to look at her own writing experience over the spectrum of her writings. By making this comparative assessment, she will be in a better position to understand what writing approach works best for her.
"You've learned some ways to revise your writing (like slotting, movability, expansion, and sentence combining). Do you use one of these ways more often than the others? How do you decide when to use one of these strategies?"	These questions involve Shelley in the process of analyzing and evaluating the merits of her own revision strategies.
"You have had many chances to read your piece to other people. What things do you find out after you read your piece to someone?"	Shelley is encouraged to use the conference dialogue as an opportunity to reflect on the composition process.

FIGURE 15.3

External Design Questions

External Design Questions	Types of Thinking Elicited
"Who will be your audience?"	This question encourages Shelley to imagine her audience as she writes and as she reflects on her written piece.
"What do you want your readers to learn from your written piece?"	Shelley is asked to consider the impact of her writing on her audience. The question assumes that her writing has purpose, and it challenges her to articulate her message.
"What writing genre will best communicate your ideas to that audience?"	The Critical Friend presupposes that several writing genres could work, although not equally well. Sometimes young writers get stuck in only one genre. This question gets Shelley to look at alternative genres for getting her message across (e.g., play, diary, newspaper article, poem, limerick, poster, advertisement, letter, or autobiography).

FIGURE 15.4

Internal Design Questions

Internal Design Questions	Types of Thinking Elicited
"As you reread your piece, what words and phrases are especially important for the message you want to get across to the reader?"	All these questions presuppose that there is not just one way to style a sentence or a paragraph. They challenge Shelley to think of how she has made word choices. They give Shelley an opportunity to consider the fine-tuning of her composition.
"Are there any nonessential words, phrases, or paragraphs that could be eliminated from the piece without detracting from the content?"	
"Are there words, phrases, or paragraphs that might be moved to another place in your piece in order to give it greater clarity?"	
"Are there ideas that you think are too sketchy and that need expansion? Are there sections that are too wordy and need reduction?"	
"What opening strategy did you use to grab your reader's attention?"	These questions presuppose that Shelley cares about capturing and retaining the attention of her readers and that deliberately crafted wording can do just that.
"What variety of transition words did you use between paragraphs to keep your reader's interest?"	

and internal. External design questions ask the author to pay attention to his or her audience and to use that knowledge to decide in what genre the piece should be written. Internal design questions deal with the composition style of a piece. These questions encourage the author to evaluate his or her word strategies (Figures 15.3 and 15.4). I have described the writing conference as a feedback spiral that joins together a writer and a Critical Friend. The challenge of conferencing is to engage the student in a process that focuses on the writer rather than the written product. The conference plants seeds that promote metacognitive thinking in writers so they focus on the processes behind their writing, not just on the emerging product.

In its ideal form, the writing conference models for student writers the type of self-critique that is most important to adopt. By introducing questions in a supportive and affirming manner, conferencing trains the student to be self-modifying, self-renewing, and self-taught. This is its highest calling.

PART VI

The Developmental Continuum of Personal Mastery

The Developmental Continuum of
Personal Mastery

ARTHUR L. COSTA AND BENA KALLICK

The only person who is educated is the one who has learned
how to continue to learn and change.

—CARL ROGERS

A learning organization requires all of its members to see themselves as continual learners working toward personal mastery. Yet as people gain experience and competence, it becomes increasingly difficult for them to place themselves in the position of acquiring new skills and competencies. They are concerned because they know that new learning often requires valleys before arriving at peaks.

For example, in learning how to use the word processor, many people experience the following scenario. First, they read a manual that seems unintelligible—unintelligible because it contains a whole new vocabulary, a new set of options and commands, and menus that are not clearly understood. Although they have been assured that writing will be made simpler with a word processor, it feels far more complex. Every time they sit down to write using this new machine, they assume that what would normally take one hour might easily take three. They must be prepared to persevere rather than fall back on familiar but supposedly less efficient ways. Finally, after personal mastery, come three observations:

- Writing is, indeed, more efficient and effective.
- Using the word processor has changed the way they now think about writing.
- Perhaps other options and programs could be used to add style to the text—importing graphics, for example.

Learning in an information age will require continual personal mastery of new skills and competencies as job descriptions expand, change, and shift. And collectively, the organization will have varying levels of expertise to draw from.

Although many schools set outcomes intended to recognize and celebrate diversity as a value in their learning communities, they may not learn sufficiently how to make use of varied personal mastery to maximize profit from the group. Unless we really understand that each of us brings a different talent, ability, and knowledge to the learning environment, we will never reach that outcome. It requires thinking of learning from the perspective of strength rather than deficiency, a paradigm at the heart of our shift in reassessing assessment. We must be able to accept the fact that each of us is a novice in some aspects of our learning and that each of us brings expertise to the learning community. Our role as educational leaders in the classroom, among the faculty, and in the larger school community is to continually find ways for people to bring what they know to the environment and to find ways to stimulate the new learner in everyone.

An example of this point is nicely made with the concept of shared decision making—a place where different group members have different perspectives and knowledge to bring to the group. Or we might consider the sailing experience of a group of educators. A number of years ago, a schooner set forth into Boston Harbor with several teachers and administrators on board. Roland Barth set up the event so that participants would have the experience of guiding a ship through the harbor as a metaphor for teamwork. An Outward Bound instructor on board helped teach various participants skills for setting the ship on course. As we set forth, the unequal knowledge base in the group was clear. That inequality was not based on hierarchical position in the school organization but on knowledge of sailing. Traditional leadership roles in school gave way to captains of the sea.

When the Outward Bound instructor told the group at 11 a.m. that they would be on their own for the rest of the trip, a growing uneasiness spread among the crew. What? There would be no designated captain? Each novice thought, "I only learned a small skill. How am I supposed to function in this large harbor with such a small amount of knowledge?" The experts were equally uncertain. They knew that they were able to bring the ship safely to shore, but it wouldn't reflect teamwork if they took over. The ensu-

ing struggle within individuals and groups led to a number of novices going to the galley and preparing lunch, a number of apprentices asking for assistance, a number of practitioners with modest sailing knowledge coming forward, and the experts finally taking leadership.

After we were safely in the harbor, we had a debriefing session. It was at this time that people expressed their concerns. Novices felt literally and metaphorically at sea. No one came forward to help them enter the culture, and they were so uncertain about what to do that they went to an area that felt more comfortable: the kitchen. The dialogue between the experts who could have become teachers but faced the dilemma of not having been designated as such and the novices who could have been learners but were not designated as such provides the perfect metaphor for a learning organization.

MULTIPLE CONTINUUMS

It is simply not enough to say that we respect diversity and various kinds of knowledge brought to our learning environment. We must provide appropriate structures that help novices to learn what they do not know and experts to become the novice's teachers. If we place too high a premium on expertise in only one area, we may shut out the potential teachers in many other significant areas. Consider Howard Gardner's theory of multiple intelligences (1983) or the work from group dynamics suggesting different inclinations for working in groups. Consider also the work from learning styles. It also suggests that if learning is described on a continuum, it reinforces the possibility of learning without embarrassment or inadequacy. As soon as learners in the classroom see the teacher attempting to learn something new (a novice), they will realize that she, too, is learning. When the Spanish-speaking student is invited to share his expertise about language and learning a second language, he, too, is an expert.

We have often heard the comment "knowledge is power." It has never been more accurate than in this information age. Information is data; knowledge is making sense out of the data. All learners will have to make sense out of new data at an ever-increasing rate. All learners will bring different experiences to the database and will become more or less expert in making sense of information depending on how many opportunities encourage them to know the power of knowing. Our present system makes the reward of knowing a scarce resource. We create finish lines and reward systems that fly in the face of a continuously increasing information base.

We need to think about a continuum that describes learning from two perspectives:

- What developmental stage is the learner at on the continuum (for example, novice or apprentice)?
- What is the quality of the work the learner produces at that stage?

Consider, for example, a rubric designating the difference between exemplary work and unacceptable work, as in Figure VI.1. This suggests a matrix that helps us to see not only where the student is on the developmental continuum but what the student chooses to produce given his or her developmental capability. Both kinds of information are necessary to describe learning. Our goal is to align such a matrix with report cards and portfolios and thus provide descriptive information to parents, students, administrators, and boards of education that shows consistency in forms of reporting.

CONTINUING TO LEARN HOW TO LEARN

In a focus group of business people, parents, and high school students, the moderator asked, "What is it you want to know from a reporting system that will acquaint you with an individual being considered for employment?" A person in charge of personnel in a major insurance company responded, "I don't really look for report cards or transcripts. Basically I have two questions that tell me more than anything else. First, describe something that you do really well. Second, describe something that you don't do particularly well and tell me what you're doing about it."

This person recognizes that as long as you're prepared to do some learning, being a novice means only that you're at a new beginning—not that you're inade-

quate or lacking in some way. The story also suggests that you're never "there." Our traditional summative reporting system, therefore, delivers a false message to students. Rather than providing an incentive for further learning, we shut students down.

Art recently asked his 9th grade granddaughter, Shawn, what she was learning in social studies. "We're learning about the Constitution," she responded. "Great! Tell me three things you've learned about the Constitution," Art inquired. "I can't. I've forgotten it already," she replied. "Shawn, how could you forget it already?" Art challenged. "Well," she replied, "we've already had the test!"

This anecdote exemplifies how some students today may have developed a view of learning as an episodic process of covering some topic, passing a test on it, forgetting it, and proceeding to the next topic.

If you employ feedback spirals, never reaching an end product, summative assessment is irrelevant. If you assume lifelong learning, summative assessment assumes finality that dissuades one from starting anew. Living in an information age, in learning organizations, and in a learning society, humans will have to perceive themselves as continual learners.

The Walt Disney Company is known to have four levels of competency for their employees:

Unconscious Incompetence: They don't know that they're doing their task incorrectly.

Conscious Incompetence: They are aware of the fact that they've made an error or are doing the task incorrectly.

Conscious Competence: The awkward performance of a task, having to think about it as they are performing it.

Unconscious Competence: The easy flow of mastery of the task performance at the level of automaticity.

What distinguishes the Disney Corporation, however, is that when employees achieve the level of Unconscious Competence in one role, they are switched to a new job so that they start the learning process anew.

FIGURE VI.1

A Developmental Continuum

ANALYTIC CRITERIA

Understanding the Problem:
- understands the question the problem poses
- chooses information that is relevant to the problem
- when using graphic/pictorial representation, accurately interprets the problem
- can restate the problem in own terms

Reasoning Strategies and Mathematics Procedures:
- chooses appropriate and applicable strategy
- draws from past knowledge and experience
- communicates reasoning process logically and sequentially
- chooses the appropriate and most efficient mathematical procedure
- sees more than one way of looking at problem
- develops system for checking accuracy and precision

Communication:
- results are presented clearly, coherently, and accurately
- uses tools of mathematical communication (e.g., graphs, notation such as +/−)

K–2 GRADE TASK: Some ladybugs have 5 spots. Some ladybugs have 7 spots. Some ladybugs have 2 spots. Show 18 spots.

Developmental Continuum

NOVICE	APPRENTICE	PRACTITIONER	EXPERT
Limited awareness of the problem. Drawing does not connect to the problem. Attempts to do the task without any strategy for how to begin. Random or weak organization of problem.	Shows appropriate use of numbers. Attempts to use equations although has incorrect solution. Shows clear understanding of problem. Random or weak explanation of strategy.	Understands problem. Uses appropriate equations. Correct solutions. Describes strategy.	Generalizes from previous math experiences. Experiments successfully to create multiple solutions. Elaborates on process or strategy used.

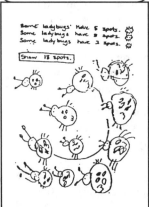   

Perhaps another metaphor can illuminate this paradigm shift. Do you remember when you first learned to ride a bicycle? You may have had training wheels fitted to each side of your bike so that balancing would be easier, and you could devote your limited attention to steering and pedaling. Even so, there were spills and bumps. Just getting on the bike was an awkward maneuver.

It was a memorable day when you graduated to riding without those beginner's accoutrements. With a little more time and practice you may have become a serious bike rider. You could get to places in your neighborhood, to school, to visit friends, to deliver papers, and, perhaps later, to work. Bike riding was fun but, more important, it was a mode of transportation.

For some enthusiasts, bike riding became more than just that interim means of transportation between walking and having an automobile. You'd affix your bike to the rack on your car and take your bike out on weekends to explore the byways. You may have joined a bicycle club and entered rallies, purchased a helmet and stretch pants, begun using the language of "derailleurs" and "tenacious oils," and dreamed of titanium Serrotis.

Entering the Olympics in bicycle competition means perseverance and practice: devotion of time and energy to serious workouts, coaching, competitive racing, training, qualifying, and on to the medals. It involves employing the scientific principles of bicycling. It means deep concentration, developing style and rigor. It means world-class mastery.

The metaphor of mastering the bicycle may be analogous to the developmental continuum: from the novice stage using training wheels, through the free-roaming "graduate" and serious "aficionado" stages to the world-class Olympian level. There are certain attributes of participation, competence, knowledge, skill, intellectual process, and emotional attachment that distinguish each stage from the one before it. Each stage implies accomplishment of a certain level of skill, but with that achievement comes a new stage of complexity and standards to be met. Even with the mastery of the highest level, athletes are never satisfied with their accomplishments; they always try to beat the existing records.

The motto of the Nike Corporation is "There is no finish line." Similarly, educators must shift their paradigm of summative assessment and replace it with the concept of developmental stages along a continuum toward ever-increasing levels of achievement and skillfulness.

The number of levels may vary depending upon how finite the distinctive attributes of each stage are described. The labels given to that stage are also arbitrary but should connote increasingly higher levels of mastery. Figure VI.2 contains one way of describing four levels along a developmental continuum—from the entry level of novice through the next levels that we call apprentice and practitioner to the highest level being expert.

Obviously the distinctions among these levels are not as clear and precise as described above. An analogy may be made to waves and tides. While the tide is moving in the direction toward the shore, each wave is not necessarily higher than the previous one. While there is a general direction of growth, each performance may not include every attribute of that stage. Even Olympic athletes have their bad days! (For further information on developmental rubrics, see Kallick and Brewer 1993 and Marzano, Pickering, and McTighe 1993.)

Teachers, too, are in a continual state of personal mastery. The distinctions between the teacher in training, the beginning teacher, and the experienced or master teacher are fairly distinguishable. In an effort to assist mentors in enhancing the work of the new teacher, the California State Department of Education Beginning Teacher Project has described the distinguishing characteristics of each stage. The characteristics have less to do with time than with learning new skills, attitudes, and intellectual processes (Garmston and Bartell 1991).

Furthermore, organizations, just as individuals, proceed through stages of growth on the never-ending journey toward that elusive level of mastery. Carl Glickman (1994), Michael Fullan (1993), and other researchers looking at the process of organizational change describe schools along a continuum as "traditional," "transitional," and "transforming." School staffs are described as moving from "isolated" to

FIGURE VI.2

Defining a Continuum: Novice to Expert

Novice: Shows limited awareness of
the problem.
- Is willing to engage in the task.
- Attempts task without strategy for how
  to begin.
- Organizes the problem in random or
  vague ways.

Apprentice: Shows a clear understanding
of problem.
- Attempts to use strategies, though may not
  use them appropriately.
- Explains strategy randomly and uses vague
  or unclear terms.

Practitioner: Is able to perform the task.
- Perceives solutions from one perspective.
- Persists in solving problem but is not always
  concerned about accuracy.
- Is bound by rules of problem solving.
- Describes strategies used to solve problems.

Expert: Operates at a metacognitive level—is
able to describe strategies and processes and
explain why they are used.
- Expresses efficacy and confidence in own
  abilities.
- Spontaneously employs the Intelligent
  Behaviors (Costa 1991).
- Draws from and employs a repertoire of
  strategies beyond the context in which they
  are learned or normally performed.
- Can teach the strategies or processes
  to others.
- Generates alternative and creative
  solutions to the problem.
- Generalizes from previous experiences.
- Experiments successfully to create
  multiple solutions.
- Elaborates on process or strategy used.

"congenial" to "cooperative" to "collaborative and col-legial" in the ways staff members interact and support each other. Covey (1989) describes a continuum from "dependence" to "independence" to "interdependence and a sense of community."

The purposes of establishing such developmental continuums with accompanying criteria are:

- So that learners (be they teachers, students, or school staffs) may know the objective criteria for each level of accomplishment and evaluate their own performances.
- So that such performances may be diagnosed and/or judged objectively by students themselves and by teachers, parents, or other panels so that further learning strategies can be geared for constant improvement.
- So that students may choose the appropriate levels of performance as their aspiration and understand the goals and criteria toward which they may strive.
- So that school staffs and communities can discuss, reach agreements on, and constantly revise their expectations and high standards.
- To provide standards to be improved upon, plateaus that can be transcended, and aspirations that can be exceeded.

References

Covey, S. (1989). *The Seven Habits of Highly Effective People: Powerful Lessons in Personal Change*. New York: Simon and Schuster.

Fullan, M. (1993). *Change Forces*. New York: The Falmer Press.

Gardner, H. (1983). *Frames of Mind: The Theory of Multiple Intelligences*. New York: Basic Books.

Garmston, R., and C. Bartell. (April 1991). "New Teacher Success: You Can Make a Difference." California State Department of Education, California New Teachers Project. Sacramento, Calif.: Commission on Teacher Credentialing.

Glickman, C. (1994). *Renewing America's Schools*. San Francisco: Jossey-Bass.

Kallick, B., and R. Brewer. (1993). *Exemplars: Math Performance Tasks, Volumes 1-10*. Underhill, Vt.

Marzano, R., D. Pickering, and J. McTighe. (1993). *Assessing Student Outcomes*. Alexandria, Va.: Association for Supervision and Curriculum Development.

From Paradigm to Practice VI: Personal Mastery

The Developmental Continuum

As we consider the developmental continuum, we are faced with a common question: "How do we watch a flower grow?" It is so difficult to see progress. It seems that as soon as we achieve one level of mastery we are striving toward the next. In the following chapters, teachers demonstrate the powerful use of portfolios as a way of helping their students observe their own growth. These portfolios are organized so that they show developmental change over time and ask students to reflect on that change.

Pat Monahan describes knowing what to look and listen for in portfolios. Darlene Johnson and Sandra Silverman begin with students and their teachers in an effort to demonstrate a continuum of growth throughout the primary years. Braden Montgomery asks his secondary students to reflect on themselves as continuously improving learners and writers. In addition, Victoria Bernhardt addresses portfolios and assessment of school improvement.

16 Criteria for Assessing School Improvement

Victoria L. Bernhardt

> What gets measured gets done.
> —Tom Peters

A comprehensive school portfolio is an excellent organizer of all information necessary to make informed decisions about any or all parts of a school. The school portfolio is useful to schools whether or not they are involved in systemic school improvement efforts. The school portfolio does not, however, stand alone. Ultimately, its utility depends upon the categories used and the criteria applied to measure the process, product, and progress of the school's efforts with respect to these categories.

Assessment criteria can facilitate the process; keep staff focused on one vision and one overall plan;

keep staff informed about how they and the process are performing; and guide next steps. The important thing is to do the assessing. Even imperfect measures provide an accurate strategic indication of progress or lack thereof (Peters 1991).

CHOOSING CRITERIA FOR ASSESSMENT

Systemically improving the manner in which a school operates is a complex and multidimensional process. It requires a complete understanding and appreciation of the complexities and interrelationships of each component of the organization in order to alter the whole, or even one part, effectively. Only by understanding the underlying principles, processes, and paradigms of the parts of the whole can staff members understand and plan for the magnitude of effort required by systemic school improvement.

This chapter was originally published in *The School Portfolio: A Comprehensive Framework for School Improvement* by Victoria L. Bernhardt, © 1994 by Eye on Education Publisher, P.O. Box 3113, Princeton, NJ 08543. Reprinted with permission.

Criteria for assessing the improvement process and progress must provide for the simultaneous assessment of each changing part as well as for the assessment of the whole. There are three basic routes available for choosing assessment criteria. A school can create its own criteria, or adopt existing criteria, or adapt existing criteria.

Creating Criteria

Creating criteria is a positive approach because it requires everyone in the organization to assist with the development of the criteria. This leads to staff buy-in, commitment, personal knowledge, and personal meaning. The downside is that developing criteria is extremely difficult and time-consuming—as any teacher who has developed comprehensive rubrics for student assessment can attest. The writing of comprehensive criteria will generally take a minimum of one year.

Adopting Existing Criteria

It's best to adopt existing criteria when certain conditions exist:

- Everyone on staff understands what the criteria are measuring and why.
- They agree that the criteria are congruent with what the school needs and wants to measure.
- They understand how to use the criteria correctly.
- They commit to using the criteria thoroughly and completely.
- They acknowledge the creators.

The *Education for the Future Continuous Improvement Continuums* are examples of adoptable criteria.

Adapting Existing Criteria

Taking existing criteria and adapting them to include additional elements important to the school is also an accepted approach. Keep two cautions in mind: Make sure the developers of the chosen criteria did an extensive amount of research and testing to ensure that the criteria work. Avoid diluting existing criteria to make it easier for the school to rate itself high on the assessment scale.

GUIDELINES FOR ASSESSMENT CRITERIA

It is ideal when the users of any assessment criteria are also the developers of the criteria. For many practical reasons, this is not always possible. If creation is out of the question, there are quality criteria available to adopt. When considering adapting or adopting existing criteria, users must understand, agree with, and commit to using the criteria in total. Whether your school develops, adopts, or adapts assessment criteria for its school portfolio and school improvement efforts, the criteria must be:

- **Focused on what is important: the students.** The purpose of systemic school improvement is to improve the preparation of students, the primary clients of the school, and to rebuild the school organization to serve students' needs. Any criteria for assessing comprehensive school improvement must focus on students.
- **Simple to use.** The goal is to spend time reflecting on progress, implementing the "big picture," and discussing next steps rather than on conducting cumbersome assessments.
- **Indicative of what needs to happen.** A straight forward measurement device must be unambiguous and direct, assess the target, and easy to understand. It makes clear the steps that need to be achieved to move forward.
- **Set up for self-assessment.** For assessment to have maximum impact, the people whose progress is being assessed should do the assessing. Very few people external to the process can come in, judge the value of a school's progress, and then inspire those involved to do more or do things differently. Therefore, the criteria must be set up for self-assessment.
- **Challenging, but achievable.** The objective is not only to make the outcomes against which progress is judged achievable (so there can be a true feeling of accomplishment), but also to make them challenging enough to effect real improvement.
- **A working contract as opposed to a form-driven exercise.** Excellent assessment criteria encourage ongoing conversations about things that are important rather than demanding activities that require conforming to rules and paperwork.

• **Comprehensive in scope.** If the overall concern is systemic school improvement, it does no good to measure only those elements on which the school wants to focus, ignoring the comprehensive learning organization. This does not lead to systemic improvement, and it is an error common to many unsuccessful improvement efforts. It is important to measure everything to see how changes and progress in any specific area effect the entire organization. Unless all parts of a school are considered simultaneously, the school's efforts will form circles around the whole issue and will never get to the real issue. Staff will end up tired, overworked, and uninterested in further change. For example, many schools beginning systemic improvement efforts assume they know enough about their clients and that they do not need to analyze existing data or gather additional information on students, parents, or the school in general. However, one small rural school district in northern California learned why the information was important to gather.

> The entire school community knew that changes needed to be made within their local school system. Each year for several years, they watched 80 percent of their graduates go off to college in the fall. Of that group, 40 percent returned by Christmas, and almost 95 percent returned by the end of spring—to stay. The problem was discussed widely among teachers and the school community. They determined that the problem centered around the students' lack of experiences and social skills. Students had not been exposed to other environments and did not have the social skills to function in another environment. Everyone also knew that students didn't show respect for the people they knew, so they could not possibly know how to interact positively with people they didn't know.
>
> The district began an extensive restructuring effort centered around working with all students K–12 on developing social skills, manners, and showing respect for others. Additionally, the teachers planned

to work out educational exchanges in other communities to help students gain experience and exposure. At the urging of a consultant brought in to assist with planning a restructuring retreat, staff reluctantly conducted a telephone survey of graduates to ask them why they dropped out of college. Almost without exception, the graduates reported the following: "They made us write. I was going to flunk out 'cause I can't write!" Needless to say, the entire restructuring effort changed immediately, and every kind of information imaginable was gathered for further analyses. Comprehensive criteria that reflected all aspects of the school were established to ensure that no shortcuts would be taken as they developed a continuum of learning that would prepare their students for the world of work.

EDUCATION FOR THE FUTURE'S CONTINUOUS IMPROVEMENT CONTINUUMS

One existing set of assessment criteria that meets the guidelines described above is the *Education for the Future Continuous Improvement Continuums.* (All seven rubrics appear in *The School Portfolio: A Comprehensive Framework for School Improvement.*) These continuums take the theory and spirit of continuous school improvement, interweave educational research, and offer practical meaning to the components that must change simultaneously and systemically.

The *Continuous Improvement* part of the title refers to the cycle of evaluating and improving this complex system on a continuous basis. *Continuum* is defined as "a continuous extent, succession, or whole, no part of which can be distinguished from neighboring parts except by arbitrary division" (*American Heritage Electronic Dictionary* 1992).

Organization of the Continuums

The *Education for the Future Continuous Improvement Continuums* are a type of rubric that represent the theoretical flow of systemic school improvement. The continuums are made up of seven key, inter-related, and overlapping components of systemic change—Information and Analysis, Leadership, Student Achievement, Quality Planning, Professional Development, Partnership Development, and Continuous Improvement and Evaluation. It is important that all seven components are used simultaneously. A school can defeat the purpose of systemic improvement by adopting only one or two continuums.

These rubrics, extending from one to five horizontally, represent a continuum of expectations related to school improvement with respect to an approach to the continuum, implementation of the approach, and the outcomes that result from the implementation. A "one" rating located at top left of each continuum describes a traditional school that has not yet begun to improve. A "five," located on the right of each continuum, represents a school that is one step removed from "world class quality." The elements between one and five describe how that continuum is hypothesized to evolve in a continuously improving school. The "five" in outcomes in each continuum is the target.

Vertically, the approach-implementation-outcome statements are hypotheses. In other words, the implementation statements describe how the approach might look when implemented, and the outcomes are the "pay-off" for implementing the approach. If the hypotheses are accurate, the outcomes will not be realized until the approach is actually implemented. A reduced version of the Leadership Continuum is shown in Figure 16.1.

Adopting the Continuous Improvement Continuums

The *Education for the Future Continuous Improvement Continuums* provide an outstanding outline for comprehensive school improvement. They are used here to illustrate how to make the school portfolio an effective assessment tool that can assist schools with systemic school improvement. Before adopting these criteria, staff should, at minimum, read the descriptions and the highest level of each continuum. If staff members agree with, and can commit to, the

outcome and the hypothesis represented in the highest category, they will probably agree with the hypotheses described between one and five.

Schools using the continuums have found them to be extremely effective in providing guidance and understanding of the principles and processes of systemic school improvement and in ensuring that all components of the organization are being considered and are improving at the same time. Schools particularly find them to be useful in helping staff share a school vision, assess their efforts to achieve that vision, and provide accountability. A brief description of each of the continuums follows. (The research behind each continuum is described in *The School Portfolio*.)

Information and Analysis is a critical element in planning for change and in supporting continual school improvement. Schools must analyze existing data and collect additional information to understand how to meet the needs of their clients, to understand the root causes of problems, to assess growth, and to predict the types of educational programs that will be needed in the future. The intent of this continuum is to establish systematic and rigorous reliance on hard data for decision making in all parts of the organization. This continuum assists schools in thinking through appropriate information to gather on an ongoing basis and analyses to make that will prevent implementing changes piecemeal or in a manner that does not get to the root causes of the problems at hand.

Leadership focuses on creating a learning environment that encourages everyone to contribute to making sure schools have accumulative, purposeful effects on student learning. A quality leadership infrastructure emphasizes the prevention of problems such as student failure as opposed to short-term solving or covering up of problems and makes the school change effort conceivable in a school. This continuum assists schools in thinking through shared decision making and leadership structures that will work with their specific population, climate, and vision.

Student Achievement describes processes for increasing student achievement—the school's "Constancy of Purpose." The intent of this component is to support schools in moving from a fire-fighting approach to one of systemic prevention of student

FIGURE 16.1

Education for the Future
Continuous Continuums for Leadership

	ONE	TWO	THREE	FOUR	FIVE
APPROACH	Principal as decision maker. Decisions are reactive to state, district, and federal mandates. There is no knowledge of continuous improvement.	Leaders are seen as committed to planning and quality improvement. Critical areas for improvement are identified. All faculty feel included in shared decision making.	Leadership team is committed to continuous improvement. Leadership seeks inclusion of all school sectors and supports study teams by making time provisions for their work.	Leadership team represents a true shared decision-making structure. Study teams are reconstructed for the implementation of a comprehensive continuous improvement plan.	A strong continuous improvement structure is set into place that allows for input from all sectors of the school, district, and community, ensuring strong communication, flexibility, and refinement of approach and beliefs. The school vision is student-focused, based on data, and appropriate for school/community values and meeting student needs.
IMPLEMENTATION	Principal makes all decisions, with little or no input from teachers, the community, or students. Inspect for mistakes is the leadership approach.	School values and beliefs are identified; the purpose of school is defined; a school mission and student essential learnings are developed with representative input. A structure for studying approaches to achieving essential student learnings is established.	Leadership team is active on study teams and integrates recommendations from the teams' research and analyses to form a comprehensive plan for continuous improvement within the context of the school mission. Everyone is kept informed.	Decisions about budget and implementation approach to the vision are made within teams, by the principal, by the leadership team, and by the full staff as appropriate. All decisions are communicated to the leadership team and the full staff.	The vision is implemented and articulated across all grade levels and into feeder schools. Quality standards are reinforced throughout the school. All members of the school community understand and apply the quality standards. Leadership team has systematic interactions and involvement with district administrators, teachers, parents, community, and students about the school's direction.
OUTCOME	Decisions lack focus and consistency. There is little staff buy-in. Students and parents do not feel that they are being heard. Decision-making process is clear and known.	The mission provides a focus for all school improvement and guides the action to the vision. Teachers and community are committed to continuous improvement. Quality leadership techniques are used sporadically.	Leaders are seen as committed to planning and quality improvement. Critical areas for improvement are identified. All faculty feel included in shared decision making.	There is evidence that the leadership team listens to all levels of the organization. Implementation of the continuous improvement plan is linked to essential student learnings and the guiding principles of the school. Teachers are empowered.	Site-based management and shared decision making truly exist. Teachers understand and display an intimate knowledge of how the school operates. Teachers support and communicate with each other in the implementation of quality strategies. Teachers implement the vision in their classrooms and can determine how their new approach meets student needs and leads to the attainment of essential student learnings.

failure. Teachers move from being providers of information to researchers who understand and can predict
the impact of their actions on student achievement.
Students change from being recipients of knowledge
delivery to goal-setting self-assessors who produce
independent, quality work. This continuum assists
schools in thinking through who students are and
understanding the why behind the curriculum, instruction, and assessment, as opposed to describing and
recommending approaches.

Quality Planning by schools must be strategic or
change efforts will not be implemented. A well-defined
and well-executed school improvement effort is based
on a strategic plan that provides a logical direction for
change. This continuum assists schools in developing
the elements of a strategic plan: a mission that
describes the purpose of the school; a vision that represents the long-range goals of the school; goals that promote the mission; an action plan; procedural steps
needed to implement the goals, including time lines
and accountability; outcome measures; and a plan for
continuous improvement and evaluation.

Professional Development helps staff members,
teachers, and principals change the manner in which
they work—how they make decisions; gather, analyze,
and use data; plan; teach; monitor achievement;
evaluate personnel; and assess the impact of new
approaches to instruction and student assessment.
Professional development provides individuals with
opportunities to continually improve their personal
performance and to learn new skills for working with
each other in reforming their culture and workplace.
This continuum assists schools in thinking through
and planning for appropriate professional development activities that will help them reach their school's
vision.

Partnership Development with the school's community must benefit all partners. This continuum assists
schools in understanding the purposes of, approaches
to, and planning for educational partnerships with
business and community groups, parents, other
educational professionals, and students covered in this
continuum.

Continuous Improvement and Evaluation of all operations of the school is essential to schools seeking systemic improvement in the manner in which they do
business. This continuum assists schools in further
understanding the interrelationships of the components of continuous improvement and in improving
their process and products on an ongoing basis.

WHO DOES THE ASSESSMENT?

The *Education for the Future Continuous
Improvement Continuums* are set up for self-assessment.
Therefore, school staff members do the actual assessments of where the school is on each continuum. The
process of assessment is instructive and is highly beneficial for anyone involved with the school's continuous
improvement efforts.

Who specifically does the assessment varies by
school. Some schools want the entire staff to make the
assessments together. Larger schools may find this
approach far too time-consuming and difficult to manage. In those cases, a team of teachers might be asked
to conduct the assessment on behalf of the teachers
they represent and then bring those assessments to the
staff for discussion. In most schools, each person
makes an assessment of where he or she believes the
school is at the given time, and then, as a group, staff
members discuss discrepancies in the ratings and come
to consensus on an overall rating. The discussion is
very informative for determining staff's understandings of the continuums, outcomes, progress, process,
and next steps. One school charts individual assessment results on a scatter graph. Staff discuss causes of
any variations and then determine a collective
response. In any case, it is preferred that everyone in
the school be familiar with the assessment process and
know when the assessment is taking place so that
every member of the school staff can contribute to the
process.

HOW OFTEN SHOULD PROGRESS BE ASSESSED?

With its open structure, assessment of a school's
progress on the criteria may be performed at any time.
The important thing is to establish definite times when
everyone knows school progress will be assessed and
documented. *Education for the Future* schools found it

helpful to assess their progress three times during the first years they used the continuums. With three assessment periods, a school is able to keep continuous improvement in the forefront; to monitor processes and progress; and to analyze, for future reference and planning, such things as which elements of the school process are easiest to change, which elements take extra effort, and which elements can leverage other elements.

Each time an assessment is made, display the results for each continuum in a bar chart or other type of graph so everyone can see the progress over time. Figure 16.2 shows a school's ratings on the approach, implementation, and outcomes on the student achievement continuum in September, January, and May. From the chart, one can see that the school increased in all three areas each time it conducted an assessment. Initially, implementation and outcomes lagged behind approach, but they caught up by the end of the year. The chart also indicates that by the end of the year, school staff could see the benefits of their efforts (outcomes increased).

One can look at wording in the student achievement continuum to understand the meaning behind the ratings. When all categories are graphed, it is easy to see where additional effort must be placed and what is holding back progress in some areas.

As in any self-assessment, it is important to encourage staff to describe honestly where they are on the continuums. Wherever the school is in the school improvement process is where it is. If any kind of negative consequences result (for example, dollars from the district are withheld because of poor results), the self-assessment process will become less than honest, staff may become adverse to risk, and the work related to improvement and the entire improvement effort will become obstructed. The beauty of the school portfolio is that it will describe why progress was or was not made on any continuum. The description provides valuable information about the impact of external and/or internal influences on progress.

MONITORING IMPLEMENTATION THROUGH STAFF-DEVELOPED RUBRICS

It is very easy to adopt new strategies. It is very difficult to implement them, especially consistently and congruently throughout the entire school. Effective leadership teams make the actual implementation of new strategies throughout the school a priority. Leadership teams ensure that professional development activities are structured to lead to actual implementation using components like peer coaching and collaborative action research. While some schools use a combination of teacher portfolios, peer coaching, and/or teacher action research to support the implementation of new strategies, others have gone one step beyond to monitor implementation with the use of staff-developed rubrics.

Based on the same philosophy as the *Education for the Future Continuous Improvement Continuums*, staff-developed rubrics can monitor, guide, and assess the implementation of new strategies both at

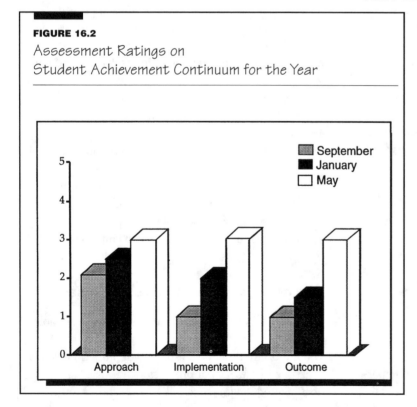

FIGURE 16.2

Assessment Ratings on
Student Achievement Continuum for the Year

the classroom level and collectively at the school level. At the top of the scale, these rubrics describe how classrooms will look with respect to instruction, assessment, curriculum, and outcomes when the vision is implemented. The other points on the scale represent the continuum of implementation. The benefits of using implementation rubrics are fourfold:

• Rubrics require teachers to describe in writing the way the classrooms will look when the strategy is implemented. This requires a shared understanding of the vision and seriously thinking through strategies for implementation.

• Teachers assess where they are on the continuums three or more times a year. This self-assessment approach is extremely powerful for reflecting on the critical processes that are being implemented and for establishing plans for improvement. The assessment also adds an element of accountability to the implementation efforts.

• The rubric approach effectively communicates to the school community that implementing a new strategy is comprehensive and complex, that it takes time, and that one cannot go from low implementation of a particular strategy to full implementation in a very short period of time.

Rubrics make it very clear to the school community where they are headed and to what they have committed.

17 Attending to the Rhythms and Intonations of Learning: Listening for Changes in Students' Portfolios

PATRICK MONAHAN

The infant learns to pay attention to speech, he listens for critical sound changes, he attends to the rhythms and intonations of talking long before he knows what it means.

—DE VILLIERS AND DEVILLIERS

Several years ago, I entered a graduate program in the teaching of writing and became a parent all at once. For a time, these events ran parallel courses, and I became interested in my daughter's growing capacity to talk. Books such as *Early Language* by Peter and Jill de Villiers and *Children's Minds* by Margaret Donaldson offered me a lens on my daughter's development. I was struck by how actively she pursued her learning. All her energies were focused upon it. As a high school English teacher, I wondered whether my students participated in their literacy development with any of the fervor I observed in my daughter.

What, I wondered, could I do to promote more engagement in their learning?

The emergence of literacy, I also discovered, was deeply connected to the growing capacity of children to become conscious of language. "The first step is the step of conceptualizing language—becoming aware of it as a separate structure, freeing it from its embeddedness in events" (Donaldson 1978, p. 90). "Along with flexibility comes greater reflection; there is a steady improvement in the ability to think about language, to treat it as an entity, and to gain conscious control over the medium itself" (de Villiers and de Villiers 1979, p. 4). To what extent were my students aware of their developments as readers and writers? And while reading and writing, did they consciously control their actions?

I discovered these were very good questions for which my students had few answers. When I asked them when they had first learned to write, few could pinpoint a moment. When I asked what project had taught them the most, they often couldn't remember. And when I asked them what teacher had been most instrumental in their learning, they could barely remember a name. At the end of these questions, some students replied that they hadn't really learned to write. One student insisted that he couldn't write, pointing out that his work hadn't improved much since the 3rd grade. So struck was I by his reply that I asked him and his classmates to gather every possible sample of their writing in earlier grades. The student who adamantly believed he had never learned to write surprised us all the next day by bringing in a huge box of his writing that his mother, a teacher, had saved. Students and I explored that box for several days, recreating the path of learning for this student who believed he hadn't learned at all.

As I have come to understand this activity, which I now repeat in my writing classes, I am attempting to free learning from its "embededness in events." Curriculums swirl around children in a frenzy: six classes a day, three assignments a night, a test and a paper due on Friday. Children become so caught up in these activities that they sometimes miss or mistake their learning.

I was first attracted to portfolios by their opportunities for reflection. "Reflection makes visible much in learning that is otherwise hidden, even from student writers themselves" (Campand Levine 1991, p. 197). Dennie Palmer Wolf (1989) writes, "Reflections . . . come from moments when teachers ask students to return to their collections of work . . . noticing what is characteristic, what has changed with time, and what still remains to be done" (p. 37). Portfolios offer students a way to remember and understand their pasts, define and appreciate their accomplishments, and shape their goals for the future. The reflective comments of Rachel, a senior in high school, demonstrate this capacity to place her learning in such a context:

> From my summer reading through short
> stories and on into drama, when I would
> go home to complete the assigned reading
> I would just . . . read. I would read careful-
> ly, remembering most of what I had read,

but I did not really analyze. On the independent reading assignment I was forced
to change my style of reading. Because I
had to search for just the right quote that
demonstrated a major theme in the novel,
I began noticing things. Not only was
there one good passage that embodied the
novel, there were several. I was just over
one-fourth of the way through my next
novel when a breakthrough happened. A
passage just seemed to jump out at me. A
class discussion had been in the back of
my mind as I was reading and I made a
connection. As I read on I noticed more
passages. All of a sudden I was reading
critically, thinking while I read—and it
was amazing that all sorts of things began
popping out of me. I hope I can continue
to read "smarter" in the future. It's easier
to draw conclusions about characters
when one notices little passages that
provide a window into their lives.

Rachel's commentary illustrates her developing understanding of the differences between comprehension and interpretation. Her delight in this new bit of learning is magnified by her sense that she has achieved it independently. It is not the product of direct instruction, although the assignment encouraged such an insight, as Rachel points out.

As I review the reflective commentaries of students, I now see entries such as Rachel's as representing an important transition, where learning is the product of their independent activity and not my direct teaching. Perhaps another student commentary will illustrate this very important movement from teacher-directed to student-owned learning. After the return of her draft on *King Lear*, Laura expressed frustration with me. As the writing unfolded and the events of her life proceeded, however, she came to think differently about the project, which she explained at the end of the quarter in her portfolio.

> When my paper was returned to me, it
> was covered with blue pen and basically
> said that my ideas were wrong. I remem-
> ber writing that Goneril and Regan should

have taken care of their father because they owed him and because it was the custom to do so. Mr. Monahan said that gratitude and custom didn't seem very good descriptions of love. I came home that weekend and tried to make sense out of what he had told me. I remember how frustrated I was because I thought he was just trying to make me write about his ideas. After struggling for a long time, I had a breakthrough. I wrote it down in my notebook because it came so suddenly I was afraid if I hadn't written it down it would've disappeared. Children should take care of their parents because they love them and feel responsible for their well being.

My grandma is in a nursing home right now. She's gone through some rough times and has had a few minor strokes. When my mom is not working, she spends a lot of time with my grandma. Even though my grandma may not recognize her sometimes, my mom feels she should be there by her side. She never says she's too tired, or it doesn't matter any more. Now I realize she's not going because she owes her or is obligated to do so. She goes because she truly loves her.

Laura's understanding of *King Lear* is anchored in the experiences of her personal life and has taken on a resonance much larger than simply her understanding of a work of literature. A portfolio offers students opportunities to place curricular activities in the much larger context of their lives. Later in the semester, Laura composed a childhood-experience poem titled "Me and My Shadow." In the poem, she describes herself as "a little sun kissed girl in bright shorts and a T-shirt" walking beside her grandmother, who is smiling "as if she enjoys the chatty grandchild who is skipping beside her." And when she describes her grandmother's eyes, she writes, "There's no place I'd rather be." In her portfolio, Laura reflected on this poem:

When I was little I always used to visit my grandmother in Florida. She was an Avon lady and she always let me help her deliver the little packages, talk to her friends and collect the money. She made me feel important and taught me to be independent. More than that, she was my best friend. We went to the beach together and at night had ice cream sundaes. As I grew older, I grew out of enjoying such simple times. I wanted to spend my summers at home so my little sister took my place. Last week my grandmother passed away. I was so terribly sad because I still wanted to be her little grandchild. I read this poem at her funeral mass. I hope that she heard it. I now realize she was a bigger part of my life than I had ever thought.

When Laura submitted her portfolio for the second quarter, she dedicated it to her grandmother. Other students also added dedications at the quarter. Such self-sponsored additions signal the movement toward ownership. The inclusions of photographs, drawings, cartoons, and clippings seem to emerge naturally as portfolios grow during the school year. Some of these additions probably result from students seeing and reading the portfolios of others. However, some, such as Laura's, are heartfelt indicators that curriculum matters.

In describing the positive qualities of self-assessment, such as those found in portfolios, Dennie Palmer Wolf (1989) writes, "the promise lies in the demonstration of how demanding and thoughtful we can be about shaping work that matters to us" (p. 35). Clearly, Laura's work matters to her, and the beauty and simplicity of her poem demonstrate the care with which she composed it. Here then is a dynamic that manifests itself as portfolios unfold. In reflecting upon their work, children must ask themselves how the work matters and what of consequence has happened. And, as they develop answers to these questions, they may come to value the work more highly and place greater demands upon themselves for future performance. Another highly desirable transition in portfolios is the movement from a description of work to a description of important work.

In her opening commentary on second quarter work, Kim described her approach to the quarter: "I vowed to myself that the start of the second quarter would mark the beginning of academic excellence for me. Things haven't worked out as planned yet. The papers I have submitted haven't reflected my learning, and I'm not particularly proud of any assignment. In the works I reflect on here, I want to pinpoint exactly what caused them and how they can be remedied." Kim's words indicate that she was disappointed in her work, yet her language also suggests how important her work has become to her. She knows that she must look closely to discover the behaviors that will improve her performance. What is perhaps most startling about these comments is that Kim received an A for the quarter. Her assessment, therefore, was not linked to my assessment of her work.

Some teachers worry that their assessments of student work will interfere with students' assessments of their own learning. Fearing that students will highlight work that received high grades and devalue work that received low grades, some teachers withhold grades. I have come to understand the transition from my assessment to their assessment as an important one, which signals their growing ownership of the processes of learning. Rather than withhold grades, I encourage students to work with small samples of their work, describing how a paragraph or section of a larger paper represents an important step in their learning. Once students move beyond the whole project that has been graded, they are free to see their work in their own terms.

Another way around this problem is to see the portfolio as a means to transform work that did not meet expectations. Through their commentaries, students have the opportunity to demonstrate that the work, though unsuccessful, has been instrumental in their learning. Hedda had difficulty interpreting "Storm Warnings," a poem by Adrienne Rich. She explained her problem as a matter of perspective: "I was doing a line-by-line analysis of the poem. In this poem that method was not going to work because the poem had a shift in point of view. I think that getting away from the line-by-line analysis is extremely important because poems have several hypocrisies that in a sense disguise the meaning, and doing a line-by-line analysis makes it easier to get caught up in the interpretive traps." Hedda understands that the meanings of poems often evolve and that lines sometimes misrepresent or contradict a poet's meanings. Accepting such circumstances, Hedda recognizes a need to step outside the poem in order to focus on its larger purposes.

Another indicator that the work matters can be found in the connections students make between the ideas they encounter in their study and their personal lives and beliefs. In writing about suffering in *Crime and Punishment*, Margaret argued that suffering alone does not lead to salvation. She explained the derivation of her thesis in her portfolio:

> I look at my father's forehead and see his suffering everyday. I can never imagine the pain and trauma he goes through every day. What is it like to be strong, independent and healthy in one moment, and in the next to be weak, handicapped and dependent? My family knows suffering, but unlike Marmeladov we don't believe this is going to lead to salvation. Christ and Job suffered, but they had something more than Marmeladov; they had faith. Our family has seen more than the average problems, but that doesn't mean we have the right to give up.

Margaret enjoyed the portfolio because it provided her with a forum to think about her curriculum in the larger context of her life. She observed, "When I write a paper, I'm not satisfied with deciphering the author's message. I relate that message to my life and, hopefully, gain a better understanding of my own beliefs. If I do not learn something that enhances the quality of my life, either spiritually, emotionally, or for pure enjoyment, then the work has been futile." Another important transition in portfolios is the movement from a distant curriculum to one situated in the experiences of learners. As portfolios make such bridges possible, they assist children in conferring personal meaning upon their instructional activities.

Portfolio advocates such as Roberta Camp and

Denise Levine have noted the highly personal nature of some students' reflections and have suggested that such reflections represent an important stage in their development. Camp and Levine (1991) write, "[Reflection] is particularly critical for young adolescents who are attempting to make sense of their world and their place in it, to understand themselves and the nature of their relationships with others, and to clarify their values and establish habits of mind" (p. 203). Certainly Laura's relationship with her grandmother had a profound influence on her reading and writing during the term, and her portfolio provided her with a means to write about that relationship. In her portfolio, however, she did not become entirely focused on her personal experiences. In other entries she comments upon using verb tenses, trusting her interpretive intuitions, seeing the distinctions between analytical and descriptive writing, and using quotations. Laura tells the story of her work, and with some samples of her work the story is rich indeed.

Learning is personal, and portfolios reveal the unique dimensions of children's learning. They "can become a window into students' heads, a means for both the staff and students to understand the educational process at the level of the individual learner" (Paulson, Paulson, and Meyer 1991, p. 61). One of the important transitions in a portfolio is the inclusion of descriptions of thinking, where students outline the processes of private thought that have led them to their work. Often in commentaries about their best work, students reflect on the mental work that led them to their successes. Eve describes her thinking that led to a successful interpretation of "Storm Warnings."

> I read the poem ten times before beginning my essay. Then, I tried to imagine the scene and the feelings being described. The line that made much impact on my thinking was "These are the things we have learned to do." The light bulb went on in my head, and the meaning of the poem came to me. This was because of a personal experience. A few days before I was talking to a school counselor. She asked me how things were, and I replied, "Normal." She then said that normal is very subjective and not always good, because people who live in abusive situations have gotten so used to it that it becomes normal. This conversation immediately came to mind when reading that line. I then looked in the poem to see if there was enough support to write of an abusive environment.

Eve's reading of the poem demonstrates her abilities to transfer her learning from one arena of her life to another. More importantly, it demonstrates her capacity to enter into a fictional situation and to carry her experiences with her in her efforts to understand it. Perhaps most notable are her comments on imagining the "feelings" of the poem and noting the line which had an "impact" on her. So much learning in schools is centered in the cognitive domain, but in the portfolio Eve was free to write not about imagery and stanza structure but her personal experience of the poem, which resulted in her interpretation of it. As such, the portfolio served to validate her approach to the poem and to admit her feelings to the classroom. Perhaps it is this quality of portfolios that so surprises teachers and convinces them of their worth.

Another characteristic of Eve's reflection is the ability she displays to control her thinking, consciously and deliberately. These are extremely important qualities. Margaret Donaldson (1978) writes, "What is going to be required for success in our educational system is that [a student] should learn to turn language and thought in upon themselves. He must become able to direct his own thought processes in a thoughtful manner. He must become able not just to talk but to choose what he will say, not just to interpret but to weigh possible interpretations" (p. 90). Portfolios assist students in making such a transition, turning thought in upon itself. As children reflect upon their products, they exhibit their control over their intellectual processes and develop a sense of mastery in their work. Margaret's reflections on a simple list poem she has written entitled "Things on the Refrigerator" show her remarkable control over the work:

> When I was required to write my own poetry, I incorporated some skills I use to

interpret poems. For example, poems usually undergo some sort of progression, whether it be from general to specific, least important to most important, or obvious to detailed. In my poem, I went from trivial to most valuable. I began with the useless Publisher's Clearing House Sweepstakes and ended with a sentimental picture.

Meanings of poems are usually found in the last stanza or the last lines. By placing "The faded picture of a lifelong friend," in the last line, I hoped to hammer in the idea that things on your refrigerator are a slice of your life. Although everyone has useless items on it, there are those items that hold great value.

When I picked out items to put in my list, I tried to make them personal, but I wanted everyone to be able to relate to them. For example, my original last line was, "An old picture of Mr. and Mrs. G, friends for a lifetime." I realized that no one knew who Mr. and Mrs. G were and what kind of impact they had on my life. Thus I made it more general, so everyone could remember their lifelong friend.

A teacher reading Margaret's poem would not be aware of the sophisticated thinking that led to its construction. More importantly, Margaret may not have been fully aware of the quality of her thinking until she described it in her portfolio. Portfolio commentaries are filled with examples of surprise, where students are genuinely enthusiastic about their own learning behaviors. Perhaps this is the transition that is most exciting in portfolios, when children suddenly are made aware of how they have topped themselves. Jen's most recent portfolio submission certainly illustrates such surprise and personal satisfaction. One entry contains two samples of writing: one drawn from freshman year, the other from senior year. In her freshman paper, she explained why Laura is the most important character in "The Glass Menagerie."

She is also the main character because of the fact that, without her, the story would have less meaning. True if Tom or Amanda were gone, the story would be less, but without Tom you have Amanda trying to get Laura a better life. Without Amanda, you still have Tom's problems and Laura's, but without Laura, you only have a conflict of mother pushing son. But this is my opinion.

Jen most surely giggled when she placed this paper in her portfolio, and she showed her humor by pasting in two newspaper clippings, one reading "FRESHMAN" in bold type above the essay and another "MIRACLE" by the grade of C. She then inserted a part of her introduction from an essay on *Crime and Punishment*:

> Within Dostoevsky's *Crime and Punishment* exists a complex character named Rodion Raskolnikov. Portrayed with dual personality, Raskolnikov sometimes acts in one manner and then suddenly in a manner contradictory. In order to emphasize this dual personality, Dostoevsky creates two other characters in the novel who represent the opposing sides of Raskolnikov's character—Sonia and Svidrigailov.

In her commentary, Jen writes about her achievement in this second essay:

> After slaving over 500 pages, I wanted a **real** topic. I could have just picked an easy one, but I decided to reach and trust my instincts. This topic of dual personalities was interesting and challenging. I used all the concepts I had learned, trusting myself and my ideas, "I" versus "One," and not rushing. I took my time on this paper and gave the book a chance to settle in my head. I got so much out of this book! As I try and trust myself, I learn that I am capable of greater things.

Two more important transitions are signaled in Jen's commentary. The first is her appreciation of her development as a learner over time. Dennie Palmer Wolf (1989) has suggested that one of the principal aims of portfolios is "that students . . . become informed and thoughtful assessors of their own histories as learners" (p. 35). Jen is amazed and delighted by her growth as a reader and writer. The other transition derives from Jen's repeated use of the word trust. She has become a self-directed learner, confidant in her abilities to select her own paper topics and certain enough that good ideas will come to her if she has the patience to wait for them. Portfolios reveal to students their strengths and aid in their development of confidence. This confidence gives them the power to take control of their learning.

I am just beginning to understand my role as teacher in a curriculum supported by portfolios. I have come to what Leon Paulson calls "the intersection of instruction and assessment" (Paulson et al. 1991, p. 61). What can I do next, I ask, to encourage additional progress in my students and at the same time showcase their accomplishments? I have a few ideas.

First, students need multiple performances to develop a set of skills. Too often, students write one type of essay and then are asked to begin another. Consequently, they have insufficient time to develop their skills and few opportunities to observe their growth and development. In the class from which the samples in this chapter have been drawn, students had multiple opportunities to complete each type of project. For example, they wrote four in-class essays on poems. In early efforts, many students had difficulty, some not managing their time well, others heading into their writing without planning, still others overlooking important lines or images. As they discussed these strategies in class and wrote more essays, they became comfortable with the work and discovered a set of strategies that worked well for them. With multiple opportunities to develop and practice skills, students were better able to see and appreciate their growth and to describe it in their portfolios.

Second, these students had numerous opportunities to make independent choices in the curriculum. For example, students generated lengthy lists of possible topics for writing on literature studied with the class and then developed original questions for themselves. Such freedom allowed Jen, for instance, to write on dual personalities in Crime and Punishment. This freedom also allowed Margaret to write about suffering, a topic which connected closely with her family circumstances and about which she cared deeply. Another form of independent work was an independent reading program initiated with students during the summer prior to their entrance into the course. Writing interpretations of independently studied literature each quarter provided students such as Rachel with an opportunity to showcase their skills. Another type of independent work required students to work ahead in literature, writing interpretations of chapters, scenes, and characters not yet studied in the large group. In addition to providing independent learning opportunities, this type of activity prepares students to participate actively in class discussions. Through independent work, particularly challenging work, children have opportunities to develop, practice, and assess their developing competencies.

Perhaps the most successful independent activity, the one most often highlighted by students in their portfolios this year, was the opportunity to write their semester examination questions, framing an original question that might be answered by drawing material from three of the works they had studied during the term. Bridget selected King Lear and two novels she had read independently: Dinner at the Homesick Restaurant and A Thousand Acres. In her portfolio she explained the genesis of her question: "After reading Lear, I was astonished at the excessive favoritism displayed by the parents in the play. When I read Dinner, I was amazed at the number of similarities. And in A Thousand Acres the topic arose again. After the third reading, I realized the signs of favoritism, the problems it causes, and the way it destroys a family. I was eager to write about it." She framed her question in this way:

> Novels written about families tend to center around the parent/child relationships. It is usually clear that there is one child whom the parent loves more than the others. In three works of literature, discuss

the problems caused by this unbalanced love, or favoritism. Identify the forms favoritism takes and the reactions of other siblings. Lastly show how favoritism has the capability to destroy family bonds and speculate about actions which could prevent it.

Bridget worked on her question for several days, revising it three or four times before I approved it. Still, she did not remark upon my involvement in her portfolio. It was her question, and though I had helped her make it, the work remained her own. Part of her sense of independence derived from her option to draw into her essay works we had not discussed in class. As she crossed the boundaries of each work in her comparisons and contrasts, also, she was entering uncharted territory.

Another activity that seemed to promote learning and led to a great many portfolio entries was the opportunity both to analyze a type of literature and to create it. As students analyzed poems, they also created them. As they read stories, they also wrote them. Such creative writing opportunities did not take tremendous amounts of class time: a week of in-class poetry writing, a few days on fiction writing. Yet the results were very powerful, as Margaret's commentary on her refrigerator poem has already suggested. Not only did such activities result in greater appreciation of literature, they seemed to encourage students to see interpretation as a creative activity itself, one that could be fun for them.

Additionally, students seemed to benefit from activities that caused them to think about their intellectual processes. While writing their essays on *Crime and Punishment*, for example, students kept a journal, talking/writing for a few minutes about their plans prior to each writing episode and then for a few minutes after each episode. Such an activity had a noticeable effect upon students who hurry into their writing without planning as well as upon students who don't pause to assess their work once they complete it. Samples of these journals appeared often in portfolios, and in their commentaries students reflected upon the positive and negative behaviors they observed in their own composing processes.

A fourth idea, which seemed especially profitable for some students, was to include in their portfolios self-sponsored writing or work that had been completed for another course or at another time. I had worked with several students on college admissions essays, and to my surprise, these essays often appeared in portfolios. I came to see these self-sponsored projects as much more important for students than I had imagined, and consequently saw my work with them on these projects as more meaningful. Students also added work from other curricular areas, and I recognized quickly that such inclusions encouraged transfer of thinking. I supported and praised such additions.

A fifth type of classroom activity that improved portfolios was the opportunity to read and evaluate other students' work. At the end of the first quarter students read several portfolios and then brainstormed possible criteria for evaluation. On the next day they identified four criteria and formally evaluated one student's work. The criteria selected by students were organization, creativity and personality, quality and thoughtfulness of reflection, and demonstration of growth. This evaluation appeared to encourage students in their efforts, and many completely restructured their portfolios for the second quarter.

As I talk about the important transitions I see in students' portfolios, I am reminded of the important transitions in my own teaching. I question the worth of each project more now, wondering how it will look and feel in students' portfolios. I recognize each comment I write on students' essays may come back to me in a portfolio, and I wonder if I will be pleased with myself. Often I am not. And yet there is a richness here. Each comment I put on a paper, each interaction in a hallway, and each lesson I teach has the power to teach well or badly. I'm beginning to know the difference.

I also know what I haven't learned to do well yet. I haven't learned to talk with students about their portfolios. I marvel at much of the work that I receive, but I haven't quite figured out what to do with it. It seems to have an instructional power of its own, and though I am learning to attend to its rhythms, I haven't yet discovered how to use it. I need to find time to talk with students about their portfolios, to tell them what I see in their work that they perhaps haven't seen, and to help them set goals and priorities in their learning.

My daughter is now 12. Her teacher has asked her to make a portfolio. I hope the one she makes fits the one described by Leon Paulson: "A portfolio, then, is a portfolio when it provides a complex and comprehensive view of student performance in context. It is a portfolio when the student is a participant in, rather than the object of assessment. Above all, a portfolio is a portfolio when it provides a forum that encourages students to develop the abilities to become self-directed learners" (Paulson et al. 1991, p. 63).

References

Camp, R., and D. Levine. (1991). "Portfolios Evolving." In *Portfolios: Process and Product*, edited by P. Belanoff and M. Dickson. Portsmouth, N.H.: Heinemann.

de Villiers, P.A., and J.G. de Villiers. (1979). *Early Language*. Cambridge, Mass.: Harvard University Press.

Donaldson, M. (1978). *Children's Minds*. New York: W.W. Norton & Company.

Paulson, F.L., P.R. Paulson, and C.A. Meyer. (February 1991). "What Makes a Portfolio a Portfolio?" *Educational Leadership* 48, 5: 60-63.

Wolf, D.P. (April 1989). "Portfolio Assessment: Sampling Student Work." *Educational Leadership* 46, 7: 35-39.

18 Seeing the Child Through Portfolio Collection

DARLENE JOHNSON AND SANDRA SILVERMAN

H uge, bold letters dominate the pages. They are the beginning pieces in a collection of work that spans the first three years of Sammie's portfolio. As my colleague and I sift through the papers, we discuss the changes that have come about since Sammie first began to write in kindergarten. We were her first teachers—her only teachers—and looking back on the history of her writing we remark on the changes that have taken place since Sammie first entered our school.

LOOKING THROUGH SAMMIE'S PORTFOLIO

Sammie began as an avid writer of bold, indistinguishable letters that often resembled her name. Random letters and oversized forms filled the pages and were virtually indecipherable to adults. Yet Sammie displayed the undaunted confidence of one who knows she has written something important, and her work reflected this confidence. In the heart of the

collection were themes of justice and inequality, with touches of magic and fantasy, all woven together with wild horses and majestic unicorns. There were beasts with long manes, arching necks, and prancing hooves.

As we reflect on the collection that spans three years, documenting Sammie's development as she becomes a fluent writer, we see the path she took to get there. The vast array of work within the collection allows us to follow her course to controlling the tools of her language. She began as a literary nymph, full of stories to tell, writing them any way she could, always being the only one who could read them. When asked about them, Sammie would read, "Once upon a time in a far off land, there lived a mermaid named Jessica . . . " (Figure 18.1).

Sammie reached a roadblock during her second year of school when she began to read and found that her invented writing was different from the writing in the stories she was reading. Hers wasn't "real writing,"

FIGURE 18.1

Sammie's Story

9-89

she would tell us. Gradually the fluency of her writing stopped, and Sammie refused to write for a while until she could write like the "real" authors did. She still told elaborate stories that went on for hours and drew upon the rich language of the fairy tales read to her at home and at school. But she was now aware of the fact that her spoken words didn't match those she had written. Her stories changed from reams of print to illustrations with a few "real" words used as labels (Figure 18.2). She hadn't drawn in kindergarten, but now her pages were filled with elaborate horses and unicorns that told the stories her bold letters used to

tell. At the time it wasn't apparent to us that Sammie was transitioning into a new phase of literary fluency. As she struggled with the conventions of writing, she replaced letters with drawings to tell her stories.

Slowly, as Sammie became comfortable with invented spelling, she began to move back into writing, sharing her stories intermittently during the children's journal-sharing sessions. She had trouble reading them back, sometimes forgetting the words she had written. Her writing during this period became partially readable and would lapse into an inventiveness that could be decoded by Sammie only if you caught her immediately after she had written. She had begun the long journey that children often make as they struggle with correctness and readability. Her parents and teachers were a constant support during this difficult period, always willing to listen to the next story, always encouraging her to forge ahead with her wonderful ideas and supplying the links when needed.

Sammie was making a transition, and her writing revealed the disequilibrium it placed her in. It is important to note here that children often are regarded as needing remedial help during these places in their development. We seldom see children and their work beyond the narrow span of one year at a time, so our judgments about them are based upon bits and pieces of work within this frame. The portfolio collection allowed us to see a broader view of Sammie as she moved through this difficult period (Figure 18.3). By closely looking at Sammie's work from both school and home, we were able to build on her strengths and see a more complete picture of her development. We found that single pieces of work did not always display a child's growth. It is the connecting pieces and the teacher and student reflections that provide the larger picture.

Not only did the portfolio provide us with a view of the patterns that surrounded Sammie's writing

FIGURE 18.2
Sammie's Transition

development, it revealed her interests, themes, and feelings. Sammie writes about what she finds important. Her themes of fairness and concern for the underdog reveal unique qualities in her character. Being extremely tall for her age, she was often ostracized from games and play. She spent her days pretending she was a horse and would wander across the playground prancing and whinnying.

Sammie's work as a whole revealed deep thought and kindness. The separate pieces that span the three-year period unravel the developmental journey to literacy that is seldom visible when our view is limited to shorter time periods. The three-year collection allowed us to build a case in support of Sammie's strengths without confining our picture of her to one particular year in her school life.

BEGINNING TO COLLECT CHILDREN'S WORK

Intrigued by our experience with student portfolios such as Sammie's, we decided to form a teacher-research group and look more closely at our children's work. We were three teachers, each with her own distinct style, who had collectively agreed to begin portfolios and to look at children's written work as the evidence of their learning and growth. We were sure our collective inquiry would move our abilities to interpret student work to higher levels.

Gretchen: Examining Writing Genres

Gretchen began by collecting writing samples from all the children in her 4th grade class. Her portfo-

FIGURE 18.3

Sammie's Further Development

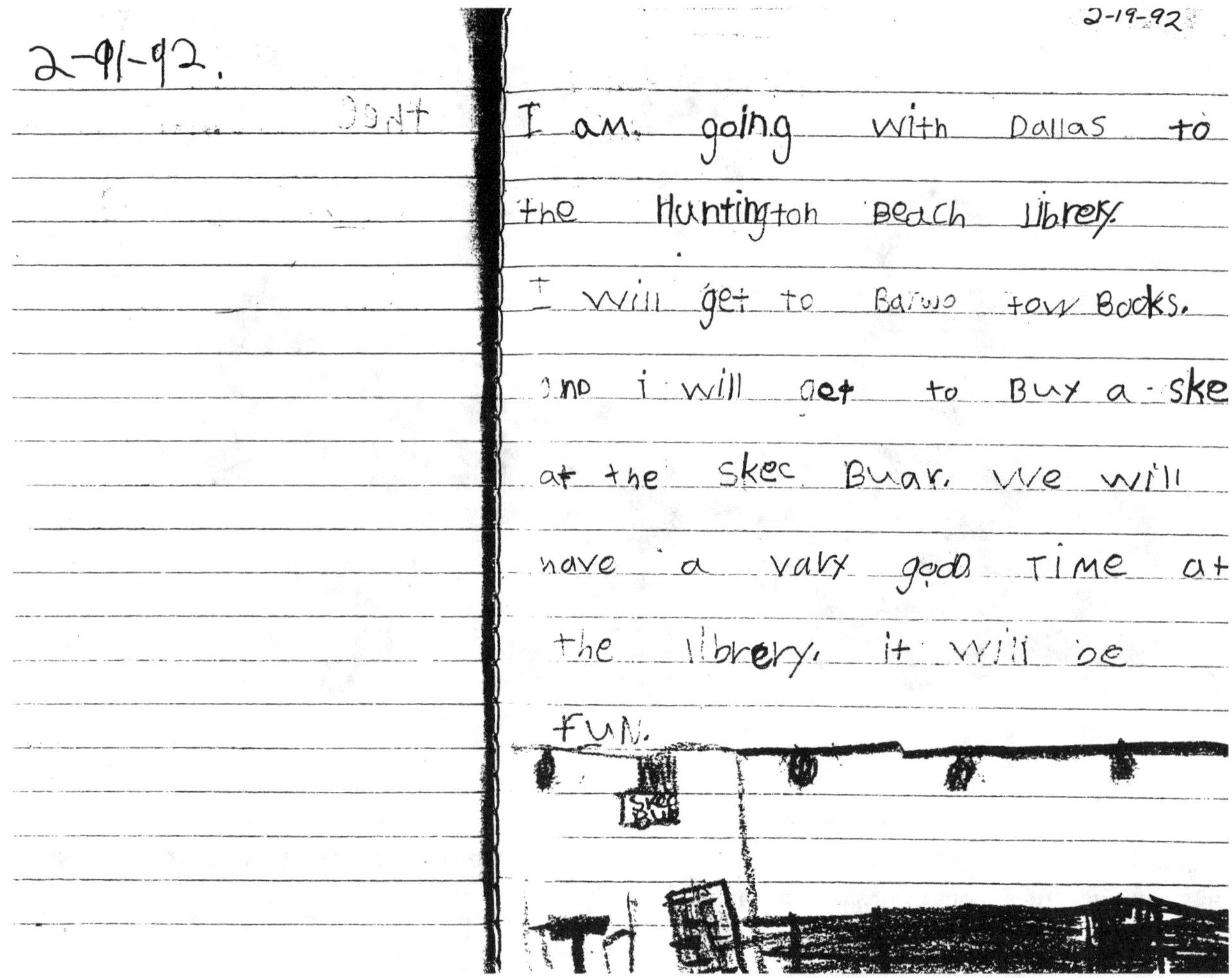

2-91-92.

2-19-92

Dant

I am going with Dallas to the Huntington Beach Librey. I will get to Baruo tow Books. ino i will aet to Buy a ske at the skec Buar. we will have a valry godd Time at the librery. it will be fun.

lios were made from legal folders and housed in a file box in the classroom cupboard. Her collections focused mainly on different types of writing. They included outlines, rough drafts, and edited pieces, and they ranged from the beginning idea of a story all the way to the finished product.

Gretchen believed it was important to include writing at different places in its development to show the progression of the story as it is revised and honed into a finished piece. Her portfolio collections con-

sisted of works in progress with a smattering of finished pieces. She admits to being overwhelmed by having to look at all the students at once and believes that it didn't all pull together until spring. "By spring, I knew what I wanted to do. Then it was a matter of pulling all the kids together and talking with them about what should be included. If I had it to do over, I would have started small, with 5 to 10 kids rather than the whole class . . . but what did I know?"

Gretchen's dilemma is one faced by many upper-grade teachers. Her students produced volumes of work, and she was faced with the task of managing the storage and review of 32 collections at a time. She learned from the first year and decided to start small the second year, focusing on five or six children. She also developed a successful management system. By meeting with seven children a day to discuss their work, she was able to spend more time with them looking over what they had written. She also became adept at analyzing the growth she saw within the pieces. This was often done aloud, with the children producing a self-review of their work.

Sandy: Emerging Readers and Writers

Sandy did start small. She initially selected five children to observe because of their vastly different approaches to reading and writing. She became fascinated by the fact that these five young children already had unique strategies that ranged from phonetic to visual to nonverbal, even a child who seemed to have no strategies in place at all. As she began the observation, her interest radiated out from the original five children, and she noticed on a whole new level the variety of things happening as children in her classroom learned to read and write.

She found that her predetermined questions had initially motivated her to look more deeply at the work of her students, yet they actually put a restricted frame around her ability to see the spontaneous learning that was happening all around her. "When my focus shifted away from seeking evidence for my research question and back onto my students, I found that my observations of the other children seemed more perceptive." Sandy had shifted from teacher-centered questioning to learner-centered questioning. She still confined her collection to five children, but her collections were now used with different criteria. The collections, which were housed in her file cabinet, included scraps of paper and Post-It notes as well as children's drawings, writing, and samples from home. The children themselves often offered work to be put into their file. They delighted at getting out their portfolios, spreading the work out all over the table, and

laughing at how much they had grown up. All the pieces were tied together with notes and anecdotes detailing her observations.

Sandy had learned that the more open-minded you are in looking, the more likely you are to find a variety of visible evidence of the child as a learner. As her collections grew, she began to see distinct patterns and themes with each child that reflected the child's focus and development as an early writer. Her return to focus on the child rather than her question expanded the world of children's thinking for Sandy.

Darlene: Learning From the Journal

In the grade 1–2 class, Darlene began to collect writing and drawing samples from her 2nd grade children. This gave her a chance to focus on a small group of 10 children while still keeping the 1st grade children in mind for later collections. As a member of the teacher research group, she had decided to keep her own journal documenting the children's daily journal sharing sessions. She was concerned that the writing seemed to consist of a stiff process style rather than the free, open flow that is characteristic of most children's writing. "I wanted to see what would happen as the year progressed. If I allowed them to share without intervening in their dialogue, would they move to a more natural type of writing?"

As she began to observe, she noticed a series of patterns and influences. Christina began to write stories about the daily adventures of "The Fish." She had a fish tank at home and her stories chronicled the adventures of the Belsey, a species of tropical fish: "The Fish Goes To Japan," "The Fish Makes Money, "and "The Fishes Happy Halloween." As Christina shared her stories with the group, Darlene noticed that other children's stories began to take on some of the characteristics of Christina's stories. Holly wrote about "The Mouse," Marlena wrote about "The Horse," and La Shaun began writing about "The Cat." This pattern continued. The children had internalized Christina's form and style and began to develop their own special stories patterned after that style. When Marlena and Holly began to write stories that consisted almost completely of dialogue, other children began to use dialogue and eventually quotation marks. The introduction of chapters and "to be continued" all seemed to reveal themselves during the journal-sharing sessions.

As I became aware of these patterns, I also began to notice what I call "first use" pieces: that is, pieces in a child's writing development that show the first use of something. Marlena began to use the exclamation point in her stories after I discussed the use of the exclamation point in the *Daily News*. These benchmark pieces began to provide Darlene with a bulk of data to include in her written statements that accompanied the collections. These data were extremely valuable in providing the evidence to show progress in writing development.

Darlene had learned to pay close attention to the dialogue held by the children about their writing, and to provide the interaction to encourage the children's own style to emerge. She also learned that the journal-sharing sessions provided a rich environment for learning and growth. The children influenced each other's writing in subtle ways that would not have been noticed if Darlene hadn't kept a journal of the sessions. Her journal provided rich anecdotes and the thread that connected Christina's fish to Holly's mouse, revealing the growth in story development within the class.

THE POWER OF OBSERVATION

Although the three of us approached portfolio assessment from different perspectives, we collectively agreed that the most important aspect when building collections of work is the observation. We found that the more we were able to set aside time to observe children interacting and working, the more we were able to see the learning taking place around us. As we set aside time to watch and listen to conversations, we began to see the children from a different perspective. We became more aware of links that existed between the earlier pieces and the most recent, and we began to make notations about these links on the pieces themselves. These notations became our reflections on the pieces we included in the portfolios—reflections enhanced by our observations.

THE SECOND YEAR

As we moved into the second year of portfolio assessment, our collections began to broaden. Initially we had selected primarily drawings and writing samples. We now began to add math diagrams, science pictures and notations, and conversations children had as they worked. How children solved problems collaboratively and on their own became a central focus. We realized that the focus on thinking and learning allowed us to collect across the disciplines rather than focus on each discipline as a separate area.

As our questions became more open-ended, we were encouraged by how much more of the child we were able to see. Darlene began to use story problems several days a week for math. A revealing glimpse into the mathematical thinking of two different children came when she asked the class how they would share their five cookies with three friends. Danny's solution to "break all the cookies into three pieces" gave concrete proof of his understanding of division as well as fractions. This example provided Darlene not only with information she needed about Danny's understanding, but it also gave her a valuable piece of evidence to back up that information. Ryan's solution to the same problem revealed yet another view of how children think. His decision to "invite two more friends over" so that "when they leave I could get a Twinkie" indicates a very different place on the developmental spectrum.

The important aspect of the question asked was that it had many possible answers. The way the children chose to solve the problem became a clear indicator of their understanding and problem-solving capabilities. This example provided us with a look at two children with very different solutions to the same problem. The information gathered by the teacher provides us with an assessment of where these children are developmentally as well as mathematically.

As we continued to fill our collections with examples such as these, we struggled with the question of how to make our portfolios useful for next year's teacher. Many teachers had told us that the portfolios "just sat in the drawer all year" and were given back to children because the teacher was unable to

FIGURE 18.4

Austin's Self Portraits

decide how to use them. We agreed that staff members needed to collaboratively construct an understanding about what constitutes meaningful elements of a portfolio.

FROM THE CLASSROOM TO THE WHOLE SCHOOL

Our principal was excited about our efforts and decided to ask all the teachers to explore portfolio assessment. We were asked to share our portfolios in grade-level meetings. Several important concepts emerged from these sessions.

During the staff meeting, six teachers sat on the floor or perched on the step of the stage in Darlene's classroom. "What interests you most about portfolios?" was the question put to them. The responses varied from "I used to do it years ago" to "How do you know what to put them in?" The questions provided a back-

ground for sharing our portfolios. Soon the portfolios of Sammie, Sean, and Adrian were being scrutinized by our colleagues.

As they shuffled through the papers, the teachers noticed that samples with attached commentary were the most informative. Without actually observing the children at work, these teachers needed supporting comments to place the work in perspective and to explain the patterns of growth and development.

"ICDTE" scribbled on a page meant little until we explained that it was kindergartner Brittany's first self-written story. She was writing the idea "I see the tree" as part of an entry in her science observation journal. The teacher's annotation explained that Brittany clearly understood that the sentence was composed of four separate words—a very important concept for young children as emergent writers. It was further noted that she was able to use at least one letter to represent each word, and that the letter was phonetically linked to the word it represented. This marked a significant advancement in Brittany's thinking about written language. In general, annotated pieces such as Brittany's became clear evidence of the children's individual thinking and conceptual level. Therefore, these pieces were pivotal selections in the portfolio.

The teachers noticed that the more open-ended, least teacher-corrected works revealed the most about the stages children were passing through. The teachers began to share interesting works from the portfolios with each other. They detected patterns of the children's progress through the samples in the collections. The samples clearly demonstrated the strengths and individuality of each child and the uniqueness of each learner.

Works in progress were considered to be the best indicators of children's abilities. While student-edited work displayed a child's best effort and highest level of development, teacher-corrected work often masked the child's true level. Shalana's addition papers consistently showed equations that usually added one number to the total: 13+18=32, 11+5=17, or 9+14=24. A sample page was placed in her portfolio to show that at this time her mathematical understanding of addition was fine but that she had difficulty counting more than her fingers could hold. A corrected version of her work would have hidden this valuable bit of information.

There were certain pieces of work in the collections that virtually leapt out at the teachers in our group. Every teacher commented on the power of the annual September and June self-portraits. In September of his kindergarten year, Austin's self-portrait consisted of separate body sections, long purple stick-legs, red hair (he's actually a blond), and no arms. By June, he portrayed a full-bodied figure with arms, legs, and buttons on his shirt (Figure 18.4).

Our staff determined unanimously that the collections needed to be thinned out at the end of the year before being passed onto the next teacher. Only benchmark pieces should remain. Many of the pieces that were critical to the understanding of the child during a particular school year may not be necessary the following year. "I just want to know the most important

things," one teacher commented.

During our meeting, other questions surfaced:

- Should the work reflect final levels ("showcase"), or should the collection include beginning and intermediary work?
- Who should select the work that remains in the portfolio?* How do we best compile work that all teachers will collect and also work that shows individual strengths?
- How many pieces should be included in the finished portfolios each year?
- Are there critical types of work that all teachers would value and collect?

As we reflected on our staff meeting, it became obvious that the crucial element underlying the value of a portfolio is the degree of authenticity of the work:

- Does the collection of work truly display the individual child's growth and stage of development?
- Is the collection "real work"? What does the work reveal about the child?

Authentic work samples show children grappling with a variety of conceptual and curricular issues, as we see in the work of Sammie, Sean, and Adrian.

Sammie's Writing

In kindergarten, Sammie authored book after book, each filled with pages of her bold, pictureless writing. She very dramatically "read" her stories to the principal, the librarian, the custodian, other children, teachers, friends, and visiting guests. At the end of the rendition, she would offer her books as treasured gifts to the listener. She often designated carefully selected books to be placed in her portfolio, which also contained signs and letters she had written as well as thank-you notes from recipients of her gifts. In reflecting upon Sammie's work, it becomes clear that Sammie's mind was filled with the rhythms of literature and that all that remained to be developed were the conventions of adult written language.

Sean: "Man of Science"

In contrast, Sean was a self-described "man of science." Writing did not especially interest him; he

FIGURE 18.5

Adrian's Mathematics

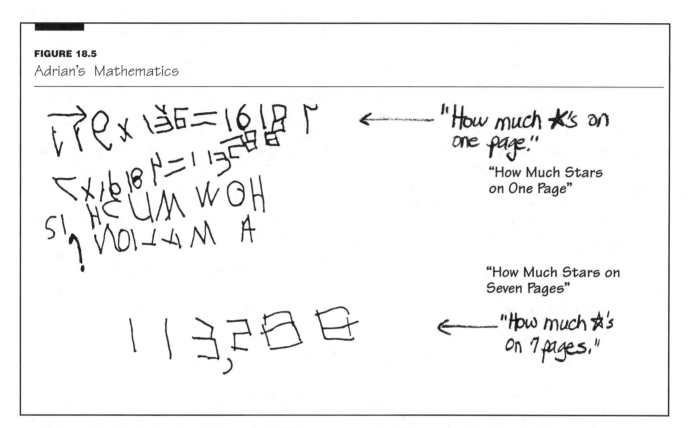

"How much ★'s on one page."

"How Much Stars on One Page"

"How Much Stars on Seven Pages"

"How much ★'s on 7 pages."

reveled in scientific exploration. While many children his age viewed scientific phenomena as akin to magic, Sean constantly sought to discover and interpret the causes for events. For example, during kindergarten sharing, Sean stood at the chalkboard and lectured the class on the concept of noon:

> This circle is the sun. It is in the differen-
> tial periphery of the molecular acid uni-
> verse. It sends light bulbs out (draws
> arrows). This, of course, is the moon. It
> sends light bulbs to the sun (more arrows).
> Here in the exact centrifugal place is noon.

Sandy transcribed Sean's dialogue and placed it in his portfolio as evidence of both his developing sense of the dynamic relationships of our solar system and his important conceptualization of scientific cause and effect. His portfolio also included signs from his science club, photos of his scientific investigations, transcripts of his conversations, and videotapes of his experiments. Reflecting on Sean's work, there is an incredible sense of his behavior as a true scientist: observing phenomena, asking questions, seeking explanations, and developing terminology.

Adrian: "Man of Mathematics"

While Sean was a "man of science," Adrian was a "man of mathematics." As a 1st grader, Adrian was still struggling to learn the names of the letters of the alphabet. He was not yet reading, and he was writing only through copied dictation. However, he was a child who truly understood multiplication at the age of six!

In the middle of Adrian's 1st grade year, Sandy read the delightful book *How Much Is a Million?* to the class. The children were fascinated by the seven pages filled with minuscule stars. The book explained that the children would have to count those pages 10 times in order to count 1 million stars. Later in the morning, Adrian showed Sandy a scrap of paper with multipli-cation equations he had written in block, calculator style numbers: 119 X 13=16,184 and 7 X 16=113,288. "This is how much stars on seven pages," Adrian announced (Figure 18.5). He explained that 119 was the number of stars in a row across the page. Later he calculated 10 pages (10 X 113,288) and explained, "It's not *really* 1 million—but close."

Adrian's portfolio is filled with scraps of paper with other mathematical equations written in crayon, diagrams of numerical processes, and math and science projects he brought to school from home. On the other hand, his writing samples are full of letters printed in uneven sizes and shapes, many erasures and cross-outs, and other evidence of his struggle with written language. For a time he signed his name "A6N." At first Sandy thought the "6" was a backward "D," but when she asked Adrian about his new signature, he explained, "A is for Adrian, and then six letters to get to the N." His absolute comfort with numbers and his discomfort with letters is clearly reflected in his work.

The portfolio collections of Sammie, Sean, and Adrian highlight the unique styles and strengths of each child through the work samples selected by teachers, parents, and the children themselves. By expanding our collections beyond a checklist of tasks or specified skills to be mastered, we were able to observe the thinking behind the work our students were doing and more clearly see the developmental stages they were passing through. We used this knowledge to identify the growth contained within each collection of work. It was through our conversations with the children and with each other that we were able to see clearly the uniqueness of each child's thinking as he made his way through the world of school.

19 Portfolios As Critical Anchors for Continuous Learning

Braden Montgomery

My first work in the portfolio shows the advantages of a revision. After analysis I found the first draft to be predictable and choppy. However, I was happy with the relationship I developed between the two main characters . . . I made them into real people instead of flat characters. The main purpose of the revision was to make the paper flow and change the ending rather drastically. I found the final draft to be much better than the original.

—LISA, 12TH GRADE

With my third selection for my portfolio, I decided to include one of my less successful pieces. It was sort of a weak attempt at a formal essay in reaction to Kate Chopin's *The Awakening*. It is a piece that has some promise to it, but overall I do not like it very much. It has been revised once, and will be revised again, so I will at least be able to get it to the point where it flows like a good piece of writing.

—BRIAN, 12TH GRADE

Two fundamental convictions reflect my growing understanding of portfolios. First, I believe that they possess the capacity to put students such as Lisa and Brian in touch with their work in ways that enlarge their thinking and expand their knowledge of themselves as learners. Such promise has been sorely lacking in schools that place a premium on rote drill and memorization of low-level learning skills while removing students from the assessment process. Second, for teachers looking for ways to actively engage students in feedback spirals, portfolios offer the best vehicle I have found for providing the formative data necessary to identify and ultimately realize meaningful goals and outcomes.

Critical Findings

The research on portfolios is extensive, growing, and, on the whole, favorable. Judith Arter, Roberta Camp, Bob Tierney, and Kathleen Yancey, Sandra Murphy and Mary Ann Smith among others have conducted extensive studies that reveal some key findings.

1. Portfolios invite reflection. The absence of metacognitive activities in school denies students the opportunity to see themselves in their work. By encouraging students to become more conscious observers of themselves, portfolios highlight the key role that self-awareness plays in becoming a more effective thinker and learner.

2. Portfolios provide alternative means of assessment. As such, they are more oriented toward a long-term portrayal of student work rather than a single snapshot. They yield what Dennie Palmer Wolf (1990) calls "autobiographical understanding." The continual feedback they provide enables teachers to make more informed diagnostic and curricular decisions.

3. Portfolios show promise in reducing the artificiality associated with schoolwork. Students are more likely to become actively engaged in learning when work is perceived as purposeful, and portfolios encourage meaningful activities. This sense of ownership is essential if students are to be the primary beneficiaries of their portfolios.

4. Portfolio programs lead teachers to pursue the same activities called for from students: reflection, self-assessment, and goal setting. Such activities encourage ongoing review of methods, requirements, and objectives. Teachers, like their students, strive to resolve key questions such as what changes occurred over time, what strategies worked best, and what assignments needed revision. This self-monitoring behavior positions teachers to grow and change along with their students, thereby changing the educational paradigm from teacher/deliverer–student/receiver to teachers and students as co-constructors of knowledge.

5. Portfolio programs tend to be unique. They don't easily transfer from classroom to classroom or from one school to another. By resisting standardization, portfolios take on a dynamic quality that allows for individual differences in program purpose. Models help, but teachers by and large shape the nature and goals of their own portfolio programs.

Portfolios the First Time Through

My first experience with portfolios was a negotiated affair; my students ultimately determined most of the guidelines and much of the content. Lacking first-hand experience with portfolios, we agreed to work together to see what discoveries we might uncover. The idea of educational collaboration, largely absent from my earlier teaching, in effect raised the level of involvement. Students assumed a more active role primarily because they felt their opinions were valued.

After a series of discussions regarding the role of portfolios outside of school (in art, journalism, and finance)—and after exploring their potential inside other classrooms—we agreed on five conditions that would guide us through our first portfolio experience:

• Each portfolio would showcase a student's best work.

• Each portfolio would include five to eight selections that revealed some diversity in writing experience.

• Each portfolio would include an introductory reflective letter. This narrative was to be the story of students' work: why they selected certain pieces, what they felt the writing revealed, what conditions contributed to their growth as writers, or what obstacles hindered their development.

• The portfolios would not be graded. Instead, students would be given credit for fulfilling the mutually agreed-upon requirements.

• The portfolio would be read by a significant adult selected by the student (teacher, administrator, guardian, parent) and then returned to me for a final review. I attached a letter to each student's portfolio explaining the nature of the project and encouraged a written response from the adult.

With this framework in place, students started shuffling through their folders, reviewing papers, consulting with classmates, making choices, and composing their letters. I must admit my enthusiasm was mixed with apprehension. I was pleased with students' energy and their high level of involvement. I was uncertain, however, as to the nature and potential outcome of some of the negotiated requirements.

I was the one, for example, who insisted that portfolios be read by an adult outside the class. I was curious about adult feedback on the project, and I wanted the notion of "other eyes" to motivate my students to take the project seriously. What I did not anticipate was the reaction of these other eyes. The parent responses especially voiced support and enthusiasm for a program that allowed them access to their children's work and encouraged them to reflect upon what they perceived as progress in their child's writing samples. Many parents commented that this was the first time they felt a partnership in their son's or daughter's secondary school experiences. As one father noted, "We're proud of Michael's work. It's gratifying to see his creativity being given a chance to flourish. The portfolio idea has given us the opportunity to see how much his writing has matured and expanded since last year."

Another area of concern involved students' reflective letters. While we had done some self-monitoring of individual pieces, we had not attempted anything as comprehensive as a portfolio narrative. Initially, students were unclear about what a portfolio commentary might look like. I addressed their uncertainty in two ways. First, I modeled. I distributed a copy of my own portfolio reflection that I was required to develop as part of my Admission to Candidacy to a doctoral program at the University of Pennsylvania. My firsthand experience enabled students to judge how one individual participated in an examination of his own work. Second, I encouraged flexibility. I suggested that the assignment was not lockstep. Students were free to arrange their portfolio in any number of ways (chronologically, by mode of discourse, from weakest to strongest) and then simply talk about individual pieces.

Student Voices

Student feedback not only confirmed the importance of reflection, it validated the activity as a necessary component to any portfolio program. My own discoveries of what students learned about their writ-ing, though significant, were matched, if not surpassed, by the range and depth of insights students revealed in their portfolio letters. They commented repeatedly on how revision and editing often led to proper structure and a clearer expression of ideas. They become more sensitive to audience and purpose, more willing to make judgments about their own work. They valued the opportunity to experiment with dialogue, with personal voice and techniques, and with modeling the distinctive styles of professional writers. They, in fact, became writers. For example, Emily commented:

> If a stranger opened my portfolio, this is what he would see: four descriptive exercises, two poems, a book review, an essay, a Journal entry, a letter, a parody, and a short story. I, however, see the explorations of a writer.

Until her senior year, Emily questioned her ability to write. Earlier courses, she claimed, were "formulaic," allowing for little or no diversity in her writing. Emily's comments detail the struggle of her first assignment: "I can vividly remember trying to write this at my kitchen table. As my eyes stared down at the mess of ink on my paper, I began questioning my ability to write. But with each exercise that followed, my quality improved and my confidence grew."

Another student, Chris, observed:

> "Him" was a paper I wasn't pleased with when I wrote it. I thought that what I was saying was fake. But then I read the paper about three weeks ago while reading every paper in my folder. It was so much different than any of the other papers. I asked myself "Would you feel comfortable reading this paper twenty years from now and remembering your father this way?" The answer was yes. The paper gives real specific insights into my father's strengths and weaknesses. I chose the paper for my portfolio because I never had the opportunity or the bravery to write something like it before.

These discoveries reveal students' potential to reflect thoughtfully over time on their own work. Their comments suggest ongoing learning; they express a pride in ownership and accomplishment. They reveal candor and a mature willingness to assess their strengths and weaknesses as writers. True, I was pleased with student commentaries such as Emily's and Chris's. However, I needed to address what Judith Arter and Vicki Spandel call "the criteria for judging merit" (1992). While the narratives my students composed often revealed powerful stories of growth and achievement, they just as often revealed an absence of critical thinking and an inability to specify concretely the nature of their growth. Some students, like Laura, did not demonstrate the readiness for meaningful self-reflection: "I wanted my paper from Vonnegut's novel *Hocus Pocus* in my portfolio just because I like it. There's nothing special about it to me. Nothing that particularly sticks out. But I did want it in there." Though others like Jason were not yet articulate, they were making strides toward the pride of ownership: "My best piece is probably the conversation between Vanilla Ice, Geoffrey Chaucer, and James Joyce. It was a lot of fun to work on and it turned out great."

Expanding the Role of Portfolios

Comments like Laura's and Jason's raise a concern regarding portfolios. While I believe portfolios can function as a showcase of a student's best work, and at times that might be their most important role, I have come to believe that portfolios should have the capacity to serve teachers and students in more purposeful ways. The full potential of portfolios and reflection will only be realized when they are linked to criteria and accountability.

A number of issues are at stake. We are concerned with developing good thinkers who possess the capacity to persist in their work, thinkers who show precision in language and thought and the ability to transfer and apply new thinking (Costa 1991). We want assessment measures that allow for a full range of student learning styles and activities. We seek assessment that promotes learning, not tests that fail to inform it (Wolf 1990). There is a need for high standards and for schools and teachers to cultivate what Rexford Brown

(1991) calls "a literacy of thoughtfulness." Portfolios can significantly reduce our dependence on narrow and simplistic forms of measurement. However, they require new thinking from teachers—a shift from assessment as a reductive process toward assessment that enriches our knowledge of student work and informs students themselves of their own strengths and areas needing improvement.

This year in an attempt to expand the role of the portfolio in my classroom, I have focused attention on identifying criteria for good work and effective reflection. While I continue to be interested in process writing, diversity, voice, and revision, my students and I spend more time on developing and practicing a language that enables us to judge writing as successful, competent, or weak. We examine models of good writing that exhibit energy, risk, or unique or unusual twists in perspectives and language. We focus attention on the larger issues of standards and goals that we would like to work toward. We talk about growth, about what knowledge is worth possessing, about how progress can be seen and articulated. By examining the portfolio letters collected from the previous year and critiquing the writing of past and present students, we hold an ongoing dialogue about what we value in writing, learning, and thinking.

Hopefully, what is being set in motion in my classroom is a portfolio system that allows students to showcase their accomplishments but also requires them to make informed decisions and judgments about the quality of their work. Reflection thus becomes purposeful and instructional, an opportunity for students to become more conscious observers of themselves. When Tammy, for example, talks about revision providing her writing with "more structure, a more dynamic opening paragraph, and a clearer and more developed series of examples," she reveals both the language and knowledge of evaluation. When Matt, on the other hand, can only conclude that his paper has merit because "Mr. Montgomery said he liked it," he fails to articulate an acceptable rationale or judgment for his choice. I do believe, however, that both Matt and Tammy and all other students can be educated to express understanding of their learning in more complete and authentic ways.

Points of Departure

For teachers and other educators just starting out with portfolios, I would like to offer the following observations for consideration.

• **Introduce the concept of portfolios and reflection early in the year—as early as possible, in fact, in a child's education.** My 12th grade students have little or no prior experience in portfolio activities, so it is imperative that they are given an opportunity to acclimate to the process and the language.

• **Be flexible and willing to experiment.** Student growth affects classroom dynamics; likewise, the goals we strive for are constantly refined and modified. Thus, questions that promote reflection must evolve. For example, at the onset of the program, the key question for students to reflect on may be as simple as "What do you like best about this piece of writing?" Midway through the year, students may be able to address more specific questions such as "Which piece of writing shows the most coherence and development?" or "Which piece shows the most precise use of language?"

• **Encourage students to write frequently in a variety of forms.** When there is little writing to select from or when one form of writing dominates, students experience difficulty seeing growth, change, or even purpose to a portfolio. As Brian observes: "At first it seemed as though my portfolio was intended to be a showcase for my best pieces of writing. But if we come to understand that it's more than that, if all of the pieces I selected were the same type of writing, it wouldn't really show much about me."

• **Be prepared to rethink the role of teacher.** Whereas I once saw myself as the focal point of the class—more out of the desire for control than anything else—I now respect and encourage student opinion and insight. While I have not reneged on my responsibility to educate, I have adopted a position more akin to coach than absolute ruler. I am convinced that no portfolio program can truly succeed when teachers seize control, leaving students with no meaningful say as to the course's content and no real sense of ownership.

• **Read the available literature on portfolios, alternative assessment, theories of learning and teaching.** While no portfolio program can be replicated in another classroom, models provide illustrations as well as the underlying justification for such programs. Reading the research provides the necessary insight and awareness to guide teachers through the inevitable troublesome stages we all experience in setting new programs in motion.

• **Take small steps and be patient.** My own evolution had its origination in the simple institution of folders and journal writing. Along the way I have tinkered with a variety of requirements and assignments. I am constantly learning. Had I attempted a wholesale imposition of portfolios without the opportunity to grow to understand their link to other critical components of my educational program, I doubt I would have come to see their true potential.

• **Finally, do not allow initial concerns of time and management to overwhelm and ultimately defeat the promise of portfolios in the classroom.** Teachers are frequently distracted by the legitimate issues of class size, daily routine, frequent meetings, conferences, and extracurricular duties. Such demands can discourage experimentation and transformation. But the combination of a teacher dissatisfied with the status quo working together with a district willing to support change can overcome most obstacles. How to keep a portfolio separate from a folder, knowing what questions to ask students about their work, deciding how many and what kind of papers to place in a portfolio, agonizing over how to grade students on their work—these are all difficult yet real and practical concerns. If we, however, think of ourselves as researchers and approach portfolios as dynamic and evolving portraits of student work, we free ourselves to take the risks that lead to the types of discoveries we encourage in students. Abundant evidence suggests that portfolios present a comprehensive and illuminating look at what our students know and value. The danger is that we will squander the opportunity to grow beyond standardized testing, beyond the "short right answer" (Karp 1985) mentality that has plagued education for decades. Portfolios, with their respect for student involvement in the assessment process, represent a chance for meaningful learning to take precedence over the "tyranny of testing" (Smith 1986). The promise of portfolios is unlimited; it demands, however, a willingness to forge an alternative direction. We owe it to our students.

References

Arter, J., and V. Spandel. (Spring 199). "Using Portfolios of Student Work in Instruction and Assessment." *Educational Measurement: Issues and Practice.* pp. 36-44.

Brown, R. (1991). *Schools of Thought: How the Politics of Literacy Shape Thinking in the Classroom.* San Francisco: Jossey-Bass.

Camp, R. (Spring 1990). "Thinking Together About Portfolios." *The Quarterly of the National Writing Project and the Center for the Study of Writing and Literacy* 12, 2: 8-14, 27.

Camp, R. (1992). "Portfolio Reflections in Middle and Secondary School Classrooms." In *Portfolios in the Writing Classroom,* edited by K.B. Yancey. Urbana, Ill.: NCTE.

Camp, R., and D. Levine. (1991). "Portfolios Evolving." In *Portfolios: Process and Product,* edited by P. Belanoff and M. Dickson. Portsmouth, N.H.: Heinemann.

Costa, A. (1991). *Teaching for Intelligent Behavior: Outstanding Strategies for Strengthening Our Students' Thinking Skills.* Bellevue, Wash.: Bureau of Education and Research.

Karp, W. (June 1985). "Why Johnny Can't Think." *Harpers,* 69-73.

Murphy, S., and M.A. Smith. (1991). *Writing Portfolios: A Bridge from Teaching to Assessment.* Markham, Ont.: Pippen Publishing Limited.

Murphy, S., and M.A. Smith. (1992). "Looking into Portfolios." In *Portfolios in the Writing Classroom,* edited by K.B. Yancey. Urbana, Ill.: NCTE.

Smith, F. (1986). *Insult to Intelligence: The Bureaucratic Invasion of Our Classroom.* Portsmouth, N.H.: Heinemann.

Tierney, B., M. Carter, and L. Desai. (1991). *Portfolio Assessment in the Reading-Writing Classroom.* Norwood, Mass.: Christopher-Gordon Publishers.

Wolf, D. (August 1990). "Assessment as an Episode of Learning." Paper presented at the Annual Meeting of the American Psychological Association, Boston, Mass.

Yancey, K.B. (1992). "Portfolios in the Writing Classroom: A Final Reflection." In *Portfolios in the Writing Classroom,* edited by K.B. Yancey. Urbana, Ill.: NCTE.

PART VII

Envisioning the World Anew: Seven Tasks Facing Learning Organizations

Envisioning the World Anew: Seven Tasks Facing Learning Organizations

Arthur L. Costa and Bena Kallick

Someday we will reflect on this era of change and think: "What was educationally significant but difficult to measure was replaced by what was educationally insignificant but easy to measure." Someday we will stop and realize how much time we've spent measuring our teaching effectiveness for subject areas and information that are no longer worth learning. Someday we will stop and recognize, as Eric Hoffer observes, that "in a time of change, learners inherit the earth, while the learned find themselves beautifully equipped to deal with a world that no longer exists."

SEVEN TASKS FOR THE "LEARNING" SCHOOL

If we expect schools to operate as holonomous organizations, entire systems will have to commit themselves to learning. To ensure the success of new assessment efforts in schools that have become learning organizations, educators will have to address at least the following seven tasks.

1. Re-establish school-site teams as the locus for accountability. For too long, the assessment process has been external to teachers' goal setting as well as curriculum and instructional decision making. School effectiveness, student achievement, and teachers' competence have often been determined by a narrow range of standardized student achievement-test scores in a limited number of content areas: reading, math, and language acquisition. Awards of excellence are granted to schools showing the highest gains in scores, and some teachers are given merit pay based on their students' performance. The test results are published in rank order in newspapers, to the delight of real estate agents who can boast, "This is a 98th percentile community." Houses are priced accordingly.

As we realize that mandates from above are obsolete, schools will decentralize. Such decentralization will also cause a change in assessment. Traditionally, decision-making authority has rested with the central administration. Not surprisingly, district offices usually request and analyze evaluation data on a macro or districtwide level, which works well for assessment of the overall district. On occasion, the central office may break data down to a subdistrict or campus level to acquire a more detailed view. But this analysis serves someone other than school-site administrators and teachers. This tendency toward district-level authority provides only limited campus- or classroom-level analysis of assessment data. To serve the needs of school-level decision makers, new and innovative strategies must be developed to incorporate staff input and participation in the assessment process. Just as site-based management assumes local involvement in instructional decision making, school-based assessment assures participation at the local campus by those responsible for instructional outcomes.

Over the years, teachers have been disenfranchised and have had little say about what tests measure. In fact, what tests do measure is usually irrelevant to the curriculum, and testing results disclose little about the adequacy of a teacher's curriculum and instructional decisions. In many ways, the desire for measurable outcomes has signaled teachers that they are incompetent to assess students themselves. In effect, they are told they cannot be trusted to collect evidence of students' growth and that their daily classroom observations are suspect and of little worth.

The accountability movement has sent educators searching for "hard data" by which to assess their efforts. What teachers observe, therefore, has been considered "soft data." We propose that the "hardest," most objective data available is collected by an enlightened teaching team that systematically and collectively gathers data over time in the real-life, day-to-day interactions of the classroom. Conversely, the "softest," most suspect data is that designed and collected by testing "experts" external to the school setting. Such "authorities" are ignorant of the school's mission, values, and goals as well as the community's culture and socioeconomics, the classroom mix of learning styles and teaching strategies, and the group dynamics in which their tests are administered.

In the restructured school, accountability will be relevant to staff members because it will require them to collect data. This feedback will be a guide to informed and reflective practice. Staff members will need training to learn how to design feedback spirals including multiple ways of gathering such data, establishing criteria for judgment, working together to develop their common understanding and reliability of observations, and reporting results.

It is acceptance and honest confrontation of the data generated in actions and experiments that builds commitment to change. When staffs administer "someone else's test," they have little ownership of the exam, what it measures, or the data it produces. Personal, professional, and team growth stem from the processes of deciding what should be taught, how it should be taught, and how it should be assessed.

2. Form new identities and roles. In the traditional school, students' typical role is to learn what the teacher chooses and then to demonstrate they've learned it on the teacher's assessment. Teachers in the traditional school view their domain as the classroom, and their major responsibility is to teach the required curriculum to their pupils. While teachers may informally and incidentally assess students' learning, the formal and "valid" evaluation of learning is performed by an agency external to the classroom.

In schools undergoing transformation, these roles are changing. A learning organization results from the transformation of the identities of participants in the process: among them, students, teachers, administrators, and staff developers. Because learning organizations honor and strive for the intellectual growth of which all human beings are capable, because learning organizations honor human diversity, and because learning organizations strive to empower others to become increasingly self-modifying, these principles will pervade the classroom, boardroom, and conference room.

Over time, students will define their role as envisioners of their own desired states, establishing goals, making plans, and clarifying outcomes for themselves. They will understand that they are in charge of developing their own strategies for achieving those goals. They will generate ways of assessing their own growth toward those ends, and they will see themselves as knowledge producers and meaning makers for themselves and others. They will know that they can contribute to a cooperative environment in which others can grow toward their desired state.

Teachers will reconceptualize their role as mediators of students' learning. Working in collaborative teams, teachers will envision those desired states for themselves, their students, and the classroom climate they share. Teachers will generate strategies for achieving those desired goals. They will view themselves as knowledge managers, knowledge producers, and meaning makers. And they will generate data as feedback to guide and assess their own, their students', and the classroom climate's progress toward these desired states.

Staff developers will envision their role as mediators of teachers', staff members', and the community's continued learning. They will generate strategies that lead teachers to be in a continual learning state. They will view themselves as knowledge producers and meaning makers, and they will generate data as feedback to assess their own, teachers', and the school environment's progress toward these desired states.

Administrators will envision their role as mediator of district- and communitywide conditions for continual learning. They will cooperatively generate strategies for achieving the vision of a learning organization, and they will generate data that help them assess progress toward that vision. Their role will be analogous to an environmental protection agency—constantly monitoring the intellectual ecology of the district and community, thus ensuring that thinking, honoring diversity, cooperation, and the intellectual growth of all participants is neither threatened nor endangered or—even worse—made extinct.

The role of district trustees belongs to community educators—keeping and protecting the value system of the district and monitoring their decisions to be consistent with these desired states.

The basic concept of establishing new identities is the investment of leadership in all stakeholders. In the traditional school, leadership is invested in a small number of professionals at the top of the hierarchy because of their training, position, and authority. In the learning organization, leadership is shared at all levels.

Such leadership functions include the following:

- coaching and serving as Critical Friends;
- participating in action research;
- making presentations to colleagues and at professional organization meetings;
- consulting with colleagues and parents in areas of expertise;
- networking with other schools, agencies, and resources; and
- facilitating team, faculty, and parent meetings.

Thus, all stakeholders in the learning organization see their role as continual learners employing feedback spirals. They work with and contribute to their team's continued effectiveness, serving as a Critical Friend to others and inviting Critical Friends to serve them in return. They contribute to the visioning process of the entire learning organization and constantly assess and monitor their own professional growth and their organization's growth.

3. Expand the range, variety, and multiplicity of assessment techniques. For too long, we have relied on a limited range of acceptable assessment measures, primarily paper-and-pencil tests. While standardized tests provide interesting information to some segments of the educational community, such test scores are inadequate to provide the complete data necessary to assess the full range of valued educational outcomes.

Enlightened, skillful teaching teams are the best collectors of data about students' growth toward the process-oriented goals of the restructured school. They are able to observe students daily in problem-solving situations that demand performance of the goals of the restructured school: cooperation, problem solving, and creativity. This type of assessment will require an expansion of our techniques:

- directly observing student performance in problem-solving situations;
- collecting portfolios of selected student work over time;
- observing performance in extended projects;
- inviting students to keep logs or journals;
- interviewing students about their own self-concept and perceptions of themselves as learners;

- making videotapes of student interactions;
- collecting writing samples over time;
- keeping checklists that record indicators of dispositions and habits of mind exhibited during group projects and discussions;
- assessing students' displays, exhibitions, and performances against a set of agreed-upon criteria;
- inviting students to display thinking skills using graphic organizers;
- engaging in child study by keeping anecdotal records;
- recording critical incidents;
- keeping checklists, logs, diaries, and journals about students; and
- employing technology to assist in collecting and recording information about students over time.

4. Systematize assessment procedures. Actually, skillful teachers already assess their students in many of the above ways. Teachers can readily describe subtle indicators of student progress: the light in a student's eye, changing voice inflections, the "aha" of discovery reflected in students' exuberance, the collaborative sharing and interdependence of group work, the serendipitous application of skills and concepts beyond the context in which they were learned, and reports from parents and other teachers of applied learnings.

What is lacking is a systematic way of collecting and reporting such evidence. Staff members need to refine their observation skills and work for inter-rater reliability. They need to identify and define terms and adopt common goals. They need to continually scrutinize the curriculum to ensure that outcomes, instruction, and assessment are aligned. Teachers, parents, administrators, and students will all need to clearly see the school's objectives and purposes so all can become more involved in collecting data, revising perceptions, and realigning practices.

Limitations of time and communication in school settings often prevent teachers in different departments, grade levels, and disciplines from meeting together. Thus, the mutual support, continuity, reinforcement, and assessment of these new goals of the

restructured school throughout the grade levels and across the subject areas has yet to be accomplished. When we consider critical reading, the scientific method, problem solving in mathematics, literacy and numeracy, modes of inquiry, and study skills, the distinctions and connections are still vague when it's time to decide which should be taught in science, which are most appropriate to math, which should be included in the social sciences, and how they all fit together.

This dilemma will continue until we consider thinking as the core of the curriculum and believe that content should be selectively abandoned or judiciously included because of its contributions to the thinking/learning process. The sooner we admit that these new processes have become the content, the sooner we will find ways to infuse and assess these goals throughout the curriculum. Our obsession with content is what separates us.

5. Re-educate legislators, parents, board members, and the community. The majority of the public does not yet value development of the intellect and continuous lifelong learning as goals of education. Business and industry leaders are increasingly supportive of schools' endeavors to educate the future generation to become better individual and group problem solvers, to develop creative capacities, to be open to new and continued learning, and to work cooperatively as team members. But many legislators, governors, and school boards—even some U.S. presidents—fail to include thinking, creativity, and cooperation in our national education goals for the 21st century.

Educators in conjunction with test makers, textbook publishers, professional organizations, business and industry leaders, parents, and the media need to mount a massive information and educational program to shift public policy and national values toward support of a more rational, cooperative, and compassionate mission statement for public education.

Educators have allowed the public to use test scores to evaluate their schools, students, and teachers without helping them see that other, more significant, nonmeasurable objectives can also be documented using a variety of reliable sources and techniques. Political decisions about testing, schooling, curriculum, and teacher competencies need to give way to more sound educational principles.

6. Assess school and classroom conditions as well as student learning.

Fritz Perls is quoted as saying, "Abnormal behavior is normal behavior under abnormal conditions." The conditions in which people work send powerful signals as to the values, mission, and purposes of the institution. Jack Frymier (1987) writes: "In the main, the bureaucratic structure of the workplace is more influential in determining what professionals do than are personal abilities, professional training, or previous experience. Therefore, change efforts should focus on the structure of the workplace, not on the teachers."

It can be assumed that teachers will more likely teach for thinking, creativity, and cooperation if they are in an intellectually stimulating, creative, and cooperative environment themselves. We must also assess the quality of the environment in which teachers, students, and administrators operate and constantly monitor the "intellectual ecology" of the workplace to ensure that intellectual growth is nurtured. Some questions by which to assess the intellectual ecology of the school environment include:

- Is the school organized for thoughtful reflection by its staff?
- Does scheduling allow for in-depth work?
- Have curriculums been developed and materials adopted to support thinking, cooperation, creativity, and the other new goals of the restructuring school?
- Are reward systems for students and the teacher assessment system aligned with the new values and mission of the restructured school?
- Do communications such as report cards, newsletters, school mottoes, and logos reflect the values of the restructured school?

7. Recognize that the ultimate purpose of assessment is nurturing the skills of self-assessment.

So much of a student's sense of "good" work depends on someone else telling them they have it right when they ask: "Did I get this right?" "Is this what you wanted?" "Is this work good enough?" If students graduate from our schools still dependent upon others to tell them when they are adequate, good, or excellent, then we've missed the whole point of what education is about. As John Dewey (1916) observes, "Experience is primarily an active-passive affair; it is not primarily cognitive. But the measure of the value of an experience lies in the perception of relationship or continuities to which it leads. It includes cognition in the degree in which it is cumulative or amounts to something, or has meaning."

We must constantly remind ourselves that the ultimate purpose of assessment is to create autonomous students who are self-analyzing, self-evaluating, self-referencing, self-renewing, and self-motivating. This requires that students develop internal feedback spirals as a means of setting goals, planning actions, gathering data about their actions, reflecting on their own values, and altering their behaviors and values accordingly.

We are not speaking of work for which there is a single right answer. We mean work that requires complex thinking, problem solving, divergent ideas, a new synthesis of one's knowledge base, or applying knowledge through performance—the kind of work that requires students to produce rather than reproduce knowledge. When we move into that zone of uncertainty in which right and wrong are a matter of shared understanding of expectations and criteria, we need responses from others. We need a mirror placed before our work that provides opportunity for reflection and constructive criticism for improvement. We need an opportunity to talk about our work with others as we develop our capacity to be sharper in our self-evaluation. The learners' task in the evaluation process is to:

- internalize external standards and expectations for good work,
- understand explicit ways to improve performance to meet those standards,
- develop a self-determined set of standards for high-quality work, and

- learn how to engage in a dialogue about appropriate standards for good work and to negotiate standards based on justifiable evaluative reasoning.

For the learner to be successful in this task, classrooms must provide opportunities for collaborative evaluation processes.

OWNING ASSESSMENT DATA

If learners are to modify their own behavior as a result of newly learned knowledge or skills, they must own the data. Change will not take place unless the learner sees the reason to change, believes that the change is worthwhile, and sees a way to integrate that change into already existing behaviors, attitudes, and knowledge. If these criteria are not met, learners may be able to reproduce knowledge in a limited way for a limited time, but integration of the new knowledge or skill by the learner will not happen.

Performing as learner is analogous to performing as teacher. To get better, you need to practice; receive accurate, descriptive responses to your work; receive sound advice from a Critical Friend; and develop the capacity to reflect on your practice and judge your performance in relationship to targets determined by yourself and others.

Improvement in the sense of being able to perform better is judged by both a Critical Friend and by self. If either source is considered untrustworthy or unreliable, the use of the evaluative data is placed in question and improvement hindered. When the gap is too great between the external sources of evaluation and the internal sources of evaluation, the learner may fall prey to one of many scenarios:

- "I will do this learning for you, but not because there is an intrinsic value for me."
- "I do not believe what you say about my work and will resist learning from you."
- "I don't know how to think about my work and feel bad about myself as a learner."
- "If I can't do what you want me to do, then I just won't work at all for you."

Any of these scenarios leaves the learner in conflict about his or her work and creates a tension that

pulls the learner away from independent, personal meaning-making toward learning for approval.

At the center of self-esteem is the question of worthiness. As Freud illuminated, one's sense of worth comes from two life-sustaining drives—the capacity to love and to work. When we ask, "What motivates the student to perform in school?" we often forget that the most significant motivating force is the student's personal meaning—the discovery of his or her capacity to do successful and good work. How one determines whether a student is doing successful and good work should be a collaborative process of standard setting. This is not the case in most educational settings. Rather, standards for successful and good work are set outside of the student's own sense of performance. The standards are presented to the student as an immutable fact, nonnegotiable regardless of the student's justifiable reasoning about his or her performance. When students are brought into a dialogue about standards, ownership of the evaluative data is more successful. The learning targets are agreed upon based on a dialogue about the quality of effort and worthiness of one's work in relation to the developing expectations of self and Critical Friend.

Our objective is to bring the learner into the evaluation process in such a way that he or she will become a partner in the learning process, a person who will be able to participate fully and autonomously in the learning experience with a sense of control over its results.

COLLABORATION BETWEEN STUDENT AND TEACHER

There are many opportunities to develop evaluation as a collaborative process in the classroom. For example, conferences provide wonderful opportunities to hear how students are thinking about their own work. The quality of conferences is far more significant than the quantity. Some schools state that a student will be interviewed at least once a month. Given a class size of between 25 and 30 students, an elementary school teacher will be required to have one conference a day. In a secondary school, it may require four or five conferences in a day. Each student is assured an opportunity to discuss his or her work with a teacher on a monthly basis. In addition, some schools require that teachers also talk with one parent every day. Regular conversations about student work are built into the daily life of school regardless of whether a student is in particular trouble, has special needs, or has done something exemplary.

Teacher conference time is provided by allowing students to do independent or group work. Some teachers provide time for student peer conferences as a regular part of their work with students. At this time, students conference with one another about their work, and the teacher pulls aside individual students for conferences. Group interviews provide another option, where the teacher pulls together a group of students and confers about their work.

The limited time with students is so valuable that teachers should think of this opportunity as one in which they have access to a primary source of information. Any information that could be gleaned from secondary sources should not consume the precious time. Most interview questions would probably start in the following way:

- How do you feel about . . . ?
- In your opinion, do you think . . . ?
- Why do you suppose . . . ?
- What was on your mind when . . . ?
- Now that you have accomplished your work, what do you think about . . . ?
- How does what you say compare to . . . in your opinion . . . ?
- What do you think would happen if . . . ?

REFLECTING ON PORTFOLIOS

One of the most significant aspects of portfolio assessment is the opportunity for students to reflect on their portfolios with another thoughtful person. The portfolio represents selections from a collection of a student's work based upon certain goals. Over the course of a few months, a student collects work, then chooses for the portfolio examples of the Intelligent Behaviors, Checking for Accuracy and Precision, and Risk Taking (Costa 1991). The examples in a writing portfolio might include:

- best final product with drafts stapled together,
- best examples of change and corrections within drafts, and
- best examples of risks taken by the learner in trying to acquire a new skill or style.

When the student chooses, he or she justifies the choice. A conference can reflect how the student has evaluated his or her work and where there are targets for growth. Sometimes the teacher will also choose best examples from the students work. In that case, the conference provides an opportunity for the teacher to share his or her best choices with the student's choices. Suppose the teacher's choices do not match the student's choices. This provides a marvelous opportunity to talk about expectations, standards, and quality of work. And what a marvelous opportunity for the teacher to understand the student's developing criteria!

BUILDING CRITERIA

The whole class can participate in the development of criteria. In any given project, students can collaborate as a classroom community in setting the standards and criteria by which they will judge the project results. The expectations should be established before the students begin their project work. In this way, students are building their capacity to critique work as well as do work.

Consider, for example, an elementary school project where a group of bilingual students focuses on building criteria for what makes a good story. The teacher and children begin to build a set of criteria for what, in their opinion, makes a good story. After they read a story together, the class discusses whether the story met their criteria. In some instances, they find that they have to expand their criteria based on their reading. In some instances, they find that certain criteria are specific to a story genre. After they become more skilled in their capacity to evaluate stories on the basis of established criteria, they decide to look at their own story writing in the same way. The students use peer conferences about their story writing as a basis for examining the story in light of the criteria. The levels of collaboration and evaluation become a powerful learning opportunity. Students eventually are able to examine their criteria for what makes a good story with some of the criteria literary critics have used. Students may converse with literary critics and inform their evaluation process through those conversations. In this way, students are working as critical thinkers, making their judgments through informed reasoning.

GROUP EVALUATION

When students work in groups, they have yet another opportunity to develop a collaborative evaluation process. Group work requires evaluating the content of the group effort as well as the group process itself. Although the criteria for good group work may be set with the class, each group may set its own criteria for good group processes. The "How Are We Doing Checklists," originally referenced in Part V, are an example of a group process evaluation form.

Students are asked to rate themselves in one of the three categories: Often, Sometimes, and Not Yet (a positive, developmental way of looking at behavior). After the student has evaluated himself or herself, the activity can expand so that all of the students in the group evaluate one another and give each other feedback about their behavior. Finally, the teacher can monitor the groups with identical charts. In this way, students have three perspectives on the same event: self, peer, and teacher. Goals can be set for new behaviors by interpreting the evaluative responses.

When a classroom is focused on thinking, the process behavior should foster better thinking. One such list of thinking traits is the Intelligent Behaviors mentioned earlier. Teachers and students might generate a set of criteria for what intelligent behavior looks like. That list can be transposed onto the "How Are We Doing?" forms.

ESTABLISHING SCHOOLWIDE STANDARDS

If teachers and students collaborate in the evaluation process, how can we begin to translate this effort into schoolwide criteria and standards? This is an excellent question for a schoolwide discussion. Usually, the discussion starts from another perspec-

tive—what standards we establish (or the state or district establishes) that we require of our students. Reversing the process by beginning in collaboration with students and working our way out from the self, the classroom, the school, and the district into the community may help us learn something new about accountability. We may learn something more about how to encourage student accountability and self-evaluation in relationship to the larger set of expectations that surround students and their work. We may also provide a more constructive framework for instruction related to student learning because teachers will stay closer to the authentic, daily performance of the work of students as they develop their criteria for evaluation.

When teachers bring the data from their classrooms to the whole-school discussion on standards and criteria setting for evaluation, the discussion remains closer to the realities of the classroom. The whole school can engage in conversations based on the work of students rather than on impressions of what ought to be. To emphasize this point, consider the following situation that occurred in an elementary school.

A group of teachers gathered writings from kindergarten through 6th grade classes. They had agreed that one of the ways they would produce a common experience for discussion would be to provide students with a writing prompt. The prompt they used was offered in early November: "Suppose you were the last turkey in the barn—describe your feelings and experience." Children were encouraged to draw as well as write, and adults were available to capture stories from nonwriters. The teachers, one from each grade, came to the meeting with their class writing samples. They were asked to switch papers so that no one scored their own set of papers. The task was to choose the best three examples of writing from their 25 or 30 samples. One of the first questions a teacher asked was, "Suppose you cannot find three best pieces?" The teacher's question reflected external standards for a good piece of writing, standards not based on the work of the children in the classroom. In fact, the task was to choose a relative measure from within the population they were given. It is not difficult to see how that attitude begins to translate to:

- expectations for students that do not match their capabilities,
- disappointment that student work is not "good enough," a feeling of lowering one's standards when accepting certain students' work, and
- difficulty providing realistic learning stretches from within the students' work.

The teachers finally got to the task and chose the three best pieces. Then, starting from the kindergarten class and moving through 6th grade, they described the characteristics that made those pieces "best." At the end of the exercise, they had an interesting story of the development of writing for these students. They could then compare that to what theorists in the writing process were suggesting. They had established a knowledge base about their students that provided a lens through with they could examine the work of other practitioners and theorists.

Instituting practices that facilitate teachers' talking about criteria, standards, and evaluation practices is one powerful way to change the accountability system. Such practices as evaluation study groups, teacher-as-researcher groups, or teachers working in partnership with one another to exchange papers all can be organized as part of staff development.

As these conversations grow out of individual schools, they can be part of the development of a school-based management system that reports to the superintendent. At the central level, the district can orchestrate school-based understandings and, through collaborative processes, can arrive at realistic expectations for students at elementary and secondary levels. The orchestration of curriculum, instruction, and assessment practices is a necessary part of school accountability.

And what about the state? It might also reverse its perspective. Rather than developing the accountability measures, it might see its role as facilitating district processes for greater accountability. The state might serve as a legitimizing agency for district practices, establishing policies regarding the criteria for a solid evaluation system or process rather than trying to establish procedures for measuring what might be differing strategies of instruction and—in some states where there is not a statewide curriculum—differing curricular requirements.

The process of collaboration should be thoughtful enough to improve learning and teaching. We know that the current process of evaluation is seen as detracting from teaching and learning. The measures that are mandated are often perceived as punitive, inauthentic, and not very descriptive of what teachers and students value. By developing collaborative processes for setting evaluation standards, we can enlarge our understanding of what it means to examine a human process as dynamic and complex as learning. We can learn to value more than one perspective regarding the question of standards. Finally, we may make our way out of an accountability process that represses rather than enhances thinking at all levels of the educational enterprise.

The highest level of *Bloom's Taxonomy* (1956) is generating, holding, and applying a set of internal and external criteria. For too long, adults alone applied criteria to student work. We need to shift that responsibility to students. Our goal of the restructured school must be to help all learners develop the capacity to modify themselves.

References

California State Department of Education Curriculum Assessment Alignment Conference. (October 16, 1989). "Beyond the Bubble." Sacramento, Calif.

Costa, A. (1991). "The Search for Intelligent Life." In *Developing Minds: A Resource Book for Teaching Thinking,* edited by A. Costa. Alexandria, Va.: Association for Supervision and Curriculum Development.

Bloom, B.S., M. Engelhart, E. Furst, W. Hill, and D. Krathwohl.(1956). *Taxonomy of Educational Objectives, Handbook I: Cognitive Domain*. New York: David McKay.

Frymier, J. (September 1987). "Bureaucracy and the Neutering of Teachers." *Phi Delta Kappan* 69, 1: 9-14.

Recommended Readings on Authentic Assessment

Aiken, L. (1987). *Assessment of Intellectual Functioning.* Needham Heights, Mass.: Allyn and Bacon.

Bernhardt, V.L. (1994). *The School Portfolio: A Comprehensive Framework for School Improvement.* Princeton, N.J.: Eye on Education.

Beyer, B. (1995). *How to Conduct a Formative Evaluation.* Alexandria, Va.: Association for Supervision and Curriculum Development.

Burke, K. (1992). *Authentic Assessment in the Mindful School.* Palatine, Ill.: Skylight Publishing, Inc.

Burke, K. (1992). *Authentic Assessment: A Collection of Articles.* Palatine, Ill.: Skylight Publishing, Inc.

Cambourne, B., and J. Turbill. (1994). *Responsive Evaluation: Making Valid Judgments About Student Literacy.* Portsmouth, N.H.: Heinemann.

Carey, L. (1988). *Measuring and Evaluating School Learning.* Rockleigh, N.J.: Allyn and Bacon, Longwood Division.

Costa, A., and B. Kallick. (1995). *Assessment in the Learning Organization: Shifting the Paradigm.* Alexandria, Va.: Association for Supervision and Curriculum Development.

Dyer, H. (1980). *Parents Can Understand Testing.* Columbia, Md.: National Committee for Citizens in Education.

Educational Testing Service. (1986). *Creativity and Divergent Thinking.* Princeton, N.J.: Test Collection, Educational Testing Service. (This bibliography describes approximately 75 tests of creative or divergent thinking. Lists test scores and availability.)

Educational Testing Service. (1986). *Reasoning, Logical Thinking and Problem Solving.* Princeton, N.J.: Test Collection, Educational Testing Service. (This bibliography includes abstracts and availability for 133 tests. The majority are aptitude measures, although three critical thinking tests are included as well.)

Ennis, R.H. (1987). "A Taxonomy of Critical Thinking Dispositions and Abilities." In *Teaching Thinking Skills: Theory and Practice*, edited by J.B. Baron and R.J. Sternberg. New York: W.H. Freeman. (This chapter is a good review of current issues with respect to assessing critical thinking.)

Ennis, R. (1986). *Critical Thinking Tests.* Champaign, Ill.: Illinois Critical Thinking Project. (Brief reviews of

| | | | | | | | | | | | | | | | | | |

major reasoning tests currently available. Includes seven general and four aspect-scientific critical thinking tests. Available from the University of Illinois, 1310 S. Sixth St., Champaign, IL 61820.)

Fulton-Fisher, C., and R. King. (1995). *Authentic Assessment: A Guide to Implementation.* Thousand Oaks, Calif.: Corwin Press.

Glazer, S.M., and C.S. Brown. (1993). *Portfolios and Beyond: Collaborative Assessment in Reading and Writing.* Norwood, Mass.: Christopher-Gordon Publishers, Inc.

Goswami, D., and P.R. Stillman, eds. (1987). *Reclaiming the Classroom: Teacher Research as an Agency for Change.* Upper Montclair, N.J.: Boynton/Cook.

Gould, S.J. (1981). *The Mismeasure of Man.* New York: W.W. Norton. (Traces society's various attempts to classify and measure its members. Disputes the concept of intelligence as a single entity.)

Groundlund, N.E., and R.L. Linn. (1990). *Measurement and Evaluation in Teaching.* 6th ed. New York: Macmillan.

Harp, B., ed. (1994, paperbound). *Assessment and Evaluation for Student Centered Learning.* Norwood, Mass.: Christopher-Gordon Publishers, Inc.

Harp, B., ed. (1995, hardbound). *Assessment and Evaluation for Student Centered Learning: Expanded Professional Version.* Norwood, Mass.: Christopher-Gordon Publishers, Inc.

Herman, J.L., P.R. Aschbacher, and L. Winters. (1992). *A Practical Guide to Alternative Assessment.* Alexandria, Va.: Association for Supervision and Curriculum Development.

Hill, B.C., and C. Ruptic. (1993). *Practical Aspects of Authentic Assessment.* Norwood, Mass.: Christopher-Gordon Publishers, Inc.

McArthur, D.L., ed. (1987). *Alternative Approaches to the Assessment of Achievement.* Hingham, Mass.: Kluwer Academic Publishers.

Norris, S., and R. Ennis. (1989). *Evaluating Critical Thinking.* Midwest Publishing Company.

Norris, S.P., and R. King. (1984). *The Design of a Critical Thinking Test on Appraising Observations.* Report, Institute for Educational Research and Development, Memorial University of Newfoundland. (Details how the authors developed and validated the Test of Appraising Observations. Included is their procedure for interviewing students in order to come up with an independent measure of quality of reasoning.)

Perrone, V., ed. (1991). *Expanding Student Assessment.* Alexandria, Va.: Association for Supervision and Curriculum Development.

Rowntree, D. (1987). *Assessing Students: How Shall We Know Them?* 2nd ed. New York: Nichols Publishing Co.

Rudner, L.M., et al., eds. (1989). *Understanding Achievement Tests: A Guide for School Administrators.* Washington, D.C.: ERIC Clearinghouse on Tests, Measurement, and Evaluation and American Institutes for Research.

Sachse, T. (1981). *Role of Performance Assessment in Tests of Problem Solving.* Portland, Ore.: Clearinghouse for Applied Performance Testing, Northwest Regional Educational Laboratory. (This bibliography includes reviews of 13 tests for school ability, life skills, problem solving, and critical thinking. Six features of each test are examined: definitions of problem solving, measurement strategy, performance assessment, reliability, uses of the test, and validity.)

Stewart, B. (1979). *Testing for Critical Thinking: A Review of the Resources.* (Rational Thinking Reports No. 2, ERIC No. ED 183588). Champaign, Ill,: University of Illinois–Urbana, Illinois Rational Thinking Project. (Twenty-five critical thinking tests are reviewed. Information on reliability and validity as well as item analysis is included. Most of the tests have a pre-1970 copyright, yet a few are still available in updated editions.)

Stiggins, R.J., E. Rubel, and E. Quellmatz. (1988). *Measuring Thinking Skills in the Classroom: A Teacher's Guide.* Portland, Ore.: Northwest Regional Educational Laboratory. (This publication addresses how to assess HOTS in the classroom and how to embed HOTS skills into everyday lesson plans. Available from Northwest Regional Educational Laboratory, 101 S.W. Main St., Portland, OR 97204.)

Tierney, R., M.J. Carter, and L.E. Desai. (1991). *Portfolio Assessment in the Reading-Writing Classroom.* Norwood, Mass.: Christopher-Gordon Publishers.

Wiggins, G. (1993). *Assessing Student Performance.* San Francisco: Jossey-Bass.

Woodward, H. (1993). *Negotiated Evaluation.* Newtown, South Wales: Primary English Association.

Worthen, B.R., and J.R. Sanders. (1987). *Educational Evaluation: Alternative Approaches and Practical Guidelines.* White Plains, N.Y.: Longman.

Wrigley, J., ed. (1992). *Guide to Assessment in Education.* London: Routledge.

About the Authors

Victoria L. Bernhardt is Executive Director of the Education for the Future Initiative, Telesis Foundation, 400 West First Street, Chico, CA 95929-9230, and Professor in the Department of Professional Studies in Education, California State University, Chico.

Arthur L. Costa is Professor Emeritus in Education Administration, California State University, Sacramento, and Co-director of the Institute for Intelligent Behavior, Berkeley, California. He is also President, Search Models Unlimited, P.O. Box 362, Davis, CA 95617-0362.

Michael Couchman is Associate Superintendent, Adrian Public Schools, 227 N. Winter Street, Adrian, MI 49221.

Theodore Czajkowski is Assistant Superintendent, Bellingham Public Schools, 1306 Dupont Street, Bellingham, WA 998225.

Charlotte Danielson is President, Princeton Education Associates, P.O. Box 7285, Princeton, NJ 08543.

Jane F. Fraser is an Education Consultant, Box 815, Westport, CT 06880, and Teacher Trainer with The Writing Project, Teachers College, Columbia University. She co-authored, with Donna Skolnick, *On Their Way: Celebrating Second Graders as They Read and Write* (Portsmouth, N.H.: Heinemann, 1994).

Patricia J. Hoffman is Assistant Superintendent, Burlington Area School District, 100 North Kane Street, Burlington, WI 53105.

Ann Johnson is Executive Director of Instruction, Ankeny Community School District, 306 S.W. School St., Ankeny, Iowa 50021.

Darlene Johnson is a Teacher at Sun View School, Ocean View S.D., 7721 Juliette Low, Huntington Beach,

CA 92647. She is a member of the UCLA Teacher Researcher Project.

Bena Kallick is an Education Consultant, 12 Crooked Mile Road, Westport, CT 06880.

Sherry King is Superintendent, Croton-Harmon School District, Gerstein St., Croton-on-Hudson, NY 10520.

Marcia Knoll is Assistant Superintendent, Valley Stream Central High School District, 1 Kent Road, Valley Stream, NY 11582.

Susan Kreisman is Assistant Principal, Central High School, 135 Fletcher Road, Valley Stream, NY 11582.

Chris Louth is Teacher, Croton-Harmon High School, 36 Old Post Road South, Croton-on-Hudson, NY 10520.

Peggy M. Luidens is an Education Consultant, 123 E. 26th Street, Holland, MI 49423.

Timothy Melchior is Principal, Memorial Junior High School, Fletcher Avenue, Valley Stream, NY 11582.

Patrick Monahan is a Teacher at Downers Grove South High School, 1436 Norfolk, Downers Grove, IL 60516.

Margo Montague is Director, Federal and Special Programs, Bellingham Public Schools, 1306 Dupont Street, Bellingham, WA 98225.

Braden Montgomery is a secondary school English Teacher with the Springfield School District, 49 West Leamy Avenue, Springfield, PA 19064.

Alison Preece is Associate Professor, Faculty of Education, University of Victoria, Box 3010, Victoria, British Columbia V8W 3N4.

Kathryn Schladweiler is Supervisor, Instructional Programs, Mason City Community School, 1515 S. Pennsylvania, Mason City, Iowa 50401.

Sandra Silverman is a Teacher at College View School, Ocean View S.D., 6582 Lennox Dr., Huntington Beach, CA 92647. She is also Coordinator of Mathematics for the San Diego County Office of Education.

William Sommers is Vice Principal, Wayzata High School, 305 Vicksburg Lane, Plymouth, MN 55447.

Robert Swartz is Professor, University of Massachusetts at Boston, and Director, National Center for Teaching Thinking, 815 Washington St., Suite 8, Newtonville, MA 02160.

Diane Zimmerman is Principal, Patwin School, 2222 Shasta Dr., Davis, CA 95616.

Index

| | | | | | | | | | | | | | | | | |

| | | | | | | | | | | | | | | | | |

INDEX TO CHAPTER AUTHORS